GENDER INEQUALITY IN LATIN AMERICA

Studies in Critical Social Sciences Book Series

Haymarket Books is proud to be working with Brill Academic Publishers (www.brill.nl) to republish the *Studies in Critical Social Sciences* book series in paperback editions. This peer-reviewed book series offers insights into our current reality by exploring the content and consequences of power relationships under capitalism, and by considering the spaces of opposition and resistance to these changes that have been defining our new age. Our full catalog of *SCSS* volumes can be viewed at https://www.haymarketbooks .org/series_collections/4-studies-in-critical-social-sciences.

GENDER INEQUALITY IN LATIN AMERICA

The Case of Ecuador

EDITED BY
PABLO QUIÑONEZ
AND CLAUDIA MALDONADO-ERAZO

Haymarket Books
Chicago, IL

First published in 2020 by Brill Academic Publishers, The Netherlands
© 2020 Koninklijke Brill NV, Leiden, The Netherlands

Published in paperback in 2021 by
Haymarket Books
P.O. Box 180165
Chicago, IL 60618
773-583-7884
www.haymarketbooks.org

ISBN: 978-1-64259-618-2

Distributed to the trade in the US through Consortium Book Sales and
Distribution (www.cbsd.com) and internationally through Ingram Publisher
Services International (www.ingramcontent.com).

This book was published with the generous support of Lannan Foundation and
Wallace Action Fund.

Special discounts are available for bulk purchases by organizations and
institutions. Please call 773-583-7884 or email info@haymarketbooks.org for more
information.

Cover design by Jamie Kerry and Ragina Johnson.

Printed in the United States.

10 9 8 7 6 5 4 3 2 1

Library of Congress Cataloging-in-Publication data is available.

Contents

PART 3
Rural and Indigenous Women in Ecuador

Acknowledgements

We are grateful to Alfonso Casanova, Bárbara Ester, Camila Vollenweider, Carlos Freire, José Álvarez-García, Lupe García, María de la Cruz Del Río Rama, Patricio Noboa Viñan, René Ramírez, Santiago Ochoa, Segundo Camino-Mogro, Shruti Iyer, Tangya Tandazo, and Xavier León for their comments and contributions. We would also like to thank David Fasenfest, editor of this series, for his support and guidance.

Figures and Tables

Figures

Tables

Acronyms

ADF	Augmented Dickey and Fuller Test
AMA	Association of Agro-artisanal Women of Ecuador (*Asociación de Mujeres Agroartesanales*)
CAME	Argentine Confederation of Medium-sized Enterprises (*Confederación Argentina de la Mediana Empresa*)
CNE	National Electoral Council of Ecuador (*Consejo Nacional Electoral*)
CODEMUF	Committee for the Development of Border Women (*Comité de Desarrollo de Mujeres de Frontera*)
CONAIE	Confederation of Indigenous Nationalities of Ecuador (*Confederación de Nacionalidades Indígenas del Ecuador*)
CONAMU	National Council of Women of Ecuador (*Consejo Nacional de la Mujer*)
COPISA	Plurinational and Intercultural Conference on Food Sovereignty (*Conferencia Plurinacional e Intercultural de Soberanía Alimentaria*)
CPI	Consumer Price Index
DCA	New York Department of Consumer Affairs
ECLAC	Economic Commission for Latin America and the Caribbean
ECUARUNARI	Confederation of Peoples of Kichwa Nationality of Ecuador (*Confederación de Pueblos de la Nacionalidad Kichwa del Ecuador*)
ENEMDU	National Survey of Employment, Unemployment and Underemployment of Ecuador (*Encuesta Nacional de Empleo, Desempleo y Subempleo*)
ESPAC	Survey of Surface and Continuous Agricultural Production of Ecuador (*Encuesta de Superficie y Producción Agropecuaria Continua*)
EUT	Time Use Survey, Ecuador (*Encuesta de Uso del Tiempo*)
FAO	Food and Agriculture Organization of the United Nations
FDI	Foreign Direct Investment
FIAN	Food First Information and Action Network
FTA	Free Trade Agreement
GDP	Gross Domestic Product
GFCF	Gross Fixed Capital Formation
GII	Gender Inequality Index
GLS	Generalized Least Squares
HCG	Human Capital Gap

HDI	Human Development Index
HIC	High-income Countries
IEE	Institute of Ecuadorian Studies (*Instituto de Estudios Ecuatorianos*)
IICA	Inter-American Institute for Cooperation on Agriculture
ILO	International Labour Organization
INEC	National Institute of Statistics and Censuses of Ecuador (*Instituto Nacional de Estadística y Censos*)
IPS	Im, Pesaran and Shin Test
LA	Latin America
LG	Labor Gap
LLC	Levin, Lin and Chu Test
LOASFAS	Organic Law on Agrobiodiversity, Seeds and the Promotion of Agriculture of Ecuador (*Ley Orgánica de Agrobiodiversidad, Semillas y Fomento de la Agricultura*)
LORSA	Organic Law of the Food Sovereignty Regime of Ecuador (*Ley Orgánica del Régimen de la Soberanía Alimentaria*)
MAG	Ministry of Agriculture and Livestock of Ecuador (*Ministerio de Agricultura y Ganadería*)
MBZ	Minimum Bradford Zone
MC	Marginal Cost
MHIC	Middle-high-income Countries
MLIC	Middle-low-income Countries
MMO	Movement of Women of El Oro (*Movimiento de Mujeres de El Oro*)
MR	Marginal Revenue
NGO	Non-Governmental Organization
OEC	Observatory of Economic Complexity
OECD	Organisation for Economic Co-operation and Development
PI	Productivity Index
PP	Phillips and Perron Unit Root Test
RIF	Re-centered Influence Function
SENPLADES	National Planification and Development Secretariat of Ecuador (*Secretaría Nacional de Planificación y Desarrollo*)
SEPS	Superintendence of Popular and Solidarity Economy of Ecuador (*Superintendencia de Economía Popular y Solidaria*)
SJR	Scimago Journal Rank
STEMM	Science, Technology, Engineering, Mathematics, and Medicine
TC	Total Citations
UB	Breitung Test
UK	United Kingdom

UN	United Nations
UNDP	United Nations Development Programme
UR	Urbanization Rate
U.S.	United States of America
USD	United States Dollar
WTO	World Trade Organization

Contributors

Rafael Alvarado
is the head of the Department of Economics of the National University of Loja (UNL, Ecuador). He is a graduate of the Catholic University of the North (Chile) and specializes in regional development, applied macroeconomics and environmental and energy economics. Rafael is the editor of UNL's journal *Vista Económica* and frequently collaborates as a reviewer for several other journals. He has published numerous articles and edited a book series in economic growth.

María Anchundia
is a lecturer and researcher at the University of Guayaquil (Ecuador). She specialized in History at the Simón Bolívar Andean University (Ecuador) and in Gender, Culture, and History at the Latin American Faculty of Social Sciences (FLACSO, Ecuador). She has published several articles on the contributions of rural women to the local and regional economy in Ecuador.

Esteban Arévalo
is a Ph.D. student at the School of Environment, Education and Development of the University of Manchester (United Kingdom). He is a recipient of the Excellence Scholarship awarded by the Ecuadorian Government. His research focuses on patrimony, history, and human geography.

Diana Cabrera
works as a lecturer at the Faculty of Economics of the University of Guayaquil (Ecuador). She is an Economics Ph.D. candidate at the Autonomous Metropolitan University (Mexico). Diana has taught at the undergraduate and postgraduate levels for several years and has been part of multiple research projects at the University of Guayaquil. Her research focuses on ecological economics and sustainable rural development.

Edwin Espinoza
is a lecturer at the University of Guayaquil (Ecuador). He graduated from the Latin American Faculty of Social Sciences (FLACSO, Ecuador), where he specialized in Development Economics at the postgraduate level. Edwin has published numerous research articles and taught at the graduate and postgraduate levels at the University of Guayaquil, where he has also participated in university-funded research projects. His research focuses on economic development, international and environmental economics.

Gabriela Gallardo
is a researcher at the National Autonomous University of Mexico (UNAM, Mexico). She is a graduate of the International Institute of Social Studies (Erasmus University Rotterdam, The Netherlands), where she specialized in Development Studies. Gabriela has extensive experience in the fields of education policy, gender, youth, and rural development. In the past, she worked as an advisor for several national and international organizations and as a research assistant at the Latin American Faculty of Social Sciences (FLACSO, Ecuador). She is the founder of the NGO *Apoyando Ecuador.*

Danny Granda
is a researcher at the Department of Economics of the National University of Loja (UNL, Ecuador), where he graduated. He has published several academic articles both at the national and international levels. He is currently the executive coordinator of UNL's journal *Vista Económica.*

Claudia Maldonado-Erazo
is a lecturer at the Polytechnic School of Chimborazo (Ecuador). She holds a bachelor's degree in Management and a master's degree in Research in Social and Juridical Sciences from the University of Extremadura (Spain), where she received the best dissertation award. She is currently enrolled as a Ph.D. student in Sustainable Territorial Development at the University of Extremadura. She has worked as a consultant for several organizations, participated in numerous international research projects, and published various articles, books, and book chapters.

Wendy Mora
is an Economist specialized at the postgraduate level in International Development Cooperation at Yeungnam University (South Korea). She has a vast experience as a university lecturer and assistant project manager, having worked with various NGOs and other organizations in Ecuador.

Diana Morán
is a lecturer at the Faculty of Economics of the University of Guayaquil (Ecuador). She specialized in Economics at the postgraduate level at the Autonomous Metropolitan University (Mexico). She has published several research pieces at local and international levels and is currently the director of a gender-focused research project at the University of Guayaquil. Her research focuses on the economics of gender, poverty, and inequality.

Sayonara Morejón

is an Economist specialized at the postgraduate level in Interdisciplinary Gender Studies at the Autonomous University of Madrid (Spain). Her research focuses on inclusive education, gender, and rights.

Carlos Moreno-Hurtado

is a lecturer and researcher at the Department of Economics of the Private Technical University of Loja (UTPL, Ecuador). He studied Economics and Law at the undergraduate level at UTPL and later specialized in Applied Research in Economics and Business at the postgraduate level at the Autonomous University of Barcelona (Spain). He has published several research articles, served as a referee at various national journals, and is currently the adjunct editor of UTPL's academic journal *Huella Económica.*

María Moreno

is a lecturer at Silva Henríquez Catholic University (UCSH, Chile). She is a graduate of the Autonomous Metropolitan University (Mexico), where she specialized in Economics and Innovation Management. María is currently the Academic Coordinator of the School of Management and Economics at UCSH. Her research focuses on sustainable development and common goods.

Ana Oña

is a Ph.D. student at the University of Lucerne (Switzerland). She studied Economics as an undergraduate and Statistics at the master's level. She has broad experience in public and private institutions in Latin America. Her research interests include health economics, applied economics, income inequality, and public policy.

Pablo Ponce

is a lecturer at the Department of Economics of the National University of Loja (Ecuador). He is a graduate of the University of Barcelona (Spain), where he specialized in Economics, Regulation, and Competition. He has published several academic articles and book chapters both at the national and international levels. His research focuses on issues of economic growth and natural resources.

Pablo Quiñonez

works as a lecturer at the Faculty of Economics of the University of Guayaquil (Ecuador). He is an Economist and holds a master's degree in Development Economics and Policy from the University of Manchester (United Kingdom). Currently, he is a postgraduate student at the Department of Social Policy and

Intervention of the University of Oxford (United Kingdom). In the past, he has worked as an Advisor for the Labor Minister Office of Ecuador and as a lecturer at the Private Technical University of Loja (UTPL). He is part of two research groups in Ecuador and collaborates as a reviewer for several academic journals in the region.

Ana Valeria Recalde-Vela

is a research consultant at FIAN Ecuador, a non-governmental organization that works with peasant and indigenous peoples in human rights and environmental issues, particularly the right to food. She is also involved in research activities with other Ecuadorian NGOs. She holds a Bachelor's degree in International Development from Leiden University (Honours College) and specialized in Agrarian Food and Environmental Studies at the postgraduate level at the International Institute of Social Studies (Erasmus University Rotterdam, The Netherlands).

Josefina Rosales

is a Sociologist who graduated from the University of Buenos Aires (Argentina), where she is also specializing in Latin American Social Studies. She is currently a teaching assistant and a part of the research groups *Popular Feminisms* and *Feminism and Marxism.* In addition, Josefina is specializing in Philosophy at the National University of Quilmes (Argentina).

Ximena Songor-Jaramillo

is a lecturer and researcher at the Department of Economics of the Private Technical University of Loja (UTPL, Ecuador). She is a graduate of the University of Alcalá (Spain), where she specialized in Applied Economic Analysis. She has published several articles and presented her research at the national and international levels. Her research focuses on economic inequality and social welfare.

Daniel Zea

is a lecturer at the University of Guayaquil (Ecuador), where he teaches Microeconomics, Macroeconomics, and Strategic Management, and is also part of a university-funded research project. He holds a bachelor's degree with honors in International Business, Finance and Economics from the University of Manchester (United Kingdom) and a master's degree in Development Studies with a major in Governance and Development Policy from the International Institute of Social Studies (Erasmus University Rotterdam, The Netherlands).

Introduction

Pablo Quiñonez and Claudia Maldonado-Erazo

In 1924, Matilde Hidalgo Navarro,[1] an Ecuadorian physician, was the first woman in Latin America to vote in a national election. Thanks to this milestone, five years later, Ecuador explicitly granted women's right to vote in its new constitution. It was the first country in the region to do so. In the following years, similar reforms occurred in other countries of Latin America, inaugurating a new chapter in the history of the fight for women's rights.

However, these struggles can be traced back to several centuries in the region. For instance, although few written pieces of evidence have survived to these days, the stories of resistance of indigenous women against the colonial power have been transmitted orally and contributed to lay the foundations of feminist thought in Latin America (Gargallo 2010). One of the earliest documented works advocating for women's intellectual and educational rights is that of Mexican nun Juana Inés de la Cruz in the XVII century (Rivera Berruz 2018). Other writers that argued in favor of women's rights include Teresa Margarida da Silva e Orta (Brazil), Flora Tristán (Peru), Rita Cetina (Mexico), and Visitación Padilla (Honduras) (Gargallo 2004).

Despite the above-mentioned rich history, it was not until the 20th century that a broader academic interest in this area emerged in the region, amidst the social movements for women liberation in the 1960s and 1970s. As explained in Chapter 4 of this volume, social scientists in Latin America first focused consistently on women's issues from the perspective of economic development. The term gender would be later introduced and gained prominence in the 1990s.

As in the U.S., modern women's movements in the region emerged in interaction to the left, responding, sometimes engaging with Latin America's left (Abbassi and Lutjens 2002). From the 1990s, in contrast to the dominant dependency theory and Marxist perspectives of the previous two decades, the 'post' impulses have gained space in the scholarship on and from the region, probably best reflecting European and U.S. tendencies (Barrett 1992).

Contrary to such a trend, Segal (1999) has argued that the core axes of cultural oppression and economic exploitation keep constructing and reconstructing themselves in the interrelated terms of gender, class, and race in the context of the totalizing control of transnational capitalism. Thus, invoking

---

1   Often referred to as Matilde Hidalgo de Procel (adding his husband's first surname after her own).

specific differences could only serve to transformative ends if it is "part of *some wider political project* seeking to dismantle these basic structures of domination" (p. 35). In line with such reasoning, this book adopts a predominantly 'social-structure' perspective to critically examine gender inequality in Latin America and, more specifically, in Ecuador.

It is true that women in this region share with women elsewhere similar fundamental inequalities in relation to men. However, there are specific conditions that differentiate them from women in developed countries and other developing nations, making it necessary to dedicate them separate attention, as discussed by Abbassi and Lutjens (2002).

In Latin America,[2] gender inequalities are rooted in a social and economic system that reproduces stereotypes, favors a sexual division of labor, and conditions women's income, political participation, and opportunities. As a result, women's autonomy and human development are harmed, which harms society. Ecuador's situation is not different from Latin America's, with women dedicating more time than men to unpaid activities, being discriminated against in wages, and relegated in politics, academia, and access to high-ranking positions, as will be discussed in this volume. Despite being the region pioneer in enfranchising women, Ecuador has lagged behind other Latin American countries in terms of gender equality in recent times.

Figure 0.1 shows the evolution of the United Nations Development Programme's (UNDP) Gender Inequality Index over the last decades for different country groups. This index measures gender inequalities in three aspects of human development: reproductive health, empowerment, and economic status. Higher index values mean greater disparities between men and women and higher losses to human development. As can be seen, the average level of gender inequality measured through this index—and the consequent human development cost—has been decreasing over the last years in Latin America, as in the rest of the world. However, even though Latin America has achieved better results than the world average and even more than the group of least developed countries, it is still far away from OECD countries.

In this context, this book draws from different areas of research to critically examine the origins of gender inequalities and their effects on the economy and the society of Latin America and, more specifically, of Ecuador. It provides insights from the perspective of political economy (Chapters 1 and 3), history (Chapter 5), macro and microeconomics (Chapters 2, 6, 7, and 10), political science (Chapter 8), rural and development studies (Chapters 9 and 11), and

---

2 Several organizations, such as the Economic Commission for Latin America and the Caribbean, consider both Latin America and the Caribbean as a whole analytical unit.

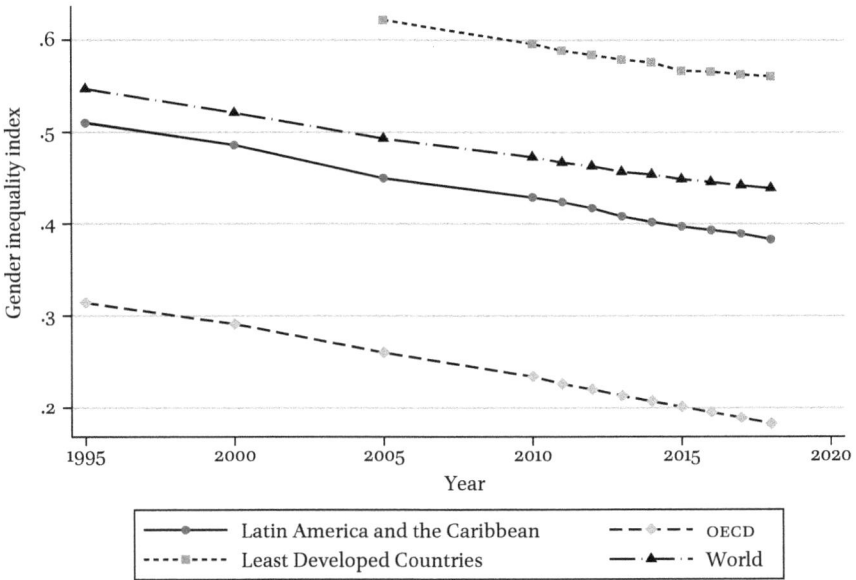

FIGURE 0.1 Gender Inequality Index
SOURCE: UNITED NATIONS DEVELOPMENT PROGRAMME (2019)

bibliometric studies (Chapter 4). The book starts reviewing the reality of Latin America, in Part 1. Then, Part 2 focuses on Ecuador. Finally, Part 3, focuses on women from ethnic minorities and rural areas of the country, for whom the problem of inequality, discrimination, and violence is even greater.

1 The Structure of the Book

1.1 *Part 1: Latin America*

Chapter 1, by Pablo Quiñonez and Claudia Maldonado-Erazo, aims to explain what shapes the gender dimension of economic inequalities, focusing on Latin America, from the perspective of political economy. In order to do so, the authors follow Frank Stilwell's (2012) framework and use the model of the circuit of capital proposed by Marx and situate gender in the sequential conditions for capital accumulation. From this perspective, gender inequalities can be seen as functional to capital expansion as they help meeting three of the requirements for its accumulation, namely the reproduction of labor power, the production of surplus value, and the realization of surplus value. This leads them to conclude that non-coordinated efforts, claims for inclusion, and the invocation of specific differences are far from solving the problem if they are not part of a broader effort that understands the structural nature of the issue. Finally, they emphasize the specific conditions that differentiate the development of capitalism and the situation of women in this region from elsewhere, as well as the cultural and institutional characteristics that have contributed to the relegation of women in Latin America over time.

In Chapter 2, Rafael Alvarado, Pablo Ponce, and Danny Granda hypothesize that the disadvantages that women face in the labor market and the formation of human capital should have had some effect on the output level of the countries in the region. Consequently, they examine the relationship among the labor and human capital gender gaps (measured as the difference in the participation in the labor market of men and women and the difference between the average years of education of men and women, respectively) and the output in Latin America in the period comprised between 1990 and 2017. By using panel data econometric techniques, the authors found that, although there does not seem to be a significant relationship between the labor gap and the real output (except for high-income countries of the region), there is a negative and significant association between the human capital gap and the real output. Their results suggest that policies aimed at reducing the human capital gap between men and women (where these still exist) or preventing them from increasing (where they have been closed) can favor output growth, both in the short and long term.

In Chapter 3, through critiquing and complementing Roswitha Scholz' ideas on value dissociation theory with the work on the emergence of patriarchal capitalism by Silvia Federici, Josefina Rosales proposes some hypotheses for explaining the phenomenon of growing precarization of women's lives and labor in the Global South—with particular emphasis on Latin America—and the multiplication and prominence of struggles for the reproduction of life in the region. The author sees the precarization of labor and life in the Global South as a mechanism of extraction of absolute surplus value under the context of a capitalist-patriarchal-racist system. Thus, she concludes that the problem of growing precarization cannot be addressed solely by cultural changes and inclusion policies. Nor the power of capital (and of wage) to demand and extract labor will be necessarily undermined solely by demanding payment for women's reproductive labor. Finally, Rosales argues that the growing power struggles for the reproduction of life and in defense of common goods have gained over the last four decades in Latin America are, in fact, a response to such incessant precarization of life.

In Chapter 4, Claudia Maldonado-Erazo and Pablo Quiñonez carry out an exploratory bibliometric study to provide an overview of the current situation and historical evolution of academic research published in high impact journals in the intersection of the areas of gender and economics in the region. The authors found that, even though these two areas have been closely linked in the research on gender issues since their very emergence in Latin America, there is an absence of a substantial number of major producers, which could be linked with the youthfulness of the subject in the region. Furthermore, and concordantly with worldwide tendencies, they found that most of the authors working on these issues were women and located at Western centers of knowledge such as the United States and the United Kingdom. Finally, it was noticed that transitory researchers in the field were predominant and that about 50% of the research had been published in journals located at the highest-impact quartile.

1.2   *Part 2: Ecuador*

In Chapter 5, Esteban Arévalo analyzes the gender imaginary in Ecuador by taking a historical journey through the events that influenced its formation. The author starts by presenting an overview of the problem of gender inequality in Ecuador. Then, through the analysis of bibliographic sources, the events that influenced the established gender ideal for women were explored chronologically. This necessarily begins in the fifteenth century with the imaginary in Spain and America. The abuse of women during the Spanish invasion and colonial society is subsequently explored in the context of the introduction of racially-based social structuring. The author argues that neither independence nor the republic brought about substantial changes for the benefit of women—only in the twentieth century was there interest in understanding gender inequality and a struggle to overcome it. His analysis then turns to the indigenous movement and Feminism, which have been influential in generating changes in women's situations. Arévalo concludes that the problem of gender inequality and violence against women is highly related to the naturalization of such an imaginary that persists in the Ecuadorian and Latin American society.

The purpose of Chapter 6, by Ximena Songor-Jaramillo and Carlos Moreno-Hurtado, was to determine gender wage differentials in Ecuador for the years 2007 and 2017 using cross-sectional data taken from the Ecuadorian National Survey of Employment, Unemployment, and Underemployment. The methodology used by the authors corresponds to a detailed decomposition of wages based on unconditional quantiles, with correction for selection bias. They found that although in 2007 the real hourly wage received by men was higher than that received by women, this gap bridged by 2017. However, they identified a statistically significant and stable factor that explains the wage gaps in the two years: discrimination against women. Although in 2017 there is a notable reduction in the magnitude of this coefficient and thus the magnitude of discrimination against women, this was proven to be a factor that structurally remains in the Ecuadorian labor market.

In Chapter 7, Diana Morán, Diana Cabrera, and María Moreno aimed to find whether there is overpricing of products through gender-related price discrimination in the Ecuadorian market. For doing so, they focused on the city of Guayaquil, one of the most populated in the country, and found the existence of a 'pink tax' in several of the categories included in their study. They argue that understanding how the capitalist system socially constructs gender identities, the sexual division of labor, the symbolism of the body, and consumption patterns renders it possible to identify a new mode of sale where prices are determined and differentiated according to the 'needs' of each gender. Thus, Morán, Cabrera, and Moreno conclude that the social construction of genders is being used by companies to impose surcharges on consumers. They maintain that drawing attention to this problem could help reduce inequality and discrimination against consumers that are developed through market instruments, and thus, their results could be used by policymakers to protect consumers, as it has happened in other parts of the globe.

Chapter 8 moves to the political arena. Here, Gabriela Gallardo sought to deepen understandings of the political representation of women in Ecuador, through interviews with female assembly members. She argues that the representation of the National Assembly of Ecuador in the period 2013–2017 is a paradigmatic case for the region and the country since at no other point in history had the number of female elected members been higher in the Ecuadorian legislature. Her research explored the model of representation from three perspectives: formal, descriptive, and substantive. This was augmented by adopting an intersectoral approach to gender, race, age, feminist identity, origin, and personal experiences. She concludes that, in the case of Ecuador, women legislators not always represent politically according to their gender. In the period under analysis, their representation was influenced by several factors, including the political context, the country's institutions, and their identity. Her results provide an important backdrop for framing a debate on the relationship between women in the legislature, their identities, and the way they represent, challenging current notions of political representation.

1.3   *Part 3: Rural and Indigenous Women in Ecuador*
Chapter 9 by Ana V. Recalde and Daniel Zea seeks to elucidate the importance of peasant women's economy in Ecuador, which, they argue, is inevitably marginalized within agrarian capitalism. For achieving their purpose, the authors

analyze various socioeconomic and political dynamics promoted by the Ecuadorian government, which threaten peasant women's economies and therefore threaten their decision-making power and ability to sustain themselves
and their families. Recalde and Zea notice that up to this day, rural societies in
Ecuador usually (but not always) maintain socially constructed, traditional
gender roles, which lead to a clear gender division of labor. This chapter reviews these roles vis-à-vis how policies and laws developed by the Ecuadorian
State affect peasant women. The authors conclude that both the current development model in Ecuador and the regulation of the agricultural sector exclude
peasant' women's economies, despite the importance of their contributions.
Women in Ecuador have been protagonists in propositioning numerous alternatives to the hegemony of productivist rural economies, even though policy
interventions have made almost no effort to fulfill the country's food sovereignty regime.

Chapter 10 by Diana Cabrera, Edwin Espinoza, and Ana Oña analyzes income inequality, working conditions, and satisfaction between genders and
ethnic groups in Ecuador. For doing so, the authors started with descriptive
statistical analysis and then delved into an econometric study. Their results
show that women's income is, in general, lower than that of men in the country. Further, both men and women of non-white ethnicities generally perceive
lower incomes and work in unfavorable conditions. In addition, people who
consider themselves *montubios* and indigenous were found to experience the
greatest job dissatisfaction. The authors conclude by making a call for action
regarding public policies aimed to improve women's and ethnic groups' access
to higher-skilled and higher-income-generating activities.

Chapter 11, by María Anchundia, Wendy Mora, and Sayonara Morejón, studies the experience of the Association of Agro-Artisanal Women (AMA) in Ecuador. The authors draw on feminist economic theory and notions of the solidarity economy to make visible the contributions of these women to the economy,
the gender-based discrimination they have faced in the process, and the importance of the principle of solidarity in economic activities. In this chapter,
the authors identify the factors that influenced the emergence of the AMA and
its continued survival, as well as its achievements and the tensions that have
been faced in the development of the organization's activities. They highlight
the contributions of women artisans both with their paid and unpaid jobs to
the economy and their ancestral practices in the use of banana fibers for processing and weaving. Further, the authors argue that the progress of women's
organizations in the Global South vis-à-vis the achievement of rights and the
enactment of policies to enhance women's productive initiatives should not be
underestimated.

References

Abbassi, J., and Lutjens, S. (2002). "Introduction. Theory, Themes, and the Realities of Gender in Latin America." In J. Abbassi and S. Lutjens (Eds.), *Rereading Women in Latin America and the Caribbean: The Political Economy of Gender*. Rowman & Littlefield Publishers.

Barrett, M. (1992). "Words and things: Materialism and method in contemporary feminist analysis." In M. Barrett and A. Phillips (Eds.), *Destabilizing Theory: Contemporary Feminist Debates* (pp. 201–219). Stanford University Press.

Gargallo, F. (2004). *Las ideas feministas latinoamericanas*. Universidad Autónoma de la Ciudad de México.

Gargallo, F. (Ed.). (2010). *Antología del pensamiento feminista nuestroamericano. Tomo I: Del anhelo a la emancipación*. Biblioteca Ayacucho.

Rivera Berruz, S. (2018). "Latin American Feminism." In E. Zalta (Ed.), *The Stanford Encyclopedia of Philosophy* (Winter 2018). Metaphysics Research Lab, Stanford University. https://plato.stanford.edu/archives/win2018/entries/feminism-latin-america/.

Segal, L. (1999). *Why Feminism?: Gender, Psychology, Politics*. Columbia University Press.

Stilwell, F. (2012). *Political Economy. The Contest of Economic Ideas* (3rd ed.). Oxford University Press.

United Nations Development Programme. (2019). *Human Development Report 2019. Beyond income, beyond averages, beyond today: Inequalities in human development in the 21st century*.

PART 1

Latin America

∴

An Overview of Gender Inequality in Latin America from a Political Economy Perspective

Pablo Quiñonez and Claudia Maldonado-Erazo

1 Introduction

Marked inequalities characterize the economic system in which we live. Income inequality—the most common economic inequality measure—has increased in most countries in the last decades (Alvaredo et al. 2018). The world's richest 1 percent have now more than twice the wealth of the poorest 6.9 billion people (Coffey et al. 2020). At the same time, despite the progress achieved on poverty reduction over the last decades, almost half of the world's population lives on less than 5.50 dollars a day (World Bank 2018).

In this context, it is not difficult to explain the rising public interest in inequality over the last years. However, for political economy, the study of inequality has always been one of the major concerns. In fact, for David Ricardo—one of the most prominent classical economists—determining the laws that regulate the distribution of the "produce of the earth" between classes is "the principal problem in Political Economy" (Ricardo 2001: 7). Nevertheless, in the last century, with the predominance of neoclassical economic theory, the field has been sometimes sided to a "somewhat modest existence" on the peripheries of mainstream academic research, as put by Sandmo (2015: 5).

As suggested by Stilwell (2012), this imbalance can and has to be redressed. If we want to understand the causes of economic inequalities and propose feasible solutions, we must look back at some crucial concepts in political economy analysis. Nevertheless, we must consider that these disparities do not only exist between rich and poor people or between classes, as traditionally depicted. There are also marked inequalities determined by the ethnic origin of human beings or by their sex (and, more specifically, by the socially constructed roles for men and women).

In such context, if we want to understand what shapes the *gender* dimension of economic inequalities—as is the purpose of this chapter, with particular emphasis on Latin America—we must adopt a (critical) political economy perspective that takes into account both dimensions of inequality (class and gender).

When we talk about gender, we refer to a concept that is particularly relevant in contemporary social sciences and, as already hinted above, used for the analysis of the identities and roles assigned by society to men and women—and their historical and cultural formation. Notably, as pointed out by Herdoíza (2015), it has proven to be especially useful for understanding the inequalities arising from such differentiation, since these are not necessarily based on biological differences.

However, despite the intrinsic and instrumental importance of eradicating gender inequalities,[1] the visibility that the issue has gained, and the progress observed in recent years, there are still gaps that need to be closed. For instance, regarding the economic sphere, all over the globe men tend to earn, on average, more than women; women are over-represented in low-paying jobs and underrepresented in senior positions, and they dedicate considerable more time to unpaid activities than men (Ortiz-Ospina and Roser 2020; Woetzel et al. 2015).

Such a generalized situation is rooted in the way we have organized our society over time. At first sight, one could point to the governing power structure in which women are subordinate to men as the primary cause. After all, patriarchal structures have been present in most parts of the world for a long time. However, it was not until the appearance of industrial capitalism and massive urbanization processes that the contemporaneous division of labor between men and women emerged. Thus, the disparities between them adopted a new nature in the context of the new mode of production.

Therefore, if we want to talk about the political economy of gender inequality (in Latin America and elsewhere), we should consider it in terms of the relationship between capitalism and patriarchy—which in turn will allow us to consider both the gender and class dimensions of inequality, as expressed in the preceding paragraphs. In this chapter, we will follow the framework proposed by Frank Stilwell (2012), who uses the Marxist model of the circuit of capital and situates gender inside the sequential conditions for capital accumulation. Stilwell argues that gender inequalities can be seen as functional for capital as they help three of the requirements necessary for its expansion to be met, namely the reproduction of labor power, the production of surplus value, and the realization of surplus value.

By doing so, Stilwell structures a very comprehensive framework for explaining the political economy of gender inequality that includes several lines

---

1   In general, the intrinsic aspect of inequality is related to the philosophical and ethical debates around inequality per se. In contrast, its instrumental aspect refers to the effects that it has on the economy and society.

of research pursued by (Marxist) feminist scholarship over the last decades. Indeed, one could not think about the contemporaneous debate on the reproduction of labor power—carried out by women inside their homes—or on the inequality conditions that women face in waged labor if it were not for the pioneering work of authors such as Margaret Benston (1969), Mariarosa Dalla Costa and Selma James (1975), Silvia Federici (2004), Sylvia Walby (1986), among others. Probably, the less visible and less explored relationship between gender inequalities and capital accumulation that Stilwell introduces is the one related to the realization of surplus value.

This approach will lead us in a different path that the pursued by some difference/cultural/postmodern perspectives that have gained predominance from the 1990s—in a sort of victory of 'words' over 'things' (Barrett 1992). Not that these do not matter, but as we will argue in this chapter, in a move towards gender equality, for real change to take place, social and economic structures must be at the center of the debate.

This chapter is structured as follows. The three subsequent sections focus on explaining how gender inequalities are functional for capital accumulation since they help meet the requirements for its expansion. Specifically, section two focuses on the reproduction of labor power, section three on the production of surplus value, and section four on the realization of surplus value. Finally, conclusions are presented in the last section.

2   The Reproduction of Labor Power

The first necessary condition for capital accumulation—and for the very existence of capital and for the functioning of any economic system—is the reproduction of labor power. This involves the birth, raising and education of children, care activities and household chores, etc. In short, all the tasks that allow the present and future workforce to be in optimal market conditions. However, it is the household, not the firm, which directly assumes its cost;[2] and, within the household, it is women who carry out most of the aforementioned non-remunerated activities.

Such sexual division of labor characterizes most societies in the world. It is often explained by neoclassical economic theory as a "simple outcome of

---

2   On this issue Marx makes an interesting point in *Das Kapital*'s chapter on Simple Reproduction: "The maintenance and reproduction of the working-class is, and must ever be, a necessary condition to the reproduction of capital. But the capitalist may safely leave its fulfillment to the laborer's instincts of self-preservation and of propagation" (Marx 2001: 821).

rational choice and economic efficiency" as individuals, pursuing their own interest, organize work in an efficient manner (Folbre 1994: 4), or as an "inevitable consequence of biological differences in procreation" by modernization theorists (Laslett and Brenner 1989: 384).

Nevertheless, these definitions fail to acknowledge, among other factors, how asymmetric power relations have influenced choices around labor division across societies and over time, and how the organization of labor (and social) reproduction goes well beyond procreation and is determined, at least partly, by economic, political, and gender struggles (Brenner and Laslett 1986).

Strictly speaking, the mere biological reproduction of the workforce does not require any specific family structure, as explained by Stilwell (2012). Yet the gendered division of labor within households that has predominated since the development of industrial capitalism has proven to serve the needs of the capitalist economy as unpaid women's domestic work ends up being a sort of subsidy for capitalist employers. Domestic labor produces use values for the reproduction of workers and their families, despite standing outside capitalist marketed production processes (Beechey 1977).

This does not mean that gender inequality or that the sexual division of labor began with capitalism. Patriarchal structures were already there, and what capitalism did was readjust these relationships to its logic and subordinate them to its specific requirements (Murillo and D'Atri 2018). Authors such as Arruzza (2014) and Federici (2018) go beyond this idea. They argue that the transformations that allowed capitalism to be born—and that meant the separation of the producers from the means of production—radically transformed the relation between production and reproduction, separating them one from another and each one of them being carried out by men (production, waged) or women (reproduction, non-waged). In turn, as the relations between men and women (within and outside households) are mediated by their relations to the capitalist conditions of production and reproduction (Gimenez 2005), the fact that women carry out most of the non-waged reproductive work has ended up affecting them in terms of autonomy, decision-making processes, etc.

Additionally, the reproduction of labor power has to be understood in the context of the broader process of social reproduction, which includes all the manual, mental, and emotional work required to provide the care necessary to uphold present life and to reproduce the next generation (Laslett and Brenner 1989). In this connection, as social reproduction has become subordinated to the commodification and alienation of labor (Bakker 2007), not only it contributes to capital accumulation but also permits the perpetuation of capitalism itself as well as the class, ethnic and gender inequalities that are crucial for its functioning.

In the 1970s and 1980s, these discussions on social reproduction had already put their focus on the domestic labor of women as such sort of subsidy on capitalist reproduction under Fordism. Nevertheless, in recent years they have been evolving to consider the progressively privatized arrangements of social provisioning and risk that have emerged in the current era of neoliberalism in the global economy, where capitalist market relations have increasingly infiltrated social reproduction—although much of the household production still has a non-capitalist character (Stilwell 2012).

If the consolidation of welfare and developmental states after World War II meant that family wages and the intervention of the state alleviated to some extent the externalization of the social reproduction costs to women in the households, the rise of neoliberalism has reprivatized social reproduction again (Bakker 2007). This increased women's reproductive non-remunerated labor and their responsibility for income generation (Elson 1991), thus increasing their total amount of work.

Moreover, in developing economies, forced international migration created a care deficit for families that women had to leave behind in their home countries, as discussed by Ehrenreich and Hochschild (2003). This resulted in more reproductive work done by other female members of the household (grandmothers and daughters, for instance), while it also meant cheap labor power for care and domestic activities in the developed world, where several of these activities had been marketized.

In Latin America, the *lost decade* and the arrival of neoliberalism meant that a growing number of women had to participate in remunerated work, but at the same time they maintained their domestic responsibilities as gendered roles, norms, and values did not change (González de la Rocha 2002). Interestingly enough, after analyzing cases in Central America and the Caribbean, Safa (2002) argued that most of the women that were driven into paid employment considered it a part of their domestic role, as their goal was to contribute with the household economy.[3]

This perception might have changed in the last decades, as more women have entered the waged labor force, and their educational level has grown considerably, yet as Figure 1.1 shows, women still carry out most of the unpaid domestic and care work in the region. Figure 1.1 displays the average number of

---

3 It has to be considered that women from poor households and ethnic groups such as African descendants and indigenes have had to work to contribute to the survival of the household way before neoliberalism hit the region, in contrast to what happened in most Western industrial societies. This meant a double burden for women as they maintained their reproductive roles.

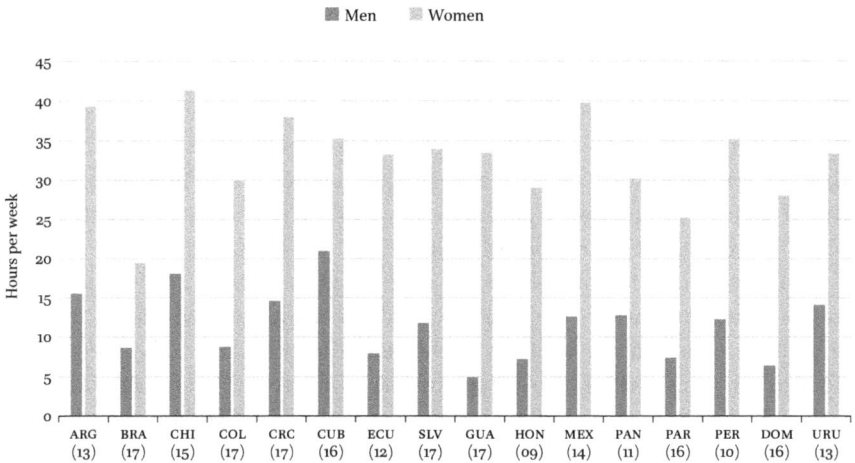

FIGURE 1.1: Hours per week dedicated to unpaid domestic and care work
SOURCE: ECLAC (2020)
NOTE: MOST RECENT YEAR FOR WHICH DATA IS AVAILABLE FOR EACH
COUNTRY. YEARS ARE IN BRACKETS.

hours that men and women dedicate per week to unpaid domestic and care work in several Latin American countries. Although there is no comparable time-series data for all the countries, all the 16 economies portrayed in the graph evidence that women are doing a disproportionate amount of unpaid domestic and care work—at least twice as men do in all countries, except Cuba—and in some cases, it exceeds the standard length of a working week (40 hours). In 2015 in Chile, for instance, women dedicated, on average, around 41 hours per week to such activities, whereas men dedicated 18. In Mexico, in 2014, women dedicated, on average, 40 hours to unpaid domestic work, while men dedicated around 12. When considering the overall level of unpaid work (not only that dedicated to domestic and care activities), a similar reality emerges.

However, if the unpaid domestic and care work performed by women had been given a monetary value, it would have been equivalent to 18% of the GDP in the case of Mexico; 16.3% in the case of Uruguay; 14.1% in the case of Peru; and 11.8% in the case of Ecuador. Moreover, in the case of Ecuador, the contribution of this activity to GDP would have been higher than that of oil extraction (11.3%) and similar to that of construction (11.8%), as pointed out by the Economic Commission for Latin America and the Caribbean (ECLAC 2016a).

Globally, the figures are compelling. Women do around 75% of all unpaid care work. Under very conservative assumptions, such work could amount to as much as 10 trillion dollars per year—around 13% of global GDP in 2015, according to Woetzel et al. (2015), or around 10.8 trillion dollars, according to a more recent estimate (Coffey et al. 2020). The accumulation of capital, a fundamental feature of the economic system in which we live, is strongly supported by the unpaid work performed by women at home.

3   The Production of Surplus Value

A second necessary condition for accumulation is the production of *surplus value*.[4] In this case, for Stilwell (2012), the central point of the debate is related to the gendered character of waged work. As he explains, women tend to be overly represented in occupations that are seen as extensions of their traditional household work, such as nursing, cooking, primary education, etc.[5] In turn, such labor market segmentation is strongly associated with gendered wage inequalities, as average wages tend to be lower for jobs that are considered as characteristically female.

But does this pattern respond to a genuine and objective choice on education and career paths, or does it reflect more complex processes of socialization that end up influencing women's decisions? If the first option were true, as mainstream economists often argue,[6] then the persistence of gender wage gaps would not be an actual problem, as they would be, in theory, reflecting gender differences in *human capital* formation (Stilwell 2019). Nevertheless, several empirical studies that have used a human capital approach for studying wage gaps have found that a considerable part of those gaps could indeed be attributable to gender discrimination, even when controlling for numerous other factors (see, for instance, Blau and Kahn 2000; Kunze 2005).

Regardless of the reduction of the gender wage gap in the last decades (Blau and Kahn 2008), the growing awareness of the problem, and the changes in legislation, the aforementioned gender differences in occupation and industry are still more important than conventional human capital variables when explaining such gap[7] (Blau and Kahn 2017).

---

4   Surplus value is a concept developed by Marx to refer to the additional value created by the wage-earner over and above the value of his labor force.

5   For a comprehensive analysis of this issue, see Witz (1992).

6   For a summary of some other recent explanations for gender differences in labor market outcomes, see Gielen and Zimmermann (2012).

7   Despite the cited study focuses on the U.S., much of what it shows can apply to other countries, as explained by the authors.

On the other hand, from a critical perspective, socialization processes originating during childhood and discrimination in labor markets and workplaces are often seen as the reasons behind such labor market segmentations. For instance, a study by Bian et al. (2017) found evidence pointing to the idea that gendered notions of brilliance are acquired early in the life of individuals and that these stereotypes immediately influence the interests of children, discouraging women later in their life to pursuit various prestigious careers. Besides, as Carli et al. (2016) summarize, there is a degree of "incongruity in the perceived traits of women with those called for in various social roles" (p. 245)—especially high-status occupational roles. As initially explained, women's roles in the labor market are often associated with their care role in the household, and, as put by Folbre (2012), whether or not biological aspects also play a role, social institutions have considerably amplified their impact.

In Latin America (and in the Hispanic Caribbean), additional cultural and historical factors are also present. As explained by Safa (2002), from colonial times, the Spanish *casa/calle* distinction—nurtured by Catholicism—meant that "women were relegated to the home and men to the street as a way of maintaining family honor and female virginity" (p. 56). However, neither the poor nor the subordinated ethnic groups followed this distinction entirely— due to the necessity of all the household members to work to contribute to the survival of the family—later on causing greater stigmatization of women's waged work than in other industrializing countries, as it was associated with these groups of the society.

In the present, despite the gaps have been reduced over the last decades, women in Latin America still perceive lower levels of wages than men irrespective of their preparation, as can be hinted by seeing at Figure 1.2, which plots the female-to-male ratio of mean urban wages according to individuals' level of education in the region (measured by years of schooling). When the overall level of income is considered and rural areas are included, the gaps become even more prominent.

Furthermore, despite economically active women in Latin America nowadays have, on average, more years of schooling than their male counterpart, their wages and overall level of income[8] are still lower than those of men. Although the income gap has been decreasing over the last decades, by 2017, women's mean income represented only 80.9% of men's income, while their average years of schooling represented 109.9% of those of men, according to data from ECLAC (2020).

---

8   Due to the high proportion of own-account workers in the region, looking at income levels— and not only at wages—is also important.

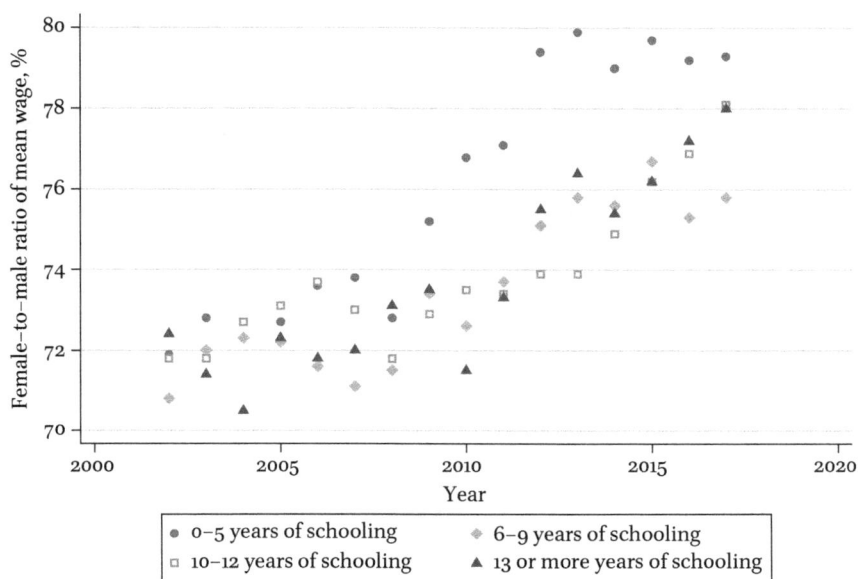

FIGURE 1.2   Female-to-male urban wage ratios in Latin America according to years of schooling
SOURCE: ECLAC (2020)
NOTE: WEIGHTED REGIONAL AVERAGES ARE PRESENTED. POPULATION AGED 15 AND OVER IS CONSIDERED.

Going back to the labor market segmentation, in South America, 78% of employed women are working in low-technology intensive areas—which among other issues, tends to mean lower wages. This problem is even more critical in Central America, where 88.2% of employed women are working on these sectors. Here, the presence of women in the *maquiladora* industry could be an explanation (ECLAC 2019). Overall, a higher proportion of women in Latin America are working in low productivity sectors (agriculture, trade, and services, as defined by ECLAC) than men. Even though the participation of both men and women in this sector has decreased over time, the proportion of men employed in low productivity sectors has diminished considerably faster than the proportion of women, as can be seen in Figure 1.3. On average, 55.2% of employed men worked on low productivity sectors by 2017, whereas 77.6% of employed women worked in the same sectors, according to ECLAC (2020).

As in most parts of the globe, the higher feminization of these sectors is associated with higher levels of wage gaps between men and women, even after controlling for variables such as age, education, presence of young children in

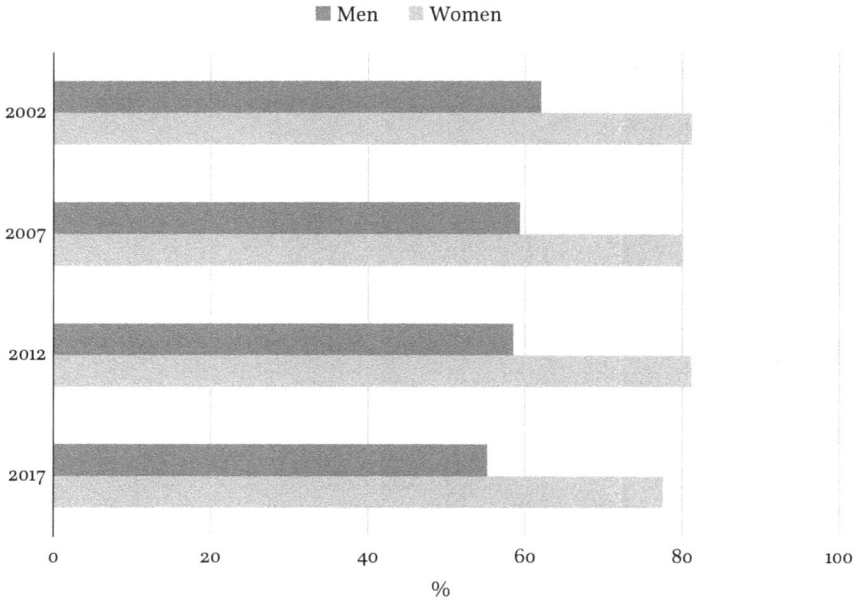

FIGURE 1.3   Percentage of the employed population working in low productivity sectors in
             Latin America
             SOURCE: ECLAC (2020)
             NOTE: WEIGHTED REGIONAL AVERAGES ARE PRESENTED.

the household, hours worked per week, etc., as estimated by the International Labour Organization (ILO 2019).

In a broader perspective, controlling for these variables is relevant as it allows comparisons between individuals with the same observable characteristics, therefore providing estimates on the equality of remuneration for 'equivalent' work (understood as work with the same characteristics).

Globally, there is a widespread awareness about this topic—a study by the World Economic Forum (2018) found, for instance, a clear and generalized perception across the globe that women earn less than men for comparable work. Additionally, although they have been disappearing across time, there are still some explicit discriminatory practices that define different wage rates for women and men (for example, in the agricultural sector) in some collective agreements and minimum wage instruments (Lexartza Artza et al. 2019).

Overall, women's wages are, on average, 24% lower than men's wages in the world (UN Women 2015). Although this distribution may be biased due to the higher incidence of part-time work among women, even after accounting for this factor, significative differences persist, with women being paid, on average, around 20% less than men (ILO 2018; Stilwell and Jordan 2007).

In an approximation focused on Latin America and the Caribbean, women's hourly wages are, on average, only 83% of what men's wages are, according to ILO's estimates (ILO 2019). This is considerably similar to ECLAC's estimate for women in urban areas in the region who work full-time and earn, on average, only 83.9% of what men earn (ECLAC 2016b).

Finally, as Lexartza Artza et al. (2019) argue, in addition to the aforementioned horizontal segregation in the labor market (i.e., the concentration of women in certain waged activities and men in different activities), the vertical segregation should be mentioned as well. The latter is related to the generalized difficulty that women experience in accessing the higher levels of the hierarchical structure in the workplace (this situation is often referred to as *glass ceilings*) concentrating them in the technical, non-strategic and less responsibility—and therefore lower-paid—positions (Ardanche and Celiberti 2011). As an example of this issue, in Latin America, fewer women are employed in senior and middle management than men, as shown in Figure 1.4, which plots the percentage of individuals in such positions who are women for seven countries of the region updated data is available. Although not even developed economies have solved this issue, most of the countries in the region exhibit a lower share than industrialized economies such as the United States (40.5%) or Sweden (39.4%).

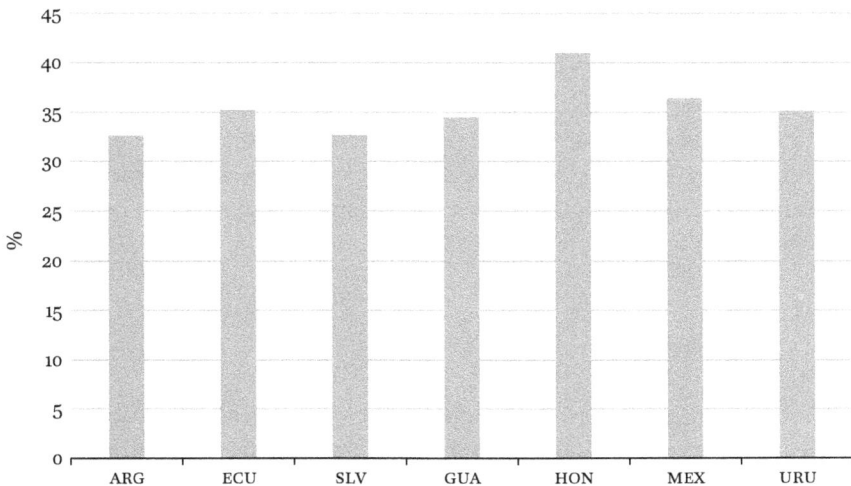

FIGURE 1.4   Female share of employment in senior and middle management, 2017
SOURCE: ILO (2020)

Furthermore, there is evidence that shows that the gender wage gap widens not only at the top but sometimes also at the bottom of the distribution, even when the characteristics of work are the same for men and women (Picchio and Mussida 2011). Thus, women are also affected by what is often referred to as *sticky floors*. It might be especially problematic in countries such as the ones in Latin America, where people at the bottom of the distribution, in general, experience more severe difficulties than in developed economies.

But how is this whole situation connected to capital accumulation? Initially, various Marxist scholars applied the idea of the reserve army of labor in this context. They argued that women might have become a common source of industrial reserve army and could be both paid wages that are lower than their labor power value and brought into (and disposed of) production as production's conditions changed (see, for instance, Beechey 1977). Nevertheless, among other criticism (see, for instance, Anthias 1980), the growing participation of women in the labor market as a permanent workforce (in contrast to what happened, for instance, during and immediately after World War II) has weakened this argument.

But even if we disregard such idea, it is clear, as Stilwell (2012) argues, that the gendered division of waged labor (but also the discrimination present in the labor market) helps to the production of surplus value—and, therefore, to capital accumulation—by keeping down the overall cost of wages. This is the direct result of the wages of women being lower than the wages of men, and the indirect result of gendered divisions among workers that undermine their collective bargaining power.

This is based on the core idea that, under normal conditions, the cheaper the labor, the greater the production of surplus value, and therefore, the higher the profits and the accumulation of capital. It is also based on the reasoning that lower levels of workers' organization and rights confer higher amounts of power to employers. This general framework has led some authors to conclude that due to the prevailing gender regime, women workers end up being a sort of cheap labor force par excellence (Wilson 2003).

4   The Realization of Surplus Value

The third condition for capital accumulation is the realization of surplus value. This means the conversion of surplus value into profit resulting from the sale of commodities that capitalist firms have produced. Here, Stilwell (2012) argues that despite both men and women are consumers (and, therefore, both contribute to the realization of surplus value), women tend to manage a larger share of the process of consumption,[9] especially that one related to day-to-day food and household items[10]—which is something evidently linked to its role in social reproduction.

In this context, advertising targets women to incentivize consumption based on widespread ideas of gender roles, thus perpetuating sexist stereotypes. This occurs because, among other things, advertising shows and reinforces aspirational social models, playing a critical socializing role (Giles 2003). In this connection, recent evidence has shown that, despite the progressive inclusion of women in different spheres, gender stereotyping in advertising still prevails in many countries around the world (Grau and Zotos 2016)–and Latin America is no exception (see, for instance, Uribe et al. 2008; Villar García et al. 2016).

But this problem does not end there. A further issue labeled as the 'pink tax' has been identified by several authors, and we consider that must be included in this discussion. A 'pink tax' refers to a situation in which products intended for consumption by women—despite being equivalent or comparable in their composition to those existing for men—tend to be more expensive than those for men. Numerous studies have identified a phenomenon of this sort for several products and services (see, for instance, Bessendorf 2015; Duesterhaus et al. 2011; Whittelsey and Carroll 1995).

Even when women are aware of the situation mentioned above and find it unfair, research has found that they may still be willing to pay such premiums (Stevens and Shanahan 2012). Such an attitude does not seem to fit in the 'rational' behavior economic assumption, but it may demonstrate that the

---

9   With industrialization and urbanization, under the logic of a male breadwinner, the role of women became focused on the management of the household consumption (Galbraith 1975). However, empirical studies on the gendered nature of household consumption are rather scant. A 2008 Boston Consulting Group study conducted in several countries provided relevant information on this issue, and their results are indeed aligned with the argument presented here (see Silverstein and Sayre 2009). But apart from this, most of the debate focuses on the u.s. case. In such context, various news, magazine articles, and business books have been previously criticized because neither they nor their cited sources provide any clear information on how such estimations were made. Nevertheless, different surveys made by private consultancies have found that more women claim to have primary responsibility for shopping decisions and for spending control in their households than men do (for a discussion on this issue, see Bialik 2011).

10 Conversely, women (especially those at the bottom of the income distribution) tend to have smaller participation in the decision on major household expenditures. For instance, in Latin America, 40% of women do not participate in such decisions (Muñoz Boudet 2011).

construction of the gendered self is partly achieved by consumer practices (Duesterhaus et al. 2011).

Although this topic has not yet been widely explored in Latin America, a surcharge paid by women, especially in personal care items—the most related with the idea of what is 'feminine'—has been identified in the context of specific areas or cities, for instance in the case of countries such as Argentina (see Confederación Argentina de Mediana Empresa 2019) and Ecuador (see Morán Chiquito et al. 2021).

5   Concluding Remarks

This chapter has tried to answer the question of what shapes the gender dimension of economic inequalities, focusing on Latin America. For doing so, we have adopted a political economy perspective that considers both the class and gender dimensions of inequality. Following Stilwell (2012), we have used the Marxist model of the circuit of capital, considering gender within the sequential conditions for capital accumulation, and arguing that gender inequalities can be seen as functional for capital as they help to guarantee that three crucial requirements for its expansion are met: the reproduction of labor power, the production of surplus value, and the realization of surplus value.

This allowed us to develop a foundational understanding of the issue that is widely applicable as women in Latin America and elsewhere share similar basic inequalities in relation to men in modern capitalism. However, some specific conditions differentiate women's situation in this region from their situation in other developing countries or the developed world. Moreover, there are differences in the historical development of capitalism within countries, making it necessaire to study each region carefully. This is why we have tried to ground the theory to the reality of Latin America.

Firstly, we analyzed how the gendered division of labor within the household that has predominated since the development of industrial capitalism has been functional to capital accumulation. This happens because labor's reproduction costs were externalized to the household (or indirectly—and only partially—to the State), thus becoming a subsidy for capitalists. For authors such as Dalla Costa and James (1997) and Federici (2018), the exploitation of female nonwage reproductive labor has been extremely effective precisely because of the lack of a wage hid it. In most countries of the region, women dedicate at least twice as many hours as men to unpaid domestic and care work, sometimes exceeding the typical duration of a working week. Under very conservative assumptions, if a monetary value were given to this work, it would have been equivalent to a considerable share of the national production, comparable, for instance, to economic activities such as oil extraction and construction in the case of Ecuador.

Secondly, we studied how the gendered division of labor and the discrimination present in labor markets are functional to the expansion of capital as they help to the production of surplus value by ensuring lower wages and diminished collective bargaining power for a sector of the population. Women's career choices and their under-representation in top-positions at work go well beyond the traditional explanations based on human capital theory and expected difficulties about reconciling a career with a family (Bian et al. 2017; Carli et al. 2016; Fogarty et al. 1981; Witz 1992). Instead, a political economy explanation is much more powerful when explaining these inequalities in outcomes.

As in various parts of the world, in Latin America, women earn, on average, less than men, even though their mean level of education is higher. They are over-represented in low productivity and informal sectors of the economy and under-represented in high-responsibility positions. However, in contrast to what happened in other regions across time, in Latin America, the model of the nuclear family living on the male breadwinner's wage has been historically limited to a reduced number of cases (González de la Rocha 2002). Work by women, youngsters, and even children has often been used by poor households—primarily indigenous, Afro-American, and ethnic minorities. In this context and considering the specific cultural and historical factors present in the region, such as the colonial Spanish *casa/calle* distinction, women's work has been stigmatized much more than in other industrializing countries, as it was associated with the least favored, as explained by Safa (2002). This became especially relevant with the increased waged labor participation of women in the last decades, and the economic restructuring that the arrival of neoliberalism meant. It took a long time for women's paid work to be seen differently (Acevedo 1995).

Thirdly, we analyzed how gender stereotypes and the attached aspirational social models are useful to incentivize consumption, given the role of women as administrators of day-to-day purchases, and incentivize certain consumer practices even when price discrimination against women is present. As in many regions of the world, in Latin America, gender stereotyping in advertising remains present, as well as some discriminatory price practices against women, based on such idealized social models. This is the less explored area of the chapter, as the research done on the field is very scant. Nevertheless, it is worth to be mentioned due to its theoretical value and to incentivize more in-depth scrutiny that widens the evidence here mentioned.

As stated at the beginning of this chapter, despite the progress achieved in eradicating gender economic inequalities, there are still several gaps that need to be closed. Nowadays, gender-based discrimination may not be a matter of individual choice for many anymore, yet it is still embedded in social and economic institutions and their usual functioning. Moreover, as gender inequalities are functional to the expansion of capital, non-coordinated efforts, the invocation of specific differences or simple claims for inclusion will not solve the problem, unless they are part of a broader political project looking for a real change in these core structures of domination, as put by Segal (1999).

This does not mean that a passive attitude should be adopted as the problem has deep structural roots. Rather, as Stilwell (2012) concludes, it means that for the movement for gender equality to be fully successful, a "struggle against the prevailing structures and interests of capital" is also required (p. 359). It does not mean either that Marxist feminist explanations for women's subordination under capitalism, such as the presented here, are exempt from the debate, as pointed out by Bhattacharya (2020), nor that the solutions are universal. As mentioned above, cultural and historical factors matter as well. In specific, in Latin America, as the relegation of women has been ideologically regarded as a part of the "natural order of things" and perpetuated by social institutions, including education, cultural praxis, and religion (Acosta-Belén and Bose 1995: 15) a deep understanding of them is also required to contribute to real change. Finally, although not analyzed here due to the specific focus of this chapter, the ethnic dimension of inequality must be considered as well, especially as women from ethnic minorities tend to be the most affected in Latin America and elsewhere.

References

Acevedo, L. (1995). "Feminist inroads in the study of women's work and development." In C. Bose and E. Acosta-Belén (Eds.), *Women in the Latin American Development Process*. Temple University Press.

Acosta-Belén, E., and Bose, C. (1995). "Colonialism, structural subordination, and empowerment: Women in the development process in Latin America and the Caribbean." In C. Bose and E. Acosta-Belén (Eds.), *Women in the Latin American Development Process* (pp. 15–37). Temple University Press.

Alvaredo, F., Chancel, L., Piketty, T., Saez, E., and Zucman, G. (2018). *World Inequality Report 2018*. Belknap Press.

Anthias, F. (1980). "Women and the Reserve Army of Labour: A Critique of Veronica Beechey." *Capital & Class* 4(1): 50–63. https://doi.org/10.1177/030981688001000105.

Ardanche, M., and Celiberti, L. (2011). *Entre el techo de cristal y el piso pegajoso. El trabajo como herramienta de inclusión en el Uruguay de 2011*. Cotidiano Mujer. www .cotidianomujer.org.uy/sitio/pdf/pub_trabajo11baja.pdf.

Arruzza, C. (2014, September). "Remarks on gender." *Viewpoint Magazine*. https://www .viewpointmag.com/2014/09/02/remarks-on-gender/.

Bakker, I. (2007). "Social reproduction and the constitution of a gendered political economy." *New Political Economy* 12(4): 541–556. https://doi.org/10.1080/13563460701661561.

Barrett, M. (1992). "Words and things: Materialism and method in contemporary feminist analysis." In M. Barrett and A. Phillips (Eds.), *Destabilizing Theory: Contemporary Feminist Debates* (pp. 201–219). Stanford University Press.

Beechey, V. (1977). "Some Notes on Female Wage Labour in Capitalist Production." *Capital & Class* 1(3): 45–66. https://doi.org/10.1177/030981687700300103.

Benston, M. (1969). "The Political Economy of Women's Liberation." *Monthly Review* 21(4): 13–27. https://doi.org/10.14452/MR-021-04-1969-08_2.

Bessendorf, A. (2015). *From Cradle to Cane: The Cost of Being a Female Consumer: A Study of Gender Pricing in New York City*. https://www1.nyc.gov/site/dca/partners/ gender-pricing-study.page.

Bhattacharya, T. (2020). "Liberating Women from 'Political Economy.' Margaret Benston's Marxism and a Social-Reproduction Approach to Gender Oppression." *Monthly Review* 71(8): 1–13. https://doi.org/10.14452/MR-071-08-2020-01_1.

Bialik, C. (2011, April 23). "Who Makes the Call at the Mall, Men or Women?" *The Wall Street Journal*, A2. https://www.wsj.com/articles/SB10001424052748703521304576278964279316994.

Bian, L., Leslie, S.-J., and Cimpian, A. (2017). "Gender stereotypes about intellectual ability emerge early and influence children's interests." *Science* 355(6323): 389–391. https://doi.org/10.1126/science.aah6524.

Blau, F.D., and Kahn, L.M. (2000). "Gender differences in pay." *Journal of Economic Perspectives* 14(4): 75–99. https://doi.org/10.1257/jep.14.4.75.

Blau, F.D., and Kahn, L.M. (2008). "Women's Work and Wages." In S. Durlauf and L. Blume (Eds.), *The New Palgrave Dictionary of Economics* (pp. 762–772). Palgrave Macmillan.

Blau, F.D., and Kahn, L.M. (2017). "The Gender Wage Gap: Extent, Trends, and Explanations." *Journal of Economic Literature* 55(3): 789–865. https://doi.org/10.1257/ jel.20160995.

Brenner, J., and Laslett, B. (1986). "Social reproduction and the family." In U. Himmelstrand (Ed.), *Sociology Crisis to Science: Volume 2. The Social Reproduction of Organization and Culture* (pp. 116–131). SAGE Publications Ltd.

Carli, L.L., Alawa, L., Lee, Y., Zhao, B., and Kim, E. (2016). "Stereotypes About Gender and Science : Women ≠ Scientists." *Psychology of Women Quarterly* 40(2): 244–260. https://doi.org/10.1177/0361684315622645.

Coffey, C., Espinoza Revollo, P., Harvey, R., Lawson, M., Parvez Butt, A., Sarosi, D., and Thekkudan, J. (2020). *Time to care. Unpaid and underpaid care work and the global inequality crisis*. OXFAM.

Confederación Argentina de Mediana Empresa. (2019). *Impuesto Rosa 2019*.

Dalla Costa, M., and James, S. (1975). *The Power of women and the subversion of the community*. Falling Wall Press Ltd.

Dalla Costa, M., and James, S. (1997). "Women and the Subversion of the Community." In R. Hennessy and C. Ingraham (Eds.), *Materialist Feminism: A Reader in Class, Difference, and Women's Lives* (pp. 40–53). Psychology Press.

Duesterhaus, M., Grauerholz, L., Weichsel, R., and Guittar, N.A. (2011). "The Cost of Doing Femininity: Gendered Disparities in Pricing of Personal Care Products and Services." *Gender Issues*, 28(4), 175–191. https://doi.org/10.1007/s12147-011-9106-3.

Economic Commission for Latin America and the Caribbean. (2016a). *Autonomía de las mujeres e igualdad en la agenda de desarrollo sostenible*. United Nations. https://repositorio.cepal.org/bitstream/handle/11362/40633/4/S1601248_es.pdf.

Economic Commission for Latin America and the Caribbean. (2016b). *Notes for Equality N°18* (Issue March). https://oig.cepal.org/sites/default/files/note_18_wage_gap_.pdf.

Economic Commission for Latin America and the Caribbean. (2019). *Women's autonomy in changing economic scenarios*. United Nations. https://repositorio.cepal.org/handle/11362/45037.

Economic Commission for Latin America and the Caribbean. (2020). *CEPALSTAT. Databases and Statistical Publications* [database]. https://estadisticas.cepal.org/cepalstat/.

Ehrenreich, B., and Hochschild, A. (Eds.). (2003). *Global Woman: Nannies, Maids and Sex Workers in the New Economy*. Metropolitan Books.

Elson, D. (1991). "Male Bias in Macro-economics: The Case of Structural Adjustment." In D. Elson (Ed.), *Male Bias in the Development Process* (pp. 164–190). Manchester University Press.

Federici, S. (2004). *Caliban and the Witch: Women, the Body, and Primitive Accumulation*. Autonomedia.

Federici, S. (2018). *El patriarcado del salario. Críticas feministas al marxismo*. Traficantes de Sueños.

Fogarty, M., Allen, I., and Walters, P. (1981). *Women in top jobs, 1968–1979*. Heinemann Educational.

Folbre, N. (1994). *Who pays for the kids? Gender and the structures of constraint*. Routledge.

Folbre, N. (2012). "Should Women Care Less? Intrinsic Motivation and Gender Inequality." *British Journal of Industrial Relations* 50(4): 597–619. https://doi.org/10.1111/bjir.12000.

Galbraith, J.K. (1975). *Economics and the Public Purpose*. The New American Library.

Gielen, A.C., and Zimmermann, K.F. (2012). "Equality and Fairness in the Labor Market." In F.D. Blau, A.C. Gielen, and K.F. Zimmermann (Eds.), *Gender, Inequality, and Wages.* Oxford University Press. https://doi.org/10.1093/acprof:oso/9780199665853.001.0001.

Giles, D. (2003). *Media Psychology.* Lawrence Erlbaum Associates, Inc.

Gimenez, M.E. (2005). "Capitalism and the oppression of women: Marx revisited." *Science and Society* 69(1): 11–32. https://doi.org/10.1521/siso.69.1.11.56797.

González de la Rocha, M. (2002). "The Urban Family and Poverty in Latin America." In J. Abbassi and S. Lutjens (Eds.), *Rereading Women in Latin America and the Caribbean. The Political Economy of Gender.* Rowman & Littlefield.

Grau, S.L., and Zotos, Y.C. (2016). "Gender stereotypes in advertising: A review of current research Gender stereotypes in advertising." *International Journal of Advertising* 35(5): 761–770. https://doi.org/10.1080/02650487.2016.1203556.

Herdoíza, M. (2015). *Construyendo Igualdad en la Educación Superior. Fundamentación y lineamientos para transversalizar los ejes de igualdad y ambiente.* SENESCYT/UNESCO.

International Labour Organization. (2018). *Global Wage Report 2018/19. What lies behind gender pay gaps.* ILO / International Labour Office. https://www.ilo.org/global/research/global-reports/global-wage-report/WCMS_650568.

International Labour Organization. (2019). *Women in the World of Work. Pending Challenges for Achieving Effective Equality in Latin America and the Caribbean.* ILO / Regional Office for Latin America and the Caribbean. https://www.ilo.org/americas/publicaciones/WCMS_736930.

International Labour Organization. (2020). *ILOSTAT database* [database]. https://ilostat.ilo.org/data/.

Kunze, A. (2005). "The evolution of the gender wage gap." *Labour Economics* 12(1): 73–97. https://doi.org/10.1016/j.labeco.2004.02.012.

Laslett, B., and Brenner, J. (1989). "Gender And Social Reproduction: Historical Perspectives." *Annual Review of Sociology* 15(1): 381–404. https://doi.org/10.1146/annurev.soc.15.1.381.

Lexartza Artza, L., Chaves Groh, M.J., Carcedo Cabañas, A., and Sánchez, A. (2019). *La brecha salarial entre hombres y mujeres en América Latina. En el camino hacia la igualdad salarial.* International Labour Organization.

Marx, K. (2001). *Capital. A Critique of Political Economy. Volume I.* The Electric Book Company.

Morán Chiquito, D., Cabrera Montecé, D., and Moreno Zea, M. (2021). "The Cost of Femininity: evidence for the City of Guayaquil." In P. Quiñonez and C. Maldonado-Erazo (Eds.), *Gender Inequality in Latin America. The Case of Ecuador* (pp. 158–179). Brill. https://doi.org/10.1163/9789004442917_009.

Muñoz Boudet, A.M. (2011, November). "América Latina: mujeres aún luchan por igualdad en trabajo y el hogar." *World Bank Blogs.* https://blogs.worldbank.org/es/latinamerica/am-rica-latina-mujeres-a-n-luchan-por-igualdad-en-trabajo-y-el-hogar.

Murillo, C., and D'Atri, A. (2018, September). "Producing and Reproducing: Capitalism's Dual Oppression of Women." *Left Voice Magazine*. https://www.leftvoice.org/on-reproductive-labor-wage-slavery-and-the-new-working-class.

Ortiz-Ospina, E., and Roser, M. (2020). *Economic inequality by gender*. Our World in Data. https://ourworldindata.org/economic-inequality-by-gender.

Picchio, M., and Mussida, C. (2011). "Gender wage gap: A semi-parametric approach with sample selection correction." *Labour Economics* 18(5): 564–578. https://doi.org/10.1016/j.labeco.2011.05.003.

Ricardo, D. (2001). *Principles of Political Economy and Taxation*. The Electric Book Company.

Safa, H. (2002). "Economic Restructuring and Gender Subordination." In J. Abbassi and S. Lutjens (Eds.), *Rereading Women in Latin America and the Caribbean. The Political Economy of Gender*. Rowman & Littlefield.

Sandmo, A. (2015). "The Principal Problem in Political Economy: Income Distribution in the History of Economic Thought." In A. Atkinson and F. Bourguignon (Eds.), *Handbook of Income Distribution* (1st ed., Vol. 2, pp. 3–65). Elsevier B.V. https://doi.org/10.1016/B978-0-444-59428-0.00002-3.

Segal, L. (1999). *Why Feminism?: Gender, Psychology, Politics*. Columbia University Press.

Silverstein, M., and Sayre, K. (2009). *Women Want More: How to Capture Your Share of the World's Largest, Fastest-Growing Market*. Harper Collins.

Stevens, J.L., and Shanahan, K.J. (2012). "Anger, Willingness, or Clueless? Understanding Why Women Pay a Pink Tax on the Products They Consume." In E. Stieler (Ed.), *Creating Marketing Magic and Innovative Future Marketing Trends* (pp. 571–575). Academy of Marketing Science. https://doi.org/10.1007/978-3-319-45596-9_108.

Stilwell, F. (2012). *Political Economy. The Contest of Economic Ideas* (3rd ed.). Oxford University Press.

Stilwell, F. (2019). *The Political Economy of Inequality*. Polity Press.

Stilwell, F., and Jordan, K. (2007). *Who Gets What? Analysing Economic Inequality in Australia*. Cambridge University Press.

UN Women. (2015). *Progress of the World's Women 2015–2016. Transforming Economies, Realizing Rights*. UN Women. https://www.unwomen.org/en/digital-library/publications/2015/4/progress-of-the-worlds-women-2015.

Uribe, R., Manzur, E., Hidalgo, P., and Fernández, R. (2008). "Estereotipos de género en la publicidad: un análisis de contenido de las revistas chilenas." *Academia, Revista Latinoamericana de Administración* 41: 1–18. http://www.redalyc.org/articulo.oa?id=71611842003.

Villar García, M.G., Mora Cantellano, M. del P., and Maldonado Reyes, A.A. (2016). "La construcción identitaria de género en las representaciones sociales de la publicidad de época en México. Una reflexión hacía la sustentabilidad cultural."

21° Encuentro Nacional Sobre Desarrollo Regional En México. http://ru.iiec.unam
.mx/3398/.

Walby, S. (1986). *Patriarchy at work: patriarchal and capitalist relations in employment.*
Polity Press.

Whittelsey, F., and Carroll, M. (1995). *Women Pay More: And How to Put a Stop to It.* New
Press.

Wilson, T.D. (2003). "Forms of Male Domination and Female Subordination: Home-
workers versus Maquiladora Workers in Mexico." *Review of Radical Political Economics* 35(1): 56–72. https://doi.org/10.1177/0486613402250194.

Witz, A. (1992). *Professions and Patriarchy.* Routledge.

Woetzel, J., Madgavkar, A., Ellingrud, K., Labaye, E., Devillard, S., Kutcher, E., Manyika,
J., Dobbs, R., and Krishnan, M. (2015). *The power of parity: How advancing women's
equality can add $12 trillion to global growth.* McKinsey Global Institute.

World Bank. (2018). *Poverty and Shared Prosperity 2018. Piecing Together the Poverty Puz-
zle.* World Bank. https://www.worldbank.org/en/publication/poverty-and-shared
-prosperity.

World Economic Forum. (2018). *The Global Gender Gap Report 2018.* World Economic
Forum.

CHAPTER 2

Labor and Human Capital Gender Gap and Economic Growth in Latin America

Rafael Alvarado, Pablo Ponce and Danny Granda

1 Introduction

Economic growth is one of the main macroeconomic aggregates that allows measuring the performance of the economic activity of a country or region. In Latin America, during the last 20 years, the growth of the economy has registered an increase of 55% according to data from the World Bank (2018), associated with different determinants such as public spending, foreign direct investment, the use of renewable energy, specialization, industrialization, and in particular due to the increase in the prices of natural resources (Alvarado et al. 2017). However, empirical literature has systematically omitted discrimination faced by women, whether in the labor market or in the educational factor (Castelló and Doménech 2002), and its implications on growth. It is well known that Latin America is one of the regions with the greatest inequality of income and opportunities worldwide. Although discrimination against women has been reduced in recent years, it has not yet been possible to eliminate educational inequality and participation in the labor market.

According to the statistics of the World Bank (2018), the percentage of women employed in Latin America increased from 39% in 1990 to 47% in 2018, while the percentage of employed men decreased from 77% to 71% in this same period. The difference between men and women in formal employment with access to social security and all labor benefits is more pronounced. On the other hand, in Latin America, the average years of schooling between men and women have undergone significant changes. According to Barro and Lee (2013), on average in 1990, the gap in years of education between men and women is 0.57, while by 2018 this has gone to 0.1 in favor of women, that is, in 1990 men registered more years of education than women and in 2018 this situation has been reversed. According to these data, it becomes important to analyze the impact of the labor gap and the schooling gap on economic growth in Latin America.

In recent years, some empirical research has been carried out on the importance of human capital and women's labor participation in the labor market. According to De Ibarrola (2009), Erten and Metzger (2019), and Heathcote et al.

(2017), the study of the participation of men and women in economic activity is essential to understand the levels of development. However, there is limited empirical evidence on the effect of the labor and human capital gap by sex as a determinant of economic growth in Latin America. In this context, the objective of this research is to verify if these gaps have had any effect on the product of the region and if the variables have an equilibrium relationship in the short and long term. The hypothesis of our research is that the reduction of the labor and human capital gap has a positive effect on the economic growth of the region. The labor gap is the difference in the participation in the labor market of men and women, while the human capital gap is the difference between the average years of education of men and women. The two variables constitute the independent variables of the model, while the dependent variable is the logarithm of the output at constant prices for 2010. The control variables include foreign direct investment, gross capital formation and urbanization rate. We use econometric strategies of cointegration with panel data, we also divide the countries according to their level of income based on the Atlas method of the World Bank (2018).

The main results of this research indicate that the reduction of the labor gap generated a positive effect on economic growth, while the reduction of the human capital gap increased economic growth only in the high-income countries of Latin America. The results of this research suggest that public policies should be aimed at reducing the labor and human capital gender gap in the long term in order to increase the region's product. Likewise, we found that there is no dependence on the cross sections, therefore, we used the unit root tests and the first generation cointegration test for panel data (Dickey and Fuller Augmented-ADF; Levin, Lin and Chu-LLC; and Phillips and Perron-PP) (Dickey and Fuller 1981; Levin et al. 2002; Phillips and Perron 1988). These results were contrasted with two non-parametric tests to ensure the robustness of the results found (Breitung-UB, and Im, Pesaran and Shin-IPS) (Breitung 2002; Im et al. 2003).

The rest of this chapter has the following structure: The second section contains the review of previous literature on the mechanisms that lead to educational and labor gaps affecting the output. The third section describes the statistical sources and raises the econometric strategy. The fourth section reports the results, which are discussed with the previous literature. The fifth section contains the research findings and possible policy implications.

2   Literature Review

Several studies on gender inequalities focus on analyzing wage gaps, but few analyze the labor gap between men and women, which would ultimately be the cause of wage disparities (He and Wu 2017). Gender inequality in general has been widely studied and several reports from multilateral organizations present a global perspective on the context in which this problem develops. For instance, according to the International Labor Organization, women are approximately 26% less likely to participate in the labor market compared to men and 10% more likely to be vulnerable workers (ILO 2018). The United Nations Development Program states that the Human Development Index (HDI) of women is 5.9% lower than that of men and the main causes are due to the minor income and education that women receive with respect to men (UNDP 2018). This situation is not only relevant from an ethical perspective but also has direct implications for the development of countries, since the poorest states have the highest levels of gender inequality (Dollar and Gatti 1999; Klasen and Lamanna 2009).

Some relevant research supports the theory that such inequality is due to biological causes, including the founding works of Becker (1985) and Daymont and Andrisani (1984). The former argues that women tend to give preference, time and energy to the care of the children, so they will spend less time on work activities, while the latter indicates that women choose different occupational roles and they specialize in different fields of study due to their own preferences. These postulates are rejected by other authors considering them as a justification of inequality that limits equitable access to opportunities for women. In addition, some feminist theories argue that there are no biological reasons for gender inequalities; instead they are more related to cultural assets (Mayer and Cordourier 2001).

In recent times, productive specialization and the reduction of the fertility rate have allowed women to be inserted into several economic activities, some of them highly paid, particularly in the services sector. Nevertheless, the existing factors of distribution of the labor force still condition the type of employment, access and wage differences in the labor market. Moreover, challenges long-ago identified persist until today, especially in the developing world, such as the forced tendency of women choosing jobs with lower pay in exchange for fewer penalties for labor intermittency, as studied by Blau and Ferber (1991).

Moreover, Cuberes and Teignier (2012) calculate that gender inequality creates an average income loss of 15.4% in the long run on OECD economies, while developing countries suffer from an average income loss of 17% in the long run, being gender gaps in occupational choices the cause of 44% of those losses, on average. In this context, it has been argued that due to stereotypes built as a society that give masculine and feminine directions, certain careers, activities or jobs are considered as exclusively appropriate for a given gender, causing labor segregation. The consequences for women of this occupational segregation translate into inequality in pay, lower job opportunities and few alternatives when choosing a job or career (Hegewisch et al. 2010).

In this context, many empirical studies focus on analyzing how gender disparities in employment and human capital affect economic growth. Following the research of Klasen and Lamanna (2009), we have divided the empirical evidence into two groups, the first group analyzes the existent research on labor gender gaps and economic growth, while the second group summarizes the research on human capital gender gaps and economic growth. Within this first group, we find that most studies that have been carried out on this topic suggest that reducing the labor gap significantly increases economic growth globally (Antecol 2000; Tzannatos 1999). In high-income countries, low rates of inequality in terms of access to the labor market are more pronounced. In the OECD countries, female participation in the labor market is essential to overcome the imbalances in employment (Albanesi and Şahin 2018). Similarly, in these countries the productivity of companies is higher the more opportunities there are for female labor access (Albanesi and Şahin 2018; Cuberes and Teignier 2016; Guzman and Kacperczyk 2019; Sauré and Zoabi 2014). In emerging countries such as China, labor segregation is identified as causing wage inequalities between men and women and these are more pronounced in the private sector. However, gendered labor preferences are more evident in the public sector (He and Wu 2017; Zhang and Wu 2017). Finally, in the case of Ecuador, a developing economy, there is also evidence of discrimination in the labor market against women in the form of lower wages and disparities in employment, underemployment and formality (Posso 2016).

In the second group of investigations that relate human capital gender gaps and economic growth, we find that human capital influences both the economic growth of countries and the wage gaps between individuals and constitutes a key factor in understanding gender inequalities. Francesconi and Parey (2018) find that men with a university degree receive a higher salary than the one that a woman with the same degree receives for the same job.

However, Pearlman (2018) demonstrates that such wage gaps are smaller between men and women with a university degree, so he proposes that equal access to higher education should be encouraged to eliminate these disparities. Ahmed and McGillivray (2015), meanwhile, estimate that increasing human capital reduces salary inequalities by approximately 31% in favor of women. However, it must be taken into account that there are countries where religious, ethnic and social capital factors are predominant when explaining job insecurity and gender inequalities (Blommaert and Spierings 2019).

3   Data and Methodology

3.1   *Statistical Sources*

The data on output, labor gap, foreign direct investment, gross capital formation and urbanization were taken from World Bank's World Development Indicators (2018). The labor gap measures the difference between the percentage
of the male and female employment rate. Regarding the human capital gap,
such indicator was calculated from the human capital database of Barro and
Lee (2013) and measures the difference between the average years of schooling
of men and women. In order to obtain annual data for the human capital series, the five-year data were interpolated. This strategy is useful because human capital has a linear adjustment over time, which allows interpolation of
inter-annual data without losing the consistency of the series. The analysis
covers the period between 1990 and 2018.

Table 2.1 presents the main descriptive statistics of the variables. In the case
of the variables GDP, labor gap (LG), human capital gap (HCG), urbanization

TABLE 2.1   Descriptive statistics of the variables

Variable			Mean	S.D.	Min.	Max.	N
Output	(GDP)	Overall	24.92	1.55	22.26	28.51	N = 522
		Between		1.56	22.72	28.18	n = 18
		Within		.31	24.15	25.74	T = 29
Labor gap	(LG)	Overall	3.45	.26	2.65	3.95	N = 522
		Between		.23	2.98	3.80	n = 18
		Within		.14	3.10	3.89	T = 29
Human capital	(HCG)	Overall	.32	.63	−1.23	2.17	N = 522
gap		Between		.55	−.378	1.81	n = 18
		Within		.33	−.81	1.76	T = 29
Foreign direct	(FDI)	Overall	3.29	2.63	1.00e-07	16.22	N = 522
investment		Between		1.65	1.31	7.11	n = 18
		Within		2.08	−2.28	12.41	T = 29
Log (Gross fixed	(GFCF)	Overall	23.28	1.79	1.37	27.03	N = 522
capital formation)		Between		1.40	21.45	26.06	n = 18
		Within		1.16	−1.01	24.64	T = 29
Urbanization rate	(UR)	Overall	4.21	.21	3.70	4.55	N = 522
		Between		.20	3.83	4.529	n = 18
		Within		.06	3.97	4.42	T = 29

rate (UR) and gross fixed capital formation (GFCF), there is greater variability between countries than within them; while in the variable foreign direct investment (FDI) there is greater variability within countries than between them. These facts indicate that foreign investment had greater volatility over time within countries than among the countries analyzed. For all the variables T = 29 and n = 18, so the econometric estimates are made using an exactly balanced data panel.

Latin America has experienced a sustained increase in its product in the last two decades, except for the 2008 crisis and the slowdown in the period following the drop in the price of commodities by the middle of this decade. However, this growth has not necessarily translated into social improvements. High levels of inequality are proof of that. In several countries of the region, the employment status of women has improved substantially, but the gaps between women and men persist in economic and social aspects (World Bank 2018). For example, on average, the data shows the existence of higher unemployment in women than in men, and the fact that the average human capital of men is slightly higher than that of women (World Bank 2018).

Figure 2.1 reports 4 graphs of the evolution of output, the labor gap and the human capital gap, both for Latin America as a whole (LA) and in a grouped way: high-income countries (HIC), middle-high-income countries (MHIC), and

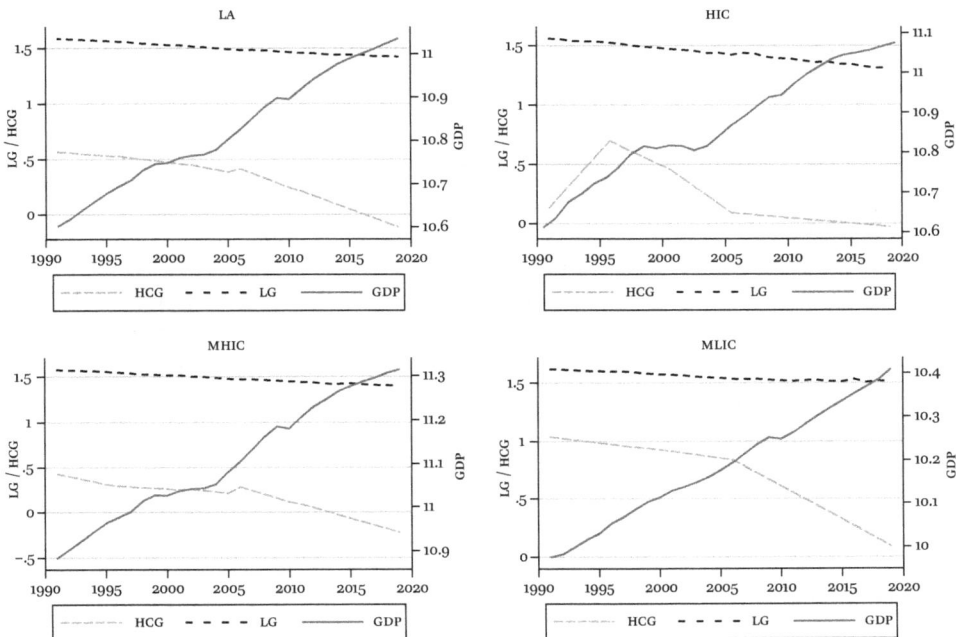

FIGURE 2.1 Evolution of output, labor gap and human capital gap

middle-low-income countries (MLIC). The existence of a positive gap indicates that men have higher human capital or higher employment rate, while a negative gap indicates a better situation for women. In the HICs, the human capital gap widened during the first half of the 1990s, and subsequently narrowed until the 2008 crisis, and then narrowed at increasingly slow rates. In the MHIC, the human capital gap narrowed throughout the period of analysis at slow rates, but in a sustained manner. While in the MLIC the gap is reduced during the analysis period, but it is more significant after the financial crisis of 2008. In parallel, the labor gap in the three groups of countries and globally is slightly reduced. In general, these stylized facts indicate that in the countries of Latin America the labor gap and the human capital gap have been reduced over the last decades, with some exceptions.

Latin America is a region where the productive structure is strongly associated with primary-export activity, with an accelerated urbanization process (Alvarado and Iglesias 2017; Alvarado-López et al. 2017), which offers a growing demand for services. Likewise, the technological adoption processes of the countries of the region attract external capitals, which mainly focus on the exploitation of raw materials, infrastructure and access to technologies with the effort of the private and public sector (electricity, roads, ports, fixed and mobile telephony, internet, and others) as indicated by Alvarado et al. (2017). In order to capture that reality of the countries of the region, it is necessary to include a set of controls: foreign direct investment, urbanization rate and gross capital formation. An additional reason for the inclusion of these variables is that the productive structure is associated with social processes, especially with the inequality of opportunities; in a region that is characterized by considerably high levels of income inequality.

3.2   *Econometric Strategy*

The main advantage of a model with panel data is that it captures the variability of time and cross-sections, which generates more robust estimators. The objective of this research is to examine the effect of the labor gap and human capital gap between men and women on the economic growth of 18 countries in Latin America. The choice of countries was due to the availability of data from all the series included in the econometric models. Equation (1) raises the basic relationship to estimate:

$$\log GDP_{it} = (\gamma_0 + \delta_0) + \gamma_1 LG_{it} + \gamma_2 HCG_{it} + \gamma_3 CV_{it} + \theta_{it} \qquad (1)$$

Where the dependent variable is the logarithm of GDP at constant prices for the year 2010; LG_{it} is the labor gap and HCG_{it} is the average human capital gap in country i in period t, respectively. The unit of analysis of our research is the country, $i = 1,\ldots,18$ over the period 1990–2017 ($t = 1990,\ldots,2017$.) The control variables (CV_{it}) are foreign direct investment, urbanization rate and gross fixed capital formation, which allow to establish whether the parameters that measure the effect of labor and human capital gaps are consistent and stable. The parameter ($\gamma_0 + \delta_0$) captures the fixed effect of time and countries. Finally, θ_{it} is the stochastic error term.

The choice between a fixed effects model was determined by a formal test. The results of the Hausman test (Hausman, 1978) indicate that Equation (1) must be estimated using a fixed effects model. While the Wooldridge test (Wooldridge 2002) suggests the presence of autocorrelation in the model and the Lagrange multiplier test of Breusch-Pagan (1980) indicates that the model has heteroscedasticity. In order to correct both structural problems in the equation, it was necessary to estimate a generalized ordinary least squares (GLS) model, which reports estimators consistent with autocorrelation and heteroskedasticity (Alvarado et al. 2017; Alvarado et al. 2018; Ponce and Alvarado 2019, among others). The next stage of the econometric strategy consists in estimating the existence of a short-term and long-term equilibrium relationship, for which it is necessary to verify if the series do not follow a trend behavior. The Pesaran test (Pesaran 2004) indicates that there is no dependence on the cross sections, therefore, we estimate the first generation cointegration tests and models. Specifically, we estimate the unit root tests of Dickey and Fuller augmented-ADF, Levin, Lin and Chu-LLC, and Phillips and Perron-PP (Dickey and Fuller 1981; Levin et al. 2002; Phillips and Perron 1988) for panel data. The results of these tests are contrasted with the results obtained in two other tests: Im, Pesaran and Shin-IPS, and Breitung-UB (Breitung 2002; Im et al. 2003). This set of tests can be generalized from Equation (1) as follows:

$$y_{it} = \alpha_0 + \lambda y_{it-1} + \alpha_1 t + \sum_{i=2}^{p} \beta_j y_{it-1} + \varepsilon_{it} \tag{2}$$

The first- and second-generation unit root test approach allows comparing the results obtained by the types of tests and verifying the robustness of the results. The dependence test in the cross sections suggests a weak dependence between the panels. In order to determine the long-term equilibrium relationship between the variables, we use the cointegration test developed by Pedroni (1999) from the following equation:

$$GDP_{it} = \alpha_i + \sum_{j=1}^{n-1} \beta_{ij} LG_{it-j} + \sum_{j=1}^{n-1} \omega_{ij} y_{it-j} + \sum_{j=1}^{n-1} \omega_{ij} HCG_{it-j} + \sum_{j=1}^{n-1} \omega_{ij} CV_{it-j} + \pi_i ECT_{t-1} + \varepsilon_{it} \tag{3}$$

In Equation (3) the parameters β, ω and π are the parameters to estimate while ECT_{t-1} is the long-term equilibrium cointegration vector. Finally, $\mathcal{E}_{it}$ is the term of stationary random error with zero mean and is the length of the offset determined with the information criterion of Akaike (1974). The short-term equilibrium was estimated using the test developed by Westerlund (2007) and applied by Persyn and Westerlund (2008).

4 Results and Discussion

Table 2.2 shows the results of the GLS regression. The results are reported for the 18 countries as a whole and for the three groups of countries according to their level of income per capita.

There are several empirical studies that highlight the importance of women's participation in the labor market, in managerial positions and in politics and the conditions that are required for women to be able to participate actively in the economy (Iyer and Mani 2019). The participation of women in the labor market assures them a source of income, directly improving the economic and social well-being of households. Likewise, the higher educational levels of women can translate into better educational levels of children, higher income levels and in general, a more productive workforce.

The results in Table 2.2 indicate that there is negative association between the labor gap among men and women and GDP, but this is only statistically significant for high-income countries. The human capital gap, on the other hand, is negatively associated with the level of output in Latin America as a whole and in two of the three groups of countries. Here, the coefficients are significant for all groups. With respect to the results of the control variables, novel results are obtained. An unexpected outcome is that the effect of foreign direct investment on economic growth is negative for the region, although only statistically significant in MLICs. This result, although surprising, is consistent with the conclusions of Alvarado et al. (2017).

Moving on, gross fixed capital formation shows a positive and significant association with the level of GDP, coherently with the logic of the growth model of Solow (1956) and Swan (1956). Henderson (2003) offers a solid argumentation of the mechanisms through which urbanization translates into greater economic growth. Regarding the expected positive relationship between the urbanization rate and economic growth, our results confirm the theoretical approach of Henderson (2003), except in HICs, where the effect is negative and significant. This result can be explained in the logic that excess economic and population concentration can have a negative effect on economic growth (Alvarado-López et al. 2017; Atienza and Aroca 2013).

Once the estimators have been obtained in a context of a basic regression, Table 2.3 reports the results of the unit root test. The underlying logic of this test is to find exactly if the series used in subsequent estimates have a trend component that can generate spurious results. The tests are performed with and without fixed effects of time. Despite the difference between the first- and second-generation unit root tests, the results are consistent among the five tests used (PP, ADF, LLC, UB, IPS). The results confirm that the series are stationary in first differences, and have an order of integration I (1). Consequently, cointegration and causality models are estimated with the variables in first differences.

Table 2.4 reports the results of the Pedroni cointegration test (Pedroni, 2001). The cointegration model was estimated to obtain the parameters within the dimensions and between the dimensions. Both results confirm the existence

TABLE 2.2   Relationship between output, labor gap and human capital gap

	LA	HIC	MHIC	MLIC
Labor gap	−0.0600	−0.568*	−0.0726	−0.140
	(−0.71)	(−2.47)	(−0.79)	(−0.95)
Human capital gap	−0.0991**	−0.260***	0.00742*	−0.00315*
	(−2.66)	(−5.08)	(2.15)	(−2.07)
Foreign direct investment	−0.00185	−0.00244	0.00217	−0.0149***
	(−0.78)	(−0.65)	(0.90)	(−3.73)
Log (Gross fixed capital formation)	0.0748***	0.730***	0.0165**	0.535***
	(6.80)	(21.82)	(2.62)	(11.58)
Log (Urbanization rate)	4.370***	−8.928***	5.525***	0.529*
	(32.41)	(−5.26)	(23.12)	(2.02)
Constant	4.977***	50.04***	1.819	10.17***
	(6.90)	(5.64)	(1.60)	(5.87)
Serial correlation test (p-value)	0.8945	0.6075	0.9378	0.7729
Observations	522	58	319	145

Note: the t statistic in parentheses; * when p <0.05, ** when p <0.01, *** when p <0.001

TABLE 2.3   Results of the unit root test

	With fixed effects					Without fixed effects				
	PP	ADF	LLC	UB	IPS	PP	ADF	LLC	UB	IPS
GDP_{it}	−24.76	−9.17	−18.88	−4.30	−20.86	−24.31	−9.17	−16.86	−2.53	−20.73
LG_{it}	−29.00	−11.01	−19.40	−6.33	−24.30	−30.98	−10.77	−22.56	−6.99	−26.87
HCG_{it}	−15.46	−3.64	−19.70	−10.28	−16.35	−17.96	−6.45	−18.31	−11.04	−17.01
FDI_{it}	−33.69	−16.30	−15.90	−5.53	−23.51	−33.58	−16.84	−12.32	−5.52	−23.32
$GFCF_{it}$	−29.54	−12.14	−16.11	−5.31	−21.41	−5.58	0.99	13.91	−2.33	−8.37
ur_{it}	−6.59	0.96	−26.66	−2.77	−12.31	−3.97	2.25	0.02	−2.36	−5.92

of a long-term equilibrium relationship between the variables. In practice, these results confirm the idea that the labor gap and the human capital gap between men and women have a long-term equilibrium relationship with the product, which move together and simultaneously over time. The results are similar for Latin America and the three groups of countries.

The long-term equilibrium reported in Table 2.4 makes it possible to verify the existence of a short-term equilibrium, for which we estimate the Westerlund test (2007). The results are not consistent in all estimators, indicating that there is not enough evidence to conclude that there is a short-term equilibrium between the included variables. This result is understandable because the effect of the labor and human capital gap between men and women must be reflected in the long term rather than in the short term (Minasyan, Zenker, Klasen and Vollmer 2019). The underlying logic behind this result is that the changes in the participation of women in the labor market and in their formation of human capital are gradual and slow in time, so that their effect on production becomes visible in the long term. In addition, the results of the policies to improve the labor insertion of women and increase the human capital of women generate benefits after several years of its application and not immediately. This result reinforces the results obtained in Table 2.2, where the effect of the labor gap was not significant in the growth of the 18 countries of Latin America as a whole or by groups of countries.

These arguments support the fact that in the short term there is no balance between the variables studied, while there is a long-term equilibrium. Finally, Table 2.6 reports the results of the Granger-type causality model

TABLE 2.4   Pedroni cointegration results

	LA	HIC	MHIC	MLIC
Within dimension Test statistics				
Panel v-statistic	-2.5^{**}	-0.974	-1.75	-1.098
Panel p-statistic	-1.411^{**}	0.07514	-1.203	-1.259
Panel PP-statistic	-15.52^{**}	-3.355^{**}	-12.56^{**}	-11.44^{**}
Panel ADF-statistic	-10.5^{**}	-3.003^{**}	-5.754^{**}	-1.625
Between dimension Test statistics				
Panel p-statistic	-0.2584	0.5733	-0.3647	-0.5931
Group PP-statistic	-17.55^{**}	-3.418^{**}	-14.57^{**}	-13.88^{**}
Group ADF statistic	-10.07^{**}	-3.021^{**}	-5.697^{**}	0.4954

Note: * when p <0.05, ** when p <0.01, *** when p <0.001

TABLE 2.5   Westerlund short term test results

Statistic	LA			HIC			MHIC			MLIC		
	Value	Z-value	p-value	Value	Z-value	p-value	Value	Z-value	p-value	Value	Z-value	p-value
Gt	-13.5	-48.7	0.000	-4.4	-2.6	0.005	-3.2	-2.1	0.01	-40.0	-87.7	0.00
Ga	-0.7	7.2	1.000	0.1	2.5	0.995	-0.9	5.6	1.00	-0.7	3.8	1.00
Pt	-10.7	-0.6	0.262	-1.3	1.8	0.971	-7.4	0.4	0.66	-18.4	-12.2	0.00
Pa	-8.3	1.4	0.933	-0.1	1.8	0.971	-8.1	1.2	0.89	-1.4	2.6	0.99

TABLE 2.6   Results of the causality test of Dumitrescu and Hurlin

Causality	Group	W-bar	Z-bar	p-value
$LG_{it} \to GDP_{it}$	LA	0.7200	−0.8400	0.4009
	HIC	1.2240	0.2240	0.8227
	MHIC	0.6609	−0.7954	0.4264
	MLIC	0.6485	−0.5558	0.5783
$HCG_{it} \to GDP_{it}$	LA	0.5409	−1.3773	0.1684
	HIC	1.0492	0.0492	0.9608
	MHIC	0.5133	−1.1413	0.2537
	MLIC	0.3983	−0.9514	0.3414
$FDI_{it} \to GDP_{it}$	LA	1.5498	1.6494	0.0991
	HIC	0.5006	−0.4994	0.6175
	MHIC	2.1927	2.7972	0.0049
	MLIC	0.5551	−0.7035	0.4818
$GFCF_{it} \to GDP_{it}$	LA	1.2121	0.6364	0.5245
	HIC	3.1064	2.1064	0.0352
	MHIC	0.6028	−0.9316	0.3515
	MLIC	1.7950	1.2570	0.2088
$UR_{it} \to GDP_{it}$	LA	1.0445	0.1336	0.8937
	HIC	1.9777	0.9777	0.3282
	MHIC	1.0159	0.0374	0.9702
	MLIC	0.7342	−0.4203	0.6743
$GDP_{it} \to LG_{it}$	LA	1.0953	0.2858	0.7750
	HIC	0.0116	−0.9884	0.3230
	MHIC	1.6599	1.5477	0.1217
	MLIC	0.2865	−1.1282	0.2592
$GDP_{it} \to HCG_{it}$	LA	1.3033	0.9098	0.3629
	HIC	3.7378	2.7378	0.0062
	MHIC	1.0544	0.1276	0.8984
	MLIC	0.8769	−0.1946	0.8457
$GDP_{it} \to FDI_{it}$	LA	1.3529	1.0586	0.2898
	HIC	0.5192	−0.4808	0.6307
	MHIC	1.7985	1.8726	0.0611
	MLIC	0.7060	−0.4649	0.6420
$GDP_{it} \to GFCF_{it}$	LA	2.1273	3.3820	0.0007
	HIC	4.2632	3.2632	0.0011
	MHIC	1.3107	0.7285	0.4663
	MLIC	3.0697	3.2725	0.0011

TABLE 2.6   Results of the causality test of Dumitrescu and Hurlin (*cont.*)

Causality	Group	W-bar	Z-bar	p-value
$GDP_{it} \rightarrow UR_{it}$	LA	1.2226	0.6679	0.5042
	HIC	0.9838	−0.0162	0.9870
	MHIC	1.1914	0.4488	0.6535
	MLIC	1.3870	0.6118	0.5407

proposed by Dumitrescu and Hurlin (2012). In most relationships there is no causality. We found a bidirectional relationship that goes from foreign direct investment to the output in the MHICs, from the output to the human capital gap in the HICs, from the output to the gross capital formation in the HICs and in the MLICs.

In general, our results are relatively similar to the conclusions obtained in other contexts. For example, Klasen and Lamanna (2009) using panel data analysis for the period 1960–2000 found that education and employment gaps reduce economic growth. The result is stronger in North Africa, the Middle East and South Asia. The results found in the long-term cointegration tests, and in the causality test, are consistent with the fact that historically women have had lower employment rates and educational enrollment rates (Hill and King, 1995). However, in recent years the educational and employment gap has narrowed (World Bank, 2018).

5   Conclusions and Policy Implications

Like several developing regions, there is a broad consensus that women in Latin America have disadvantages over men, particularly in the formation of human capital and in the labor market. In this context, we hypothesized that the disadvantages women face should have some effect on the level of production of the countries. This chapter addressed such topic through empirical research for the countries of the region. Our results offer a first look at the effect of the labor gap and the human capital gap between men and women on economic growth in Latin America. The results suggest that, in the short term, there is not a significant relationship between the region's GDP and the labor gap, but there is a negative and significative relationship between the human capital gap and the product of the region. The results were consistent after controlling for three structural aspects of Latin America: foreign direct investment inflows, the strong urbanization process and the formation of fixed capital due to the increase in the product in recent decades. The five variables move together and simultaneously in the long term, demonstrating that the effects of the gaps in economic growth impact in the long term, while, in the short term, there is no significant change.

These results suggest that the inefficiency that discrimination against women can generate, both in the labor market and in the education system, is indeed visible in the production levels of the countries of the region. However, it should also be considered that the results of the causality test indicate that for the most part there is no causal relationship.

The results have several economic policy implications. First, efforts to increase human capital of women and reduce the historical gap with men are likely to be associated with an increased level in the region's product in the long term. Likewise, foreign investment flows do not necessarily generate positive results in the product, because they mainly focus on highly volatile sectors and the technology absorption capacity of most of the countries in the region is limited. Rather, there are strong indications that the product of the countries of the region can increase significantly if there is adequate management of urbanization levels. Specifically, urbanization can be promoted in middle-high and medium-low income countries; while high-income countries must manage the costs of excessive economic and population concentration.

The present investigation has at least two limitations: there are no data on the variables used in the econometric models for all countries in the region and the available variables do not necessarily capture all the gaps between men and women. Future research may focus on measuring the effect of the human capital gap and participation in the labor market using micro data, this would ensure greater robustness of the results presented in this research. The incorporation of the variable salaries is necessary to obtain more conclusive results on the disadvantages faced by women in Latin America.

References

Ahmed, S., and McGillivray, M. (2015). "Human capital, discrimination, and the gender wage gap in Bangladesh." *World Development* 67: 506–524. https://doi.org/10.1016/j.worlddev.2014.10.017.

Akaike, H. (1974). "A new look at the statistical model identification." *IEEE Transactionson Automatic Control* 19(6): 716–723. https://doi.org/10.1109/TAC.1974.1100705.

Albanesi, S., and Şahin, A. (2018). "The gender unemployment gap." *Review of Economic Dynamics* 30: 47–67. https://doi.org/10.1016/j.red.2017.12.005.

Alvarado, R., and Iglesias, S. (2017). "Sector Externo, Restricciones y Crecimiento Económico en Ecuador." *Problemas del Desarrollo* 48(191): 83–106. https://doi.org/10.1016/j.rpd.2017.11.005.

Alvarado, R., Iñiguez, M., and Ponce, P. (2017). "Foreign direct investment and economic growth in Latin America." *Economic Analysis and Policy* 56: 176–187. https://doi.org/10.1016/j.eap.2017.09.006.

Alvarado, R., Ponce, P., Criollo, A., Córdova, K., and Khan, M.K. (2018). "Environmental degradation and real per capita output: New evidence at the global level grouping countries by income levels." *Journal of Cleaner Production* 189: 13–20. https://doi.org/10.1016/j.jclepro.2018.04.064.

Alvarado-López, J.R., Correa-Quezada, R.F., and Tituaña-Castillo, M. del C. (2017). "Migración interna y urbanización sin eficiencia en países en desarrollo: Evidencia para Ecuador." *Papeles de Población* 23(94): 99–123. http://dx.doi.org/10.22185/24487147.2017.94.033.

Antecol, H. (2000). "An examination of cross-country differences in the gender gap in labor force participation rates." *Labour Economics* 7(4): 409–426. https://doi.org/10.1016/S0927-5371(00)00007-5.

Atienza, M., and Aroca, P. (2013). *¿Es la concentración espacial un problema para el crecimiento en América Latina?* (WP2013/10; Documentos de Trabajo en Economía y Ciencia Regional, Vol. 41).

Barro, R., and Lee, J. (2013). "A New Data Set of Educational Attainment in the World, 1950–2010." *Journal of Development Economics* 104: 184–198. https://doi.org/10.1016/j.jdeveco.2012.10.001.

Becker, G.S. (1985). "Human Capital, Effort, and the Sexual Division of Labor." *Journal of Labor Economics* 3(1, Part 2): S33–S58. https://doi.org/10.1086/298075.

Blau, F.D., and Ferber, M.A. (1991). "Career Plans and Expectations of Young Women and Men: The Earnings Gap and Labor Force Participation." *The Journal of Human Resources* 26(4): 581. https://doi.org/10.2307/145976.

Blommaert, L., and Spierings, N. (2019). "Examining ethno-religious labor market inequalities among women in the Netherlands." *Research in Social Stratification and Mobility* 61(November 2018): 38–51. https://doi.org/10.1016/j.rssm.2019.01.005.

Breitung, J. (2002). "Nonparametric tests for unit roots and cointegration." *Journal of Econometrics* 108(2): 343–363. https://doi.org/10.1016/S0304-4076(01)00139-7.

Breusch, T.S., and Pagan, A.R. (1980). "The Lagrange multiplier test and its applications to model specification in econometrics." *The review of economic studies* 47(1): 239–253. https://doi.org/10.2307/2297111.

Castelló, A., and Doménech, R. (2002). "Human capital inequality and economic growth: Some new evidence." *Economic Journal* 112(478): C187–C200. https://doi.org/10.1111/1468-0297.00024.

Cuberes, D., and Teignier, M. (2012). "Gender Gaps in the Labor Market and Aggregate Productivity." *Sheffield Economic Research Paper Series*.

Cuberes, D., and Teignier, M. (2016). "Aggregate Effects of Gender Gaps in the Labor Market: A Quantitative Estimate." *Journal of Human Capital* 10(1): 1–32. https://doi .org/10.1086/683847.

Daymont, T.N., and Andrisani, P.J. (1984). "Job Preferences, College Major, and the Gender Gap in Earnings." *The Journal of Human Resources* 19(3): 408–428. https://doi .org/10.2307/145880.

De Ibarrola, M. (2009). "El incremento de la escolaridad de la PEA en México y los efectos sobre su situación laboral y sus ingresos, 1992–2004." *Revista Electrónica de Investigación Educativa* 11(2): 1992–2004.

Dickey, D.A., and Fuller, W.A. (1981). "Likelihood Ratio Statistics for Autoregressive Time Series with a Unit Root." *Econometrica* 49(4): 1057–1072. https://doi .org/10.2307/1912517.

Dollar, D., and Gatti, R. (1999). *Gender Inequality, Income, and Growth: Are Good Times Good for Women?* The World Bank.

Dumitrescu, E. and Hurlin, C. (2012). "Testing for Granger non-causality in heterogeneous panels." *Economic Modelling* 29(4): 1450–1460. https://doi.org/10.1016/ j.econmod.2012.02.014.

Erten, B., and Metzger, M. (2019). The real exchange rate, structural change, and female labor force participation. *World Development* 117: 296–312. https://doi.org/10.1016/ j.worlddev.2019.01.015.

Francesconi, M., and Parey, M. (2018). "Early gender gaps among university graduates." *European Economic Review* 109: 63–82. https://doi.org/10.1016/j.euroecorev.2018.02.004.

Guzman, J., and Kacperczyk, A.O. (2019). "Gender gap in entrepreneurship." *Research Policy* 48(7): 1666–1680. https://doi.org/10.1016/j.respol.2019.03.012.

Hausman, J. (1978). "Specification tests in econometrics." *Econometrica*, 1251–1271. https://doi.org/10.2307/1913827.

He, G., and Wu, X. (2017). "Marketization, occupational segregation, and gender earnings inequality in urban China." *Social Science Research* 65: 96–111. https://doi. org/10.1016/j.ssresearch.2016.12.001.

Heathcote, J., Storesletten, K., and Violante, G.L. (2017). "The macroeconomics of the quiet revolution: Understanding the implications of the rise in women's participation for economic growth and inequality." *Research in Economics* 71(3): 521–539. https://doi.org/10.1016/j.rie.2017.03.002.

Hegewisch, A., Liepmann, H., Hayes, J., and Hartmann, H. (2010). "Separate and not equal? Gender segregation in the labor market and the gender wage gap." *Institute for Women's Policy Research* 377.

Henderson, V. (2003). "The urbanization process and economic growth: The so-what question." *Journal of Economic Growth* 8(1): 47–71. https://doi.org/10.1023/ A:1022860800744.

Hill, M.A., and King, E. (1995). "Women's education and economic well-being." *Feminist Economics* 1(2): 21–46. https://doi.org/10.1080/714042230.

Im, K. Pesaran, M.H., and Shin, Y. (2003). "Testing for unit roots in heterogeneous panels." *Journal of Econometrics* 115(1): 53–74. https://doi.org/10.1016/S0304-4076 (03)00092-7.

International Labor Organization. (2018). World Employment and Social Outlook—Trends 2019.

Iyer, L., and Mani, A. (2019). "The road not taken: Gender gaps along paths to political power." *World Development* : 68–80. https://doi.org/10.1016/j.worlddev.2019.03.004.

Klasen, S., and Lamanna, F. (2009). "The impact of gender inequality in education and employment on economic growth: New evidence for a panel of countries." *Feminist Economics* 15(3): 91–132. https://doi.org/10.1080/13545700902893106.

Levin, A., Lin, C., and Chu, C.J. (2002). "Unit root tests in panel data: asymptotic and finite-sample properties." *Journal of Econometrics* 108(1): 1–24. https://doi .org/10.1016/S0304-4076(01)00098-7.

Mayer, D., and Cordourier, G. (2001). "La brecha salarial y la teoría de igualdad de oportunidades: Un estudio de género para el caso mexicano." *El Trimestre Económico* 68(269): 71–107. https://www.jstor.org/stable/20857050.

Minasyan, A., Zenker, J., Klasen, S., and Vollmer, S. (2019). "Educational gender gaps and economic growth: A systematic review and meta-regression analysis." *World Development 122*: 199–217. https://doi.org/10.1016/j.worlddev.2019.05.006.

Pearlman, J. (2018). "Gender differences in the impact of job mobility on earnings: The role of occupational segregation." *Social Science Research* 74: 30–44. https://doi .org/10.1016/j.ssresearch.2018.05.010.

Pedroni, P. (1999). "Critical values for cointegration tests in heterogeneous panels with multiple regressors." *Oxford Bulletin of Economics and Statistics* 61(S1): 653–670. https://onlinelibrary.wiley.com/doi/abs/10.1111/1468-0084.0610s1653.

Pedroni, P. (2001). "Purchasing power parity tests in cointegrated panels." *Review of Economics and Statistics* 83(4): 727–731. https://doi.org/10.1162/003465301753237803.

Persyn, D., and Westerlund, J. (2008). "Error-correction–based cointegration tests for panel data." *The Stata Journal* 8(2): 232–242. https://doi.org/10.1177%2F153686 7X0800800205.

Pesaran, M.H. (2004). "General diagnostic tests for cross section dependence in panels." In *CESifo Working Paper Series* (No. 1229). https://ssrn.com/abstract=572504.

Phillips, P.C.B., and Perron, P. (1988). "Testing for a unit root in time series regression." *Biometrika* 75(2): 335–346. https://doi.org/10.1093/biomet/75.2.335.

Ponce, P., and Alvarado, R. (2019). "Air pollution, output, FDI, trade openness, and urbanization: evidence using DOLS and PDOLS cointegration techniques and causality." *Environmental Science and Pollution Research* 26(19): 19843–19858. https:// doi.org/10.1007/s11356-019-05405-6.

Posso, A. (2016). "Is there discrimination against women in the Ecuadorian labour market?" *Cuadernos de Economia* 39(111): 175–188. https://doi.org/10.1016/
j.cesjef.2015.10.004.

Sauré, P., and Zoabi, H. (2014). "International trade, the gender wage gap and female
labor force participation." *Journal of Development Economics* 111: 17–33. https://doi
.org/10.1016/j.jdeveco.2014.07.003.

Solow, R. (1956). "A Contribution to the Theory of Economic Growth." *The Quarterly
Journal of Economics* 70(1): 65–94. https://doi.org/10.2307/1884513.

Swan, T. (1956). "Economic growth and capital accumulation." *Economic Record* 32(02):
334–361. https://doi.org/10.1111/j.1475-4932.1956.tb00434.x.

Tzannatos, Z. (1999). "Women and Labor Market Changes in the Global Economy:
Growth Helps, Inequalities Hurt and Public Policy Matters." *World Development*
27(3): 551–569.

United Nations Development Programme. (2018). *Human Development Indices and Indicators. 2018 Statistical Update.*

Westerlund, J. (2007). "Testing for error correction in panel data." *Oxford Bulletin of Economics and Statistics* 69(6): 709–748. https://doi.org/10.1111/j.1468-0084.2007.00477.x.

Wooldridge, J. (2002). *Econometric Analysis of Cross Section and Panel Data.* MIT Press.

World Bank. (2018). World development indicators. World Bank Group.

Zhang, Z., and Wu, X. (2017). "Occupational segregation and earnings inequality: Rural
migrants and local workers in urban China." *Social Science Research* 61: 57–74.
https://doi.org/10.1016/j.ssresearch.2016.06.020.

CHAPTER 3

Debates about Women's Precarization: Scholz and Federici

Josefina Rosales

1 Introduction

The precarization of women's lives and labor is increasing at an exponential rate across the whole world, but especially in the Global South. With maquilas, family farming, recycling and sewing cooperatives, clandestine workshops, hiring via apps, outsourcing, and labor flexibility, an overwhelming number of people in Latin America are added to the ranks of those in precarious working and living conditions, which primarily affect women and sexual dissidences,[1] especially if they are racialized.

Faced with this panorama, it is fundamental to understand how the phenomenon of the progressive and constant growth of the precarization of life emerges historically and what logic it corresponds to, if we seek to avoid the neoliberal capture of the theoretical contributions of feminist economics. It is a matter of refining interpretations so that it does not become possible to use them to derive or justify political answers that individualize, demonize, or indebt our precarious lives even more with the language of entrepreneurship, meritocracy, and financial inclusion.

When referring to the vast field of feminist economics, I am focusing especially on the theoretical contributions that arise from the denunciation and criticism of the androcentric bias of neoclassical economic theory—that assumes the characteristics of the white, adult, linked to an industrial workplace, heterosexual male as universal, as well as those of *homo economicus* and rational behavior—and instead shift the objective of the economy from the reproduction of capital to the sustainability of life (Pérez Orozco 2014, 2017).

From that perspective, another fundamental element of feminist economics is that it puts the relationship between productive/reproductive work at the center of the debate. Thus it does away with the self-sufficient appearance both of 'economic agents' by demonstrating the inherent vulnerability and

---

1 Understood as identities, cultural practices and groups not aligned with the predominant and socially accepted heterosexual norm.

interdependence of human beings as well as the irreducibility of affectivity and cooperation in social reproduction, and also of the capitalist system, which necessarily depends on plundering reproductive activities and on the nature in order to maintain its functioning and reproduction (Federici 2017; Herrero 2017).

Following this tradition's epistemological-methodological commitment to a perspective of totality, I will attempt to analyze precarization following the logic of contemporary neoliberal accumulation in the world and resistance to it in Latin America, where it has been most powerfully expressed recently. To do so, I will try to reconstruct the totality of relations that are imposed on us as societies in the Global South (class, gender, race), in the face of the fragmentary experiences we have of them (Wallerstein 1998). Therefore, I pay attention to the warnings presented by Arruzza (2014) who advocates for a 'unitary thesis' in which "a patriarchal system that is autonomous from capitalism no longer exists," in opposition to those that refer to two or three systems, each with its own logics (capitalism-patriarchy-racism) that intersect, reinforce, or even contradict one another.

This has important consequences when it comes to defining key concepts such as exploitation and oppression or determining the limits of social classes or the possible *alliances among struggles.* In this case, it is Bhattacharya (2015) who argues that if instead of only analyzing the reproduction of the economy— as if it were a system of anonymous, random, and abstract market forces— social reproduction were analyzed as a totality, the notion of the working class would lose its economistic bias that ends up reducing it to the—increasingly narrow—borders of the waged sector. Instead, it would include all of those who, having been stripped of the means of production/reproduction of their lives, participate in the total reproduction of society through their labors (regardless of whether that work was paid by capital or not).

In this context, I am particularly interested in recovering two contributions from the Marxist tradition: those of Silvia Federici (Italy) and those of Roswitha Scholz (Germany),[2] as they can help us to interpret the phenomenon of

---

2 In this context, two key antecedents of feminism with Marxist roots that make a critique of classical economics must be mentioned. On the one hand, the 'domestic labor debate'— started by Benston (1969), Dalla Costa (1972), and Delphy (1982)—that was key to identifying the material basis of gender oppression, focusing on the reproduction of labor power carried out by women—house-wives inside their homes. On the other hand, the debate between theorizations of patriarchy as a system that is autonomous from capitalism that, nonetheless, interconnects and reinforces it—made popular with the work of Hartmann (1979) and Mitchell (1971)—and those proposed in 'Sex, Race, and Class' by Selma James (1975) in which she affirms that "power relations among sexes, races, nations and generations are precisely

the increasing precarization of labor and life in the Global South and its counterpart—I hypothesize—the multiplication and prominence of struggles for the reproduction of life in Latin America. In what follows, I will contrast their theoretical contributions in order to review the categories used for analyzing the phenomenon of precarization. I am particularly interested in specifying the definitions of reproduction, labor, class, wage, and value. Critiquing and complementing the ideas on *value dissociation theory* developed by Scholz, with the historical background on the emergence of patriarchal capitalism constructed by Silvia Federici, will allow me to present some hypotheses on (a) the role of the precarization of labor and life—that disproportionately affects feminized and racialized bodies—in the accumulation strategy of contemporary neoliberalism; and, (b) the role of the struggles for the reproduction of life in Latin America—as the flipside of precarization—in the strategy of struggle of the working class.

2   **Scholz: Labor, Value and Their Dissociation**

The theory of value dissociation is elaborated in the main books and articles of German feminist Roswitha Scholz (see, for instance, Scholz 1992, 2000a, 2000b, 2013a) as well as in Briales Canseco (2013), Martínez Domínguez (2016) and Navarro Ruiz (2017). It understands capitalism as a system that is not sexually neutral and considers modern capitalist patriarchy to be qualitatively different to premodern patriarchy. Giving that both systems (capitalism and patriarchy) are inseparable, not only due to their coexistence but also because of their essence, Scholz refers to patriarchy as *a commodity producer.*

According to the so-called Value Criticism School (whose main proponents are, among others, Kurz and Scholz),[3] the history of capitalist crises is the history of the contradiction between the content and the form of global processes

---

that, particular forms or class relations" (p. 96) and by Angela Davis (1981) in 'Women, Race & Class,' accusing the monopoly capitalist system itself of being a direct beneficiary of sexism and racism.

3   The critique of value theory was developed in the *Krisis* magazine, founded in 1986 by a group of German theorists and militants coming from Marxism. By critiquing the totality of social forms and capitalist categories (value, labor, commodity, masculinity, femininity, the State), they transformed traditional Marxist political economy. In 2004, Krisis expelled Roswitha Scholz and Robert Kurz (mainly due to differences regarding value dissociation theory) who later came together and edited the *EXIT!* magazine (Von Bosse et al. 2014).

of production and reproduction.[4] They describe how, in the last four decades, during the neoliberal phase of capitalism, this contradiction was sharpened to its limit. The era of Fordism-Keynesianism, based on policies of high wages, the mass production of semi-durable goods with low prices, and massive state investment in infrastructure and social services, was largely sustained by credit and the rapid growth of 'unproductive' sectors of the economy, enabling the world to be filled with commodities and managing to hold off the outbreak of contradictions that had been expressed in the crisis of the 1930s for several decades. In contrast, the crisis of Fordism in the mid-1970s entailed a headlong rush of capital in its destructive logic.

Following Jappe (2016), when the mechanism that compensated for declining value productivity by increasing production was depleted, financing through credit changed its nature. The abolition of the international U.S. dollar convertibility to gold in 1971 dismantled the last remaining security mechanism: since then there has been no limit to the multiplication of money. However, since money is the representation of abstract labor used in successful valorization processes, that is, those that end in the realization of the surplus value contained in commodities, the multiplication of money outside of the limits of productive capital valorization have led to the creation of stock bubbles and the existence of an enormous amount of 'fictional' capital at the global level, which has already demonstrated its destructive power in the 2008 crisis.

Based on this diagnosis, Scholz goes beyond and argues that the critique of capitalism is biased by the use of forms and categories from the market world. Her critique is not directed toward surplus value itself or the uneven distribution of an abstract wealth, but to the *value form* as what constitutes the system's social character. Value (the *automatic subject*)[5] is a specific quantity of

---

4   At the same time, this contradiction is contained in the structure of the commodity, in its separation between production and consumption. Since capitalism is based on commodity production and exchange, all of its crisis are ultimately caused by the lack of a social bond besides those of commodity production and exchange themselves. Hence crises erupt as the necessary way in which the unity of the independent phases of the production process is violently imposed. That is, since the money form and the capital form represent a pure quantity, which can be increased without limits, the contradiction between the form of the social relation (an abstract quantity) and its real material existence (an always concrete and limited quantity of money), supposes not only the condition of possibility of capitalist accumulation, but also the condition of possibility of the crises themselves, which will erupt with greater violence each time the social form of the production process attempts to become independent from its material content beyond what allows for the continuity of global reproduction of society.

5   Scholz (2013b) notes that value (surplus value) relates in a self-referential process always only to itself. Gradually, the whole globe is determined by the value thus constituted, which,

human energy, that is quantified in socially valid time, expended in productive activities. Money, as the general expression of the value form (*equivalent form*), goes from being a means to an end, that as capital, makes a self-enclosed loop to valorize itself: value accumulation becomes the objective of productive activity. Value then becomes the expression of a fetishist and alienated social relationship. Sociability only takes place through products that are dead things, without any concrete or sensory content, since value is only embodied in commodities as long as they represent prior labor (the consumption of abstract social energy) and are realized in anonymous automatic markets split off from the rest of life. Therefore, it is the value form, generalized as a fundamental social relation through the universalization of commodity production, market exchange, and abstract labor, that results from the extraction of surplus value at a social level. In this way, the starting point for understanding the process of social exploitation is not social class, but value as the ultimate basis of order and cohesion in society.

However, according to Scholz—and this is where she differs from the Krisis group—value is an androcentric concept. For her 'value is man,' understanding man as the symbolic value of the public.[6] In effect, the commodity producing system expresses its social character not only in the value form, which involves abstract and productive work, but also in reproductive activities that cannot be deduced from or subsumed in that form. Each one emerges from the other, forming a logic of *ongoing value dissociation.* The field of value is production, and its logic is that of profit, which means saving time (productivity). The field of dissociation is that of life, and its logic that of care, which implies spending time. Reproductive work is together with but outside of the value form; it is its condition of possibility, its precondition, but it establishes a dialectical, irresolvable, and inseparable relationship with the value form. Therefore, the dynamics of abstract labor cannot be understood without the tasks carried out in the field of what is dissociated from value, nor can we understand value without its negation: what is not value.

At the same time, it cannot be argued that commodity producing patriarchy emerged from the sexual division of labor or from a dual division of culture. The *dialectic relationship* means that there was a process of global dissociation

---

according to her interpretation is what was called by Marx 'automatic subject.' A similar conception of the logic of value results in its notion as 'automatic subject' for authors such as Jappe (2016).

6   This idea refers to the *logic* of value and commodification as an androcentric (and biocidal) logic. As put by Herrero (2017), abandoning the androcentric and biocidal logic forces us to answer the inevitable questions: What needs must be satisfied for everyone? What production is necessary and impossible for those needs to be satisfied? What is the socially necessary labor for that?

in which the androcentric and universalist logic of identity established value as the abstract time, that is, as the equivalent, equal for exchange, and therefore reduced in its qualitative difference. The time of reproduction is non-univocal, irreducible, non-homologated. Reproductive and care activities that are carried out in the field of life cannot be subsumed to the grammar of value. They are not deduced from, although they are subordinated to, abstract labor and the wage. And they are the presupposition for thinking about the non-identical. This argument, based on Horkheimer and Adorno's (1947) *Dialectic of Enlightenment*, suggests that the masculine subject builds its enlightened universalism based on exclusion as an inherent mechanism. Therefore, the non-univocal will be the non-value as an inverse of value, that is, abstract or univocal time (number of comparable hours).[7]

Abstract labor is the form that labor power as a commodity adopts in the *dictatorship of the world of work*, whereby productive capacity becomes heteronomous. As so, it is separated from life and from the needs of those who produce and becomes an ontological principle. Ontologized, it constructs the category of labor in ahistorical and metaphysical terms. But labor as we know it emerges with capitalism, not only as a social relation, but as the internal ligament of capitalist socialization in which concrete and productive labor is such as a manifestation and representation of abstract labor. However, in the current period, labor becomes obsolete as the *automatic subject*, in its tautological dynamics, is valued (de)valuing itself. If there is less and less work, it no longer makes sense to identify the capital-labor contradiction as the unique and only one. The same applies to the critique of surplus value creating an uneven distribution of abstract wealth,[8] that is, wealth in terms of money (which is increasingly devalued).

The division between abstract labor and feminine activities of *reproduction* is a historical process connected to the genesis of capitalism. The separation of the public from the private sphere corresponded to the logic of value attached to the former and the logic of care attached to the latter—the logic of care being split from and not derived from value (but being its necessary counterpart).

---

7 Although for Scholz, this is not the main contradiction nor only logic of inequality. Abstract labor and the reproductive field, value and its dissociation, do make up the basic social form as a fragmented totality. The dialectic between value and sexual dissociation is essential and constitutive of the global social relation as a broken and contradictory relationship. This process of global and contradictory dissociation has, along with the material reproductive elements, cultural, symbolic, and socio-psychological aspects as well.

8 Abstract wealth is self-referentially accumulated as human energy quantified as socially necessary time, stripped of its quality and context, and dissociated from the needs for which it is produced.

Such division is constituted in modernity along with the capitalist production of commodities and the symbolic order of commodity producing patriarchy that institutes gender in a dualistic and hierarchical way.[9]

However, even though the division between the public and the private was founded in modernity, that does not mean that the logic of value dissociation does not cut across the public sphere as accounted for by the *feminization* of the post-Fordist labor market. Similarly, the logic of value cuts across the private sphere as certain reproductive activities are *commodified*, while also redistributing them in the female world (with migrant and lower-class women). Scholz points out that in the current state of capitalist patriarchy, women are 'doubly socialized' (Becker-Schmidt 1987) when they enter the labor market while still being responsible for reproductive work, which does not eradicate the hierarchy or excision of reproduction from abstract labor.

During contemporary globalization, a process of atomization and individuation (Beck 1992) takes place as a process of depauperization and individual responsibilization for reproduction. Faced with this context, as well as increasing pressure of global markets and the reduction of political-social spaces, patriarchy becomes increasingly brutal. This is expressed in an increase in male violence and in women becoming mangers of the crisis in the face of the erosion of work and the family: a postmodern precarious form of 'double socialization' has been produced. Traditional family relations continue to dissolve. Women, however, currently face responsibility both for money and for life/ subsistence. They are being increasingly integrated to the market without having nonetheless, a possibility of ensuring their own existence (Scholz 2000b). The crisis of daily life manifests as women administrating crisis, and does not have an emancipatory character for them. Quite the opposite: for women, it entails the double burden of being subjected to precarity and the imperative of efficiency.

3   Federici: Accumulation and Reproduction

In some of her most important books, Italian feminist Silvia Federici (2004, 2012, 2018) analyzes the role of reproductive labor as a source of value creation and exploitation. To do so, she argues that reproductive labor ensures capitalist

---

9   In the Fordist phase, the model of the nuclear family based on the dichotomous hierarchy reached its peak. Thus, the dissociation of the feminine was a precondition for the development of productive forces. That is, of the growth of relative surplus value with which wealth increases.

accumulation because it produces and reproduces the most essential commodity—labor power—and guarantees a series of activities that, although
they are not considered labor and not remunerated, are the flip side of the increase in productivity of the waged workforce. These activities are mystified as
personal services and even women's bodies are considered and exploited
as natural resources. For Federici, the genesis of reproductive labor lies in the
separation of production and reproduction, the use of the wage or the moneti-
zation of economic life, and the devaluation of women's social position. At the
same time, reproductive labor, in its nonremunerated character, is a key element for understanding the process of the construction of femininity, masculinity and gender-based hierarchies.

Federici argues that gender should not be defined in cultural terms under a
capitalist society, but as a specification of the class relation:

> if 'femininity' has been constituted in capitalist society as a work-function
> masking the production of the workforce under the cover of a biological
> destiny, then "women's history" is "class history," and the question that
> has to be asked is whether the sexual division of labor that has produced
> that particular concept has been transcended.
>
> FEDERICI 2004: 14

That is why she will defend the use of the categories 'woman' and 'reproduction' for analyzing and linking struggles.

To historicize the emergence of reproductive labor, it is important to recover the other axis of Federici's analysis (especially in *Caliban and the Witch*): the
process of *primitive accumulation*. In her perspective, this is a universal process
that takes place in every phase of capitalist development, not only in the
founding moment that establishes the structural conditions of the economic
system. As a process of the appropriation of property, relationships, and com-
munal knowledge, on the one hand, and, on the other, of the rationalization of
social reproduction and increase in the intensity of exploitation, it is repeated
in every moment of crisis as a new expansion of the capitalist relation, using
enclosure, expropriation, privatization, pauperization, criminalization, confinement or exclusion of migrants and women. In short, it uses violence as a
productive force.[10]

---

10   Referring to the well-known phrase from Marx, "Force is the midwife of every old society
      pregnant with a new one" (Marx 1946: 776) Federici will say in a footnote: "Comparing
      force to the generative powers of a midwife also casts a benign veil over the process of

These mechanisms of primitive accumulation seek to lower labor costs and hide exploitation of women and colonial subjects, using racism and sexism to denigrate those exploited by capitalism. In this way, the dynamic of capitalist development expresses the dialectic movement between accumulation and destruction of labor power.[11] Specifically, she finds these mechanisms in the witch hunts of the 16th and 17th centuries, in the processes of colonization of the Third World, and in the expropriation to the European peasantry. In other words, this process was the result of an offensive led by the ruling classes that used violence and terror to impose divisions among the working class.[12] The genocides perpetrated during colonization and the witch hunts were crucial for imposing sexual and racial hierarchies in order to break alliances and impose an international and sexual division of labor.[13]

Another mechanism was the commodification of economic life which meant an end to production for use replaced by production for the market. Production relations for the market as carriers of other social relations implied an increasing sexual differentiation of activities and the separation of production (creator of value) from reproduction. The activities involved in reproduction were considered non-labor and lacking value. They were made invisible as labor and carrying out these activities became associated with women's natural

---

capital accumulation, suggesting necessity, inevitability, and ultimately, progress." (Federici 2004: 118).

11 Another one of her major critiques of Marx is that his analysis of primitive accumulation is biased by the masculine point of view: a focus on the waged proletariat, by only observing commodity production. That is why she will emphasize changes in women's social position, observing the production of the labor force and denying the thesis of the necessity of capitalism and the progressive decrease in violence that its development would imply.

12 The figures of Caliban and the witch are taken from *The Tempest* by Shakespeare, in which Caliban is the native rebel, the witch's son, and symbol of a possible fatal alliance of the oppressed (the European proletariat, women, and colonized people), and of the dramatic counterpoint of their defeat before property and disunion imposed by Prospero. Federici analyzes this work as part of a literature that showed the European upper class's fear of the unity of the oppressed and the process that leads to the establishment of sexual and racial borders, which only become irrevocable starting in the 18th century.

13 To this respect, this process was not "simply an accumulation and concentration of exploitable workers and capital. It was *also an accumulation of differences and divisions within the working class*, whereby hierarchies built upon gender, as well as "race" and age, became constitutive of class rule and of the formation of modern proletariat" (Federici 2004: 63–64). Consequently, primitive accumulation can be seen as an "accumulation of differences, inequalities, hierarchies, divisions, which have alienated workers from each other and even from themselves" (Federici 2004: 115).

vocation, confined to them. The resultant process was that of the *devaluing* and *feminization* of reproductive labor.

According to Federici, the wage is not only used as a mechanism of commodification, but also as a tool with which capital governs and develops, as a foundation of capitalist society and an expression of the power relation between capital and workers. It has been used to exploit waged and unwaged workers. And the exploitation of the nonwage laborer has been "even more effective because of the lack of a wage hid it" as explained by Dalla Costa and James (1997: 44). That is to say, women's reproductive labor has been a mechanism for increasing the unpaid portion of the waged working day. Therefore, waged labor has depended on them, as a necessary condition to lower the cost of reproduction of the workforce.

Thus, the consolidation of the *patriarchy of the wage* was necessary so that the extraction of *absolute surplus value*, based on the extension of the working day, could be carried out simultaneously to the extraction of *relative surplus value*, based on the increase in productivity in the major productive centers of Europe and later in the United States. With wage increases in the second half of the 19th century[14]—under the 'concession' of the family wage—women were expelled from industrial work and the capitalist class invested in improving the conditions of reproduction of the one commodity that produces value: labor power. In same number of working hours, the worker of the nuclear family now produced more value. With the increase in productivity plus the extraction of labor power in nonremunerated ways from women and colonial subjects, and the nonstop privatization and exploitation of common wealth, the recovery of the rate of profit was achieved following the 1873 crisis. Simultaneously, the waged proletariat found its living conditions improved and its reproduction was guaranteed by women's unpaid work, while women's domination was ensured by making them dependent on the male wage. Thus, the male alliance to the patriarchy of the wage was consolidated.

---

14   In approximately 1870, a great reform process started in England and the U.S., from which the proletarian family was created. This process was the expression of a historical change in the politics of capital. Until 1850–1860, capitalism was based on what Marx called 'absolute exploitation.' But what we see starting in the late 19th century, with the introduction of the family wage, the male worker's wage, is that women who used to work in factories were rejected and sent home, so that domestic work turned into their main work and they became dependent (Federici 2018).

4   Discussion

4.1   *Precarization Is Not Only Explained by Patriarchal/Racist Culture*
         (That Discriminates) or by the Withdrawal of the State (That
         Excludes)

Drawing on this theoretical and conceptual analysis, we can more clearly see
the dangers involved in neoliberal capture of the explanations given by some
feminist economics perspectives about the emergence and role of increasing
precarization in the contemporary neoliberal stage. These analyses characterize the main social dynamic of patriarchal capitalism in its neoliberal stage as
the movement of states, markets, and households between economic and political inclusion and exclusion through the distribution of rights, wealth, and
care. For them, the precarization of the female workforce would correspond to
a movement of exclusion based on an unfair social organization of care. Thus,
the State's withdrawal and an unequal distribution of the time dedicated to reproductive tasks in the household would result in loss in women's productivity.

It is true that in a context in which women take on a double role, in the reproductive sphere and in the labor market, their total working time increases.
Given that current labor flexibility demands mobility and availability, women
find themselves at a disadvantage because they are burdened with hours of
reproductive work and the rigidity of care times. However, there is a weakness
in explaining precarization in terms of exclusion or discrimination: the massive entry of women and sexual dissidents into the labor market cannot be
explained as an effect of decisions made by women and dissidents, or as a result of 'empowerment.' This clashes with the current survival of patriarchal
culture (and leads to situations of gender discrimination in the market and at
home), or the unfair distribution of care work due to the withdrawal of the
State (which leads to exclusion from the labor market and, thus, from political
and social rights). It is precisely this discourse that neoliberalism uses in order
to increase the number of hours of waged labor that a family needs for its reproduction (and that makes single parent families necessarily poor) (Fraser
2013).

We have seen that the model of the nuclear family based on the (male) family wage, takes place in the context of a welfare state that was progressively and
continually eroded starting with the oil crisis in 1973. Neoliberal policies or-
chestrated by the World Bank and International Monetary Fund led to a restructuring of class relations, structural adjustment, and recolonization in a
new cycle of primitive accumulation (as put by Federici 2004) or accumulation
by dispossession (Harvey 2004). Using policies of privatization, commodification, and flexibilization, States reoriented their model to ensure the recovery

of the average profit rate by the absolute exploitation of the living (productive and reproductive capacities and common goods).

Drawing on 'unitary theory' (Arruzza 2014), which considers the capitalist-patriarchal-racist system in the totality of the relationships involved, I think that it is a mistake to dissociate the political or the cultural from the economic, as if they were discrete spheres of reality. It can be affirmed then that the massive and precarious entry of women into the labor market responds to the needs of value to valorize and commodify new regions and relationships (incorporating them into the market logic) in the face of its progressive economic devaluation. The precarization of labor and life, in this case, is a mechanism of extraction of absolute surplus value or hyper-exploitation, which mostly relies on feminized and racialized bodies of the Global South.

Therefore, it cannot be reversed solely by policies of inclusion or with a cultural shift to eliminate racial and patriarchal prejudices and thus achieve a more equal redistribution of waged and reproductive working hours between households, communities, the market, and the State. Although necessary, these actions do not target the cause of the precarization of labor and life, which increases in the context of the crisis of neoliberalism. Liberal Feminism's demand for greater inclusion in the logic of value supposes the need for more wages to guarantee the reproduction of life and for reproductive activities—that no man, woman, or youth can guarantee on their own due to the need to precariously employ themselves—to be commodified as the only way to ensure them, through the market, and survive.

At the same time, this means a greater loss of time for life and the productive and reproductive capacities that are transformed into available time for eventual and unpredictable absolute exploitation as abstract, equivalent time.

4.2   In the Face of Precarization: Wages for Reproductive Labor?

Of the two main theses elaborated by Silvia Federici, about primitive accumulation—continued in her current work on the commons—and on reproductive labor, I think that the first allows us to find more interpretative keys for understanding the dynamics and structure of contemporary patriarchal capitalism than the second.

According to her, it is through the wage that capital extracts labor from unwaged individuals, but also recognizes those who are workers and are part of the social contract. In Federici's (2012) perspective, housework is "money for capital" (p. 19) and, therefore, should be paid. At the same time, this would undermine capital's power to extract labor. This is why the proletarian housewife would be the crucial subject and reproductive labor would be a point zero for revolution. But to consider 'human capital' from this perspective, values and homologates labor as if the hours invested on production and reproduction were equal. In the words of Segato,[15] what operates here is a "convertibility among uprooted existences." Reducing value dissociation to the logic of valorization, does not lead to degenerating, denaturalizing, demythologizing, and subverting the role of women and sexual dissidents and the patriarchal social expectations about their capacities and social needs.

Although the demand for a greater part of global social wealth (still in its commercial form dissociated from the needs for which it is produced) is part of class struggle within the capital-labor relation, it is not the only (nor the most strategic) form that class struggle can adopt. The demand for payment for reproductive labor does not necessarily undermine the power of capital or the wage to demand or extract labor (that is precarized) and, as a counterpoint, accepts capital's social contract and its form of recognition that only enables subjects as long as they are waged workers.

Even though workers' demands around wage levels are a fundamental part of class struggle, we can see that other struggles for the reproduction of life are becoming increasingly central and powerful in the global fight against capital. That is because, especially in the Global South, the imperative of valorization and the growing need to translate all the capacities, time, and energy of individuals into the logic of profit and productivity (saving time), occurs in a context where conditions are increasingly more precarious. And, based on the primitive accumulation thesis, we can say that this is the condition and result of privatization and the extraction of common goods by capital in its general advance over the reproduction of life.

4.3 In the Face of Precarization, Struggles for the Reproduction of Life

As already discussed, according to Roswitha Scholz, precarization provides an index of the brutality of the patriarchy as a commodity producer. Her theory allows us to unravel the *logic* of value and its dissociation, to characterize the current moment of crisis, and to reconsider the role and tendency of waged labor (increasingly scarce and precarious, *feminized*) and of reproductive labor (increasingly *commodified*). However, its high level of abstraction does not allow us to conceptualize the role of struggles for the reproduction of life that are multiplying across Latin America.

---

15 Rita Segato in the presentation of 'Una lectura feminista de la deuda' [*A Feminist Reading of Debt*] (Cavallero and Gago 2019) in the International Book Fair, Buenos Aires, April 2019.

The historicization and conceptualization of primitive accumulation (as a mechanism that is repeated in every moment of capitalist crisis) developed in Federici's work, as well as the explanation of the emergence and functioning of the *patriarchy of the wage* during Fordism, are fundamental complements to Scholz's theoretical contribution. However, some contributions from the Global South could allow us to better refine the phenomenon of the current increase in precarization.

Bhattacharya (2015) warns of the economic bias both of the debates on reproduction and the concept of class. I believe that the multiplication and power that struggles for the reproduction of life have been gaining across Latin America over the last four decades respond to a strategic turn of class struggle in the face of the incessant precarization of life. From this perspective, the privatization of services and the public sphere, the dispossession of common goods, the xenophobic and conservative turns to racialize and feminize even more labor power and thus (hyper)exploit its *difference*—all of which have profoundly accelerated over the past forty years of neoliberalism—are nothing but the other side of increased unemployment, precarization, and progressive loss of power in the global correlation of forces between capital and labor. Therefore, struggles over the means of reproduction—such as educational and health struggles, struggles against agribusiness, against the (hyper)exploitation-oppression of feminized and racialized bodies—are an essential part of class struggle.

In Latin America, there are numerous examples of struggles in defense of common goods of Indigenous communities, feminist struggles, struggles for land and housing, against privatization, against debt, in short, struggles for the (re)appropriation of the means of (re)production of life. Although studying them exceeds the scope of this work, some theoretical contributions from Latin American authors on this matter shall at least be mentioned. For instance, Bolivian sociologist and historian Silvia Rivera Cusicanqui (2018) sketches out a *chi'ixi*[16] theory of value, that starts from the understanding of the sacred character (of connection with the whole, nature, community) that productive activity has for certain communities. Argentinian social scientist Verónica Gago has written extensively on popular economies, neoliberalism, financialization and the extractive operations of capital from a Latin American perspective (see, for instance, Cavallero and Gago 2019; Gago 2015, 2018).

---

16   The Amymara word *ch'ixi* reflects the idea of "something that is and is not at the same time." A *ch'ixi* color gray is black but not black at the same time; it is white but not white at the same time. Instead, it is both with and black (Rivera Cusicanqui 2012: 105).

Mexican sociologist Raquel Gutiérrez Aguilar writes about struggles for the commons, resistance and social transformations, and practices 'among women' that tie together the private with the public (see, for instance, Gutiérrez Aguilar 2011, 2015, 2016). Other reflections on the exploitation of the commons and the encapsulation of care as something feminine and private can be found on Quiroga Díaz and Gago (2014) and Segato (2010).

The commitment to de-commodify and de-alienate social relations, to break the logic of value and its dissociation, the separation between production and reproduction, and between people and their social capacities and needs reorients the strategic meaning of (waged, precarious, unemployed) working class struggles toward struggles to reappropriate the commons and for the reproduction of life as a whole. The struggles against monopolization, transnationalization, and privatization, against the destruction, plunder, and exploitation of nature and human lives, as well as the construction of commons from and against our precarious conditions and multiple forms of oppression are struggles oriented toward the free access and conscious management of resources of production and reproduction as long as they recuperate productive and reproductive capacities, time for life, and irreducible human energies.

References

Arruzza, C. (2014, September). "Remarks on gender." *Viewpoint Magazine*. https://www .viewpointmag.com/2014/09/02/remarks-on-gender/.

Beck, U. (1992). *Risk Society: Towards a New Modernity*. SAGE Publications Ltd.

Becker-Schmidt, R. (1987). "Dynamik Sozialen Lernens: Geschlechterdifferenz und Konflikte aus der Perspektive von Frauen." In R. Becker-Schmidt and G.-A. Knapp (Eds.), *Geschlechtertrennung—Geschlechterdifferenz. Suchbewegungen sozialen Lernens*. Verlag Neue Ges.

Benston, M. (1969). "The Political Economy of Women's Liberation." *Monthly Review* 21(4): 13–27. https://doi.org/10.14452/MR-021-04-1969-08_2.

Bhattacharya, T. (2015). "How Not To Skip Class: Social Reproduction of Labor and the Global Working Class." *Viewpoint Magazine*. https://www.viewpointmag.com/ 2015/10/31/how-not-to-skip-class-social-reproduction-of-labor-and-the-global -working-class/.

Briales Canseco, Á. (2013). "El patriarcado productor de mercancías: la teoría del valor-escisión de Roswitha Scholz." *Comunicación Al IV Congreso de Economía Feminista*.

Cavallero, L., and Gago, V. (2019). *Una lectura feminista de la deuda*. Fundación Rosa Luxemburgo.

Dalla Costa, M. (1972). "Las mujeres y la subversión de la comunidad." In M. Dalla Costa and S. James (Eds.), *El poder de la mujer y la subversión de la comunidad.* Siglo XXI Editores.

Dalla Costa, M., and James, S. (1997). "Women and the Subversion of the Community." In R. Hennessy and C. Ingraham (Eds.), *Materialist Feminism: A Reader in Class, Difference, and Women's Lives* (pp. 40–53). Psychology Press.

Davis, A. (1981). *Women, Race & Class.* Vintage Books.

Delphy, C. (1982). *Por un feminismo materialista. El enemigo principal y otros textos.* LaSal.

Federici, S. (2004). *Caliban and the Witch: Women, the Body, and Primitive Accumulation.* Autonomedia.

Federici, S. (2012). *Revolution at Point Zero: Housework, Reproduction and Feminist Struggle.* PM Press.

Federici, S. (2017). "Economía feminista entre movimientos e instituciones: posibilidades, límites, contradicciones." In C. Carrasco Bengoa and C. Díaz Corral (Eds.), *Economía Feminista. Desafíos, propuestas, alianzas.* Entrepueblos.

Federici, S. (2018). *El patriarcado del salario. Críticas feministas al marxismo.* Traficantes de Sueños.

Fraser, N. (2013, October 14). "How feminism became capitalism's handmaiden—and how to reclaim it." *The Guardian.* https://www.theguardian.com/commentisfree/2013/oct/14/feminism-capitalist-handmaiden-neoliberal.

Gago, V. (2015). "Financialization of popular life and the extractive operations of capital: a perspective from Argentina." *South Atlantic Quarterly* 114(1): 11–28. https://doi.org/10.1215/00382876-2831257.

Gago, V. (2018). "What are popular economies? Some reflections from Argentina." *Radical Philosophy* 202: 31–38. https://www.radicalphilosophy.com/article/what-are-popular-economies.

Gutiérrez Aguilar, R. (Ed.). (2011). *Palabras para tejernos, resistir y transformar la época que estamos viviendo.* Pez en el Árbol.

Gutiérrez Aguilar, R. (2015). *Desandar el laberinto: Introspección en la feminidad contemporánea.* Tinta Limón.

Gutiérrez Aguilar, R. (2016). *Horizontes comunitario-populares. Producción de lo común más allá de las políticas estado-céntricas.* Traficantes de Sueños.

Hartmann, H. (1979). "Un matrimonio mal avenido: hacia una unión más progresista entre marxismo y feminismo." *Zona Abierta* 24: 85–113.

Harvey, D. (2004). "El "nuevo" imperialismo: acumulación por desposesión." *Socialist Register.* https://socialistregister.com/index.php/srv/article/download/14997/11983/.

Herrero, Y. (2017). "Economía ecológica y economía feminista: un diálogo necesario." In C. Carrasco Bengoa and C. Díaz Corral (Eds.), *Economía Feminista. Desafíos, propuestas, alianzas.* Entrepueblos.

Horkheimer, M., and Adorno, T. (1947). *Dialektik der Aufklärung*. Querido Verlag.

James, S. (1975). *Sex, race and class*. Falling Wall Press.

Jappe, A. (2016). *Las aventuras de la mercancía*. Pepitas de Calabaza.

Martínez Domínguez, I. (2016). "La fuerza política de la teoría del valor-escisión de Roswitha Scholz." *Daimon Revista Internacional De Filosofía* 5: 699–704. https://doi.org/10.6018/daimon/272591.

Marx, K. (1946). *Capital: A Critique of Political Economy*. Unwin Brothers Limited.

Mitchell, J. (1971). *Woman's Estate*. Penguin.

Navarro Ruiz, C. (2017). "Escisión del valor, género y crisis del capitalismo. Entrevista con Roswitha Scholz." *Constelaciones. Revista de Teoría Crítica* 8–9: 475–502. http://constelaciones-rtc.net/article/view/2193/2257.

Pérez Orozco, A. (2014). *Subversión feminista de la economía. Aportes para un debate sobre el conflicto capital-vida*. Traficantes de Sueños.

Pérez Orozco, A. (2017). "¿Espacios económicos de subversión feminista?" In C. Carrasco Bengoa and C. Díaz Corral (Eds.), *Economía Feminista. Desafíos, propuestas, alianzas*. Entrepueblos.

Quiroga Díaz, N., and Gago, V. (2014). "Los comunes en femenino. Cuerpo y poder ante la expropiación de las economías para la vida." *Economía y Sociedad* 19(45): 1–18. https://www.revistas.una.ac.cr/index.php/economia/article/view/5985/5934.

Rivera Cusicanqui, S. (2012). "Ch'ixinakax utxiwa: A Reflection on the Practices and Discourses of Decolonization." *The South Atlantic Quarterly* 111(1): 95–109. https://doi.org/10.1215/00382876-1472612.

Rivera Cusicanqui, S. (2018). *Un mundo ch'ixi es posible. Ensayos desde un presente en crisis*. Tinta Limón.

Scholz, R. (1992). "Der Wert ist der Mann." *Krisis* 12: 19–52. http://ecamp.blogsport.de/images/RoswithaScholzDerWertIstDerMann.pdf.

Scholz, R. (2000a). "¡Fuera holgazanas! Sobre la relación de género y trabajo en el feminismo." *EXIT!* http://www.obeco-online.org/rst.htm.

Scholz, R. (2000b). *Das Geschlecht des Kapitalismus: Feministische Theorien und die postmoderne Metamorphose des Patriarchats*. Horlemann.

Scholz, R. (2013a). "El patriarcado productor de mercancías. Tesis sobre capitalismo y relaciones de género." *Constelaciones: Revista de Teoría Crítica* 5: 44–60. https://dialnet.unirioja.es/servlet/articulo?codigo=4761823.

Scholz, R. (2013b, July). "Feminismus—Kapitalismus—Ökonomie—Krise. Wert-Abspaltungs-kritische Einwände gegenüber einigen Ansätzen feministischer Ökonomiekritik heute." *EXIT!* https://www.exit-online.org/textanz1.php?tabelle=autoren&index=23&posnr=517&backtext1=text1.php.

Segato, R. (2010). "Género y colonialidad: en busca de claves de lectura y de un vocabulario estratégico descolonial." In A. Quijano and J. Mejía (Eds.), *La cuestión descolonial*. Universidad Ricardo Palma.

Von Bosse, H., Haarmann, P., Hausinger, B., and Ortlieb, C. (2014). "Regarding the Krisis Group Division." *EXIT!* https://www.exit-online.org/textanz1.php?tabelle= transnationales&index=3&posnr=23&backtext1=text1.php.

Wallerstein, I. (1998). *Impensar las ciencias sociales: límites de los paradigmas deci- monónicos.* Siglo XXI Editores.

CHAPTER 4

Gender and Economics in Latin America: a Systematic Analysis of Scientific Production in Scopus

Claudia Maldonado-Erazo and Pablo Quiñonez

1   Introduction

In the context of an economic and social system marked by glaring inequalities, women are and have been disadvantaged throughout history in many areas, including the academic world. Indeed, from a historical perspective, the presence of women as students and faculty in the world's universities is relatively new, and although their presence has grown markedly in recent years, women are still disadvantaged in virtually every facet of academia, even in developed countries (Shen 2013).

For example, in the European Union, despite steady progress in recent years, only a third of researchers are women; they continue to be under-represented in the publication of scientific articles, in patent registrations, and in the receipt of research grants; in 2017 only 22% of higher education institutions were headed by women; and, in 2014, women working in research and development earned on average 17% less than their male colleagues (European Commision 2019).

Of course, this unfavorable bias against women is rooted in a specific matrix of thought that tends to reinforce itself and the phenomena derived from it. Clearly this casts doubt on the notion that meritocracy prevails in the academic world. Such is the reality that, for example, numerous studies have found that even from childhood the role of a scientist is usually associated with men (Cvencek et al. 2011; Steinke et al. 2007). It is therefore not surprising that even after considering factors that could affect the level of success in an academic career, there is a great deal of evidence that shows that women's efforts and academic achievements are less valued and rewarded than those of men (Ellemers 2018; Van der Lee and Ellemers 2018).

As suggested above, focusing specifically on the publication of scientific articles, the reality is similar. A recent study that considered more than 10 million articles published since 2002, covering most of the STEMM disciplines (Science, Technology, Engineering, Mathematics, and Medicine), found that, despite recent progress, the gender gap is still far from closing and that, in certain disciplines such as surgery, computer science, physics, and mathematics, at the current rate, the gap would not be closed in this century (Holman et al. 2018).

Such a reality, which becomes more pronounced as the prestige of academic journals increases, is not exclusive to STEMM disciplines, although it is probably not as acute in other areas. For example, in the social sciences, Teele and Thelen (2017) found after reviewing 10 of the most prestigious political science journals, that the low proportion of female authors published in these journals does not simply reflect a low proportion of women researching in that domain. Rather, there is an under-representation of women in the most prominent political science journals, and most collaborative research in these journals is defined in terms of exclusively male teams.

Added to this is the fact that research aimed at making these problems visible has usually been marginalized in the academic world. For example, Cislak et al. (2018) employed a bibliometric methodology covering a wide range of social sciences, and revealed that articles concerning gender bias received less funding and were often published in journals with lower impact factors than comparable articles on social discrimination. This reflects not only explicit mechanisms of discrimination, but also more subtle mechanisms related to a negative bias in the perceived quality of gender discrimination studies (Handley et al. 2015).

There is abundant evidence that those who carry out research into gender-related areas, in different disciplines, are mostly women (Caro and Guarinos 2017; Söderlund and Madison 2015). However, gender studies have usually been pigeonholed and linked exclusively to the commitment to action of gender activists.

In addition, it is well-known that most research on gender and related issues emanates from traditional Western centers of knowledge, making being located in an American or Western European institution a crucial factor for authors to be published and cited (Wöhrer 2016). Indeed, 79.5% of the literature on women's studies between 1900 and 2013 was written by authors working in the United States and the United Kingdom (Tsay and Li 2017).

As far as Latin America is concerned, academic interest from the social sciences in the situation of women has been evident since the 1970s, especially on issues related to the field of development and the debates that prevailed at that time in the region and the wider world. However, despite the emergence of these pioneering works, generally grouped under the category of 'women's studies,' it was not until the mid-1980s that a relatively large number of studies using gender as a category of analysis emerged (Caulfield 2001). It is not surprising, therefore, that Ann Pescatello, in the early 1970s, regretted the underdevelopment, in general, of studies on Latin American women, finding a field so incipient that it was difficult for her to identify the main trends and authors (Pescatello 1972).

The progressive preference for the use of the concept of gender instead of the category of women's studies, despite the major points in common regarding the research agenda of both concepts, is due to the eminently biological character of the latter, in contrast to the nature of the former as a social construction that limits behaviors, places, and power relations between the masculine and the feminine (Abbassi and Lutjens 2002). In this sense, the use of 'gender' reflects effort by academics to avoid a certain 'essentialism' understood as the treatment of social phenomena as external and prior to the social and cultural structures, practices, and discourses that gave rise to them (Jackson 1998).

In this context, this chapter aims to shed light on the current situation and historical evolution of research published in high impact journals in the intersection of the areas of gender and economics in Latin America, which have been closely linked in research on gender issues since their very emergence in the region. To this end, an exploratory-quantitative bibliometric analysis will be carried out, considering the scientific production that is indexed in the Elsevier Group's Scopus database and that focuses specifically on issues related to gender and the economy in the region.

The remainder of the chapter is structured as follows. Section 2 presents a review of the literature on discussions of gender and economics in the region. Section 3 provides methodological details. Section 4 describes and discusses the results. Section 5 offers conclusions including limitations of this study.

2   Research on Gender and Economics in Latin America

As we know, the term gender has traditionally been used to refer to the biological differences between men and women (Castaño 1999), and it has gradually come to be considered as a series of dialectic constructions that frame specific functions and actions to each one of them, which in many cases originate from the social construction of the culture of various human groups. These constructions have shown an evident separation of activities, roles, and attitudes, associating women only with activities of the home, with submission, intuition, or as the bridge connection with nature and/or others; while men have been placed in an instance that could be considered relatively superior, because they are considered capable of executing relations with the market, power, and/or the public sphere.

Thus, a system of relations has been established around gender in which spaces of dominance (visible, masculine) and domination (invisible, feminine) have developed (Blau et al. 2002; Carrasco 2003; Vásconez 2017). It is especially from the 1970s and 80s onwards that a considerable and growing interest in the study of this phenomenon can be detected within the social sciences, and it is during this period that the concept begins to be appreciated as something that goes beyond cultural or biological issues, being rather a transdisciplinary category that takes its own form, from which comprehensions of activities, beliefs, values, and behaviors are created that are socially appreciated and different for women and men, and which should be studied (Benería and Roldán 1992).

However, the fight against such discrimination can probably be situated long before the rise of academic interest in the subject, at least in Latin America. In this region, among the first actions that put women on 'equal footing' with men was the conquest of the right to vote, which first occurred in 1924 with the vote of Matilde Hidalgo Navarro in Ecuador. Nevertheless, it is clear that, despite being able to exercise this right, the political participation of Latin American women is still restricted to this day (Desposato and Norrander 2009).

Returning to the discussion on the emergence of academic interest in the area in Latin America, it was around 1970 that the first studies on the inequality faced by women and its influence on the development of the region were recorded (Lovell 2006). This fits, in a certain way, with a second wave of the feminist movement at the international level, which between 1960 and 1970 gave rise to a systematic production of knowledge that had not occurred before then, and which allowed for a broader understanding of women's conditions (De Barbieri 2004).

However, it is difficult to study Latin American women in depth during these early years, since initial research efforts and outputs did not reach spaces of diffusion that would position them in the best way in the academic world. A lack of enthusiasm amongst scholars for feminist causes,[1] as diagnosed by Pescatello (1972), is also noteworthy. Nevertheless, this pioneering work by

---

1   In Latin America, women's studies did not emerge from a vigorous women's liberation movement (as was the case in the United States and some European countries); and, in fact, among the pioneering scholars of this discipline in the region, several did not consider themselves feminists (Navarro 1979).

Pescatello identified 70 different articles which addressed issues of the reality of Latin American women.

Interestingly, it was research in the field of development that made social science scholars in Latin America turn their attention for the first time to women's issues (Navarro 1979). At that time, the biased participation in labor, the centralization of productive roles, and the unequal levels of development that women faced in different spaces began to be brought to light (Nash and Safa 1976; Saffioti 1969).

It is also interesting to note that, during the 1970s, although several social scientists researching into Latin America worked on women's studies from a Marxist perspective (something which was then relatively common at the global level), most followed the approach of dependency theory, which was widely popular in the region at the time (Navarro 1979). Some of the most outstanding works are those by Jelin (1974), Madeira (1978), Blay (1978) and Machado Neto (1978) for Brazil; De Lattes et al. (1977) for Argentina, Bolivia, and Paraguay; Schmukler (1978) for Argentina; León de Leal (1977) for Colombia; Lustig et al. (1979) for Mexico.

With the arrival of the 1980s, research in the domain would grow considerably, projecting itself solidly towards the 1990s, and the term gender was used with increasing frequency, something very rare in the works published in previous decades. During this period, despite the marginalization they frequently faced, issues related to women's productive participation and their contributions to economic development were explored in depth (Abramo 1998; Brockman 1985; Cabral 1994; Hays-Mitchell 1997; Kidder 1999; Morales i Perez 1999; Pacheco and Blanco 1998; Rowlands 1992). Other areas explored include the sexual division of labor and inequalities in working and wage conditions (Laurie 1997, 1999; Radcliffe 1990; Raynolds 1998; Roberts and Dodoo 1995), women's participation in local, national and international political organizations (Hays-Mitchell 1995; Moreno 1996; Rico 1998; Teissedre 1997), as well as a wide variety of studies on socio-economic impacts of these phenomena (Aslanbeigui et al. 1994; Balan 1990; Chant 1991; Cravey 1997; Guendelman 1987; Molinas 1998; Psacharopoulos and Tzannatos 1993; Scott 1986).

In the 21st century, research on the subject has continued to deepen and expand (see, for example, Deere and León 2000; Esquivel 2011; Reyes 2011; Rodriguez Enriquez 2015; Salvador 2007, among others). Thus, studies on the possibilities and alternatives for development for countries of the Global South, such as those in Latin America, have been enriched by the incorporation of gender as a variable of analysis (Rodríguez Enríquez 2007) although it has not achieved the levels of dissemination that it has in the developed world.

3 Methodology

An exploratory-quantitative bibliometric analysis is undertaken, focused on scientific outputs identified concerning gender and economics in Latin America and indexed within Scopus, an international database administered by the Elsevier group.

The selection of this database is justified by its relatively long temporal coverage, an element that influences the citation data of the documentary units (Hernández-González et al. 2016).

In addition to this, Scopus supports relatively large downloads (maximum 2000 references) of metadata consisting of bibliographic information, summaries, keywords, details per author, and so on (Fernández et al. 1999). Finally, this database applies rigorous and transparent quality standards such as the Scimago Journal Rank (SJR) (Harzing and Alakangas 2016).

The article is established as the documentary unit of analysis, because this type of document is characterized for allowing rapid access to scientific knowledge (Frank 2006) which includes the most recent scholarly contributions of significant value to the research and policy communities (Goldschmidt 1986). The process used for identifying articles from this database is presented in Figure 4.1.

The sample of articles obtained from Scopus was subjected to bibliometric analyses because this allows the treatment and interpretation of different metadata collected within the database. Metadata have been established in the last decade as an important source of information for many scientific studies (Durán-Sánchez et al. 2018) and have become the principal source for the application of several types of bibliometric indicators (Spinak 1996), which arise from different mathematical models based on the relationship between two or more variables (Hubert 1981).

According to Escorcia-Otálora and Poutou-Piñales (2008), at the macro level, bibliometric indicators can be demarcated into two groups. The first group consists of activity indicators, that is, those used to understand the current state of the knowledge area; while the second group consists of impact indicators that determine the relevance of the information at an international level.

A very large number of bibliometric indicators could be constructed for any case-study context because of the permutations which are possible depending on how the sampling frame is configured, how individual indicators are mathematically formulated, and how sets of indicators are configured. As such, it ends up being essentially impossible to claim that a perfect indicator set can be established. Beyond this, the arguments of authors such as Bonilla et al. (2015) should be considered, who state that the quality and relevance of

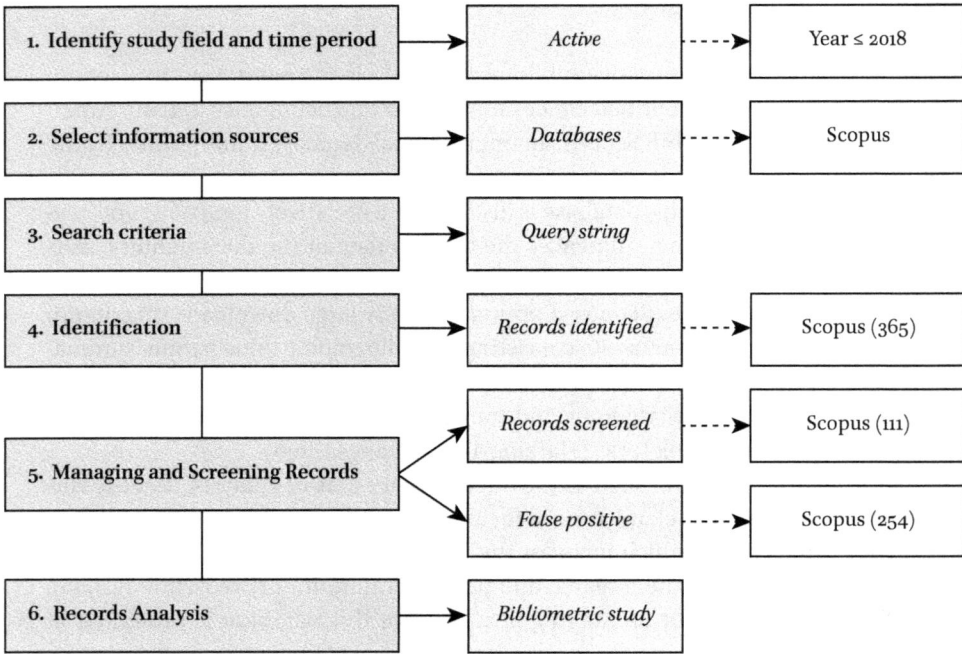

FIGURE 4.1 Sample selection

analyses carried out within bibliometric studies is in direct proportion to the combination of indicators applied to the evaluation of the metadata of each selected documentary unit.

In addition, it should be emphasized that not only is the quantity of indicators decisive for establishing the quality of the study, but it is also necessary to consider that this should be evaluated according to the needs and particularities of the study context. For this purpose Alonso et al. (2009) recommend that the choice and combination of indicators should be made according to their adaptability vis-à-vis the aims and objectives that should be achieved.

In summary, bibliometrics is an effective tool for the organization of academic information existing up to the moment due to the fact that on the one hand, it tracks the bibliographic material which directly concerns a particular subject (Álvarez-García et al. 2018; Andrés 2009); while on the other hand, it can determine the nature and extent of productive behaviors within that subject (Podsakoff et al. 2008).

Taking into consideration all the above, the bibliometric indicators to be used herein are focused on the evolution of publications, most prolific authors, most productive countries, type of institutions conducting research in this

TABLE 4.1   Search strategy

Search terms	gender, econom*, Latin America
Category title	Article title, abstract, keywords
Thematic area	All
Type of document	Article
Period of time	Publication year ≤ 2018
Language	All
Search query	(TITLE-ABS-KEY ("gender") AND TITLE-ABS-KEY ("econom*") AND TITLE-ABS-KEY ("Latin America")) AND DOCTYPE (ar)
Date of search	December 2018

area, article citations, journals with greater concentrations of articles, and co-citation and co-authorship relationships. In addition, introducing a complementary gender analysis with respect to all the indicators will enable exploring the participation of men and women within the development of these studies.

The tracking of documentary units is developed through a database search, based on the criteria and search query described in Table 4.1. The use of these criteria allows the integration of journals from the greatest number of areas of knowledge into the results, rendering searches a highly exhaustive and quality-based process (Álvarez-García et al. 2018; Corral and Cànoves 2013).

Next, management and selection of the documentary units was carried out; a process during which the data collected were refined by eliminating duplicate documents and those unrelated to the subject of the study, the latter situation generated by the inadequate use of keywords by some authors which were then used for indexing purposes by journals. The final sample consisted of 111 articles and a database was then compiled according to the analysis variables required for the application of each selected bibliometric indicator.

4   Results

4.1   *Productivity Over Time*
The sample of 111 articles extracted from Scopus were published over a 34-year period. The first indexed study on gender and economics in Latin America is Women and development in northern Belize, by Brockman (1985).

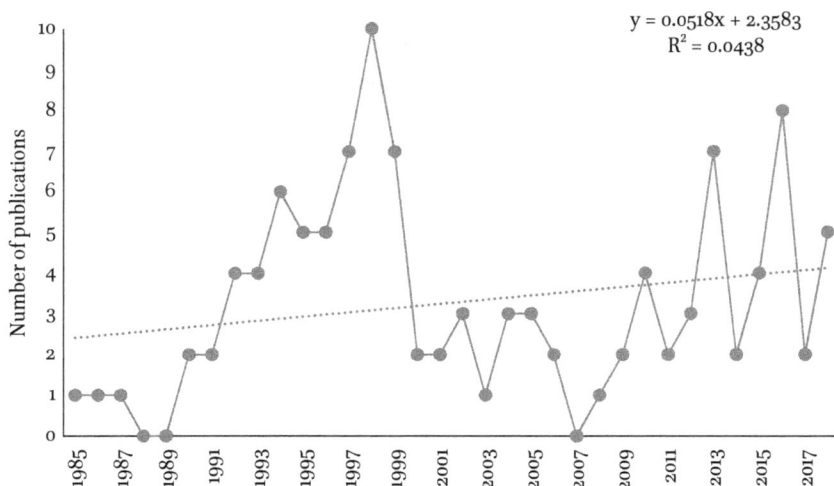

FIGURE 4.2 Evolution of publications indexed in Scopus

Figure 4.2 shows that the most productive year in terms of outputs was in 1998 when 10 articles were published. That year is an important reference for changes within Latin America as several events took place: in the case of Peru, the Ombudsman's Office expressed the importance of respecting the reproductive rights recognized in Art. 6 of that country's Constitution in response to actions taken to regulate the number of children a woman could have; in Argentina, the Salta Constitution incorporated non-discrimination by sex, promoted legal equality at various levels, and encouraged non-sexism in the language of public office; In Ecuador, 35 constitutional reforms were introduced to incorporate women's rights into the 1998 Constitution, which also highlighted the legal vulnerability of other territories where basic rights (voting, divorce, abortion, public participation, education, and so on) continued to be missing for women.

The output trends in Figure 4.2 can usefully be understood according to the three phases of behavior established by López López (1996): precursors, exponential growth, and linear growth. More specifically, in this context, the presence of two phases is identified: the first one, the precursor phase, is developed from 1985 to 1991, and during that period an average of 1 article per year was published and 62.5% of the authors were women. The presence of an incipient production of articles is related to the reduced participation of authors in this period of time, established as the period of birth for the study of the subject. The second phase, or phase of exponential growth, is presented from 1992 to

2018 with an average of 3.85 articles published per year. During this period, there was a substantial increase in the study of the subject, in addition to an increase in the total number of male authors (48, as opposed to 3 in the precursor phase); however, in proportional terms female participation increased during this second phase because 70.4% of the authors were women.

Notwithstanding the fact that academic production in this domain exhibits a non-linear trend, it is undeniable that the literature produced in relation to gender and economics was more abundant in the exponential growth phase than in the precursor phase. Whether this increased quantity also reflects increased quality is beyond the scope of this study. Relatedly, the extent to which new information is produced is an open question although it is perhaps pertinent to note that according to Price's Law, 10 to 15 years after the initiation of any subject of study, the information developed on the subject at a global level will be duplicated (Price 1956).

Importantly, it should also be stressed that the temporal evolution of academic outputs in this domain cannot be regarded as an all-encompassing proxy for the evolutionary behavior of the subject, and it is thus necessary to compare and contrast this with other indicators.

4.2   Citations

In the 34 years of evolution, a total of 1330 citations were made in relation to the 111 articles in the sample, with an average of 11.98 citations per article. Another way of expressing the citation characteristics of this sample is through the h-index; here, h=20 which means that 20 articles out of the 111 articles in the sample have obtained at least 20 citations (Figure 4.3). The highest number of citations (252) occurred in 2002, accounting for 19% of all citations to articles in the sample.

In overall terms, 63% of articles obtained between 1 and 24 citations, while 21% of the articles were uncited during the analysis period. Next, 14% (15) of the papers obtained between 25 and 100 citations and only 1% of the papers record more than 100 citations.

It can also be observed that articles published in the last 10 years lack a considerable number of citations due to the fact that these studies have not yet achieved the necessary dissemination to consolidate themselves as references of the subject, a fact that limits the amount of citations that these can attract (Merigó et al. 2015).

As shown in Table 4.2, the most frequently cited articles are as follows: Gender and the silences of social capital: Lessons from Latin America by Molyneux (2002); The impact of inequality, gender, external assistance and social capital on local-level cooperation by Molinas (1998) and The Gender Gap

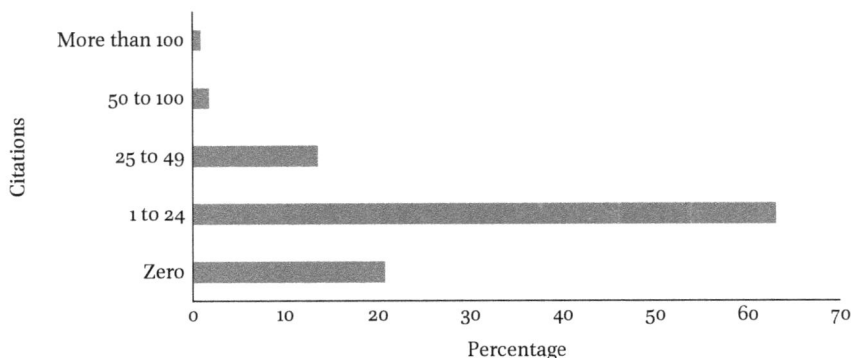

FIGURE 4.3 Distribution of citations across articles in Scopus

TABLE 4.2   Ranking of the most cited articles

Rank	Authors	Title	Year	Citations	Citations/Year
1	Molyneux	Gender and the silences of social capital: Lessons from Latin America	2002	231	13.6
2	Molinas	The impact of inequality, gender, external assistance and social capital on local-level cooperation	1998	82	3.9
3	Desposato & Norrander	The Gender Gap in Latin America: Contextual and individual influences on gender and political participation	2009	52	5.2
4	Aslanbeigui et al.	Women in the age of economic transformation: gender impact of reforms in post-socialist and developing countries	1994	41	1.7
5	Fuwa	The poverty and heterogeneity among female-headed households revisited: The case of Panama	2000	40	2.1
6	Ellis et al.	The circular migration of Puerto Rican women: Towards a gendered explanation	1996	39	1.7
7	Lovell	Race, gender, and work in São Paulo, Brazil, 1960–2000	2006	38	2.9
8	Terjesen & Amorós	Female entrepreneurship in Latin America and the Caribbean: Characteristics, drivers and relationship to economic development	2010	36	4.0

TABLE 4.2   Ranking of the most cited articles (*cont.*)

Rank	Authors	Title	Year	Citations	Citations/ Year
9	Caulfield	The history of gender in the historiography of Latin America.	2001	36	2.0
10	Cravey	The politics of reproduction: Households in the Mexican industrial transition	1997	34	1.5
11	Morgan & Buice	Latin American attitudes toward women in politics: The influence of elite cues, female advancement, and individual characteristics	2013	30	5.0
12	Raynolds	Harnessing women's work: restructuring agricultural and industrial labor forces in the Dominican Republic	1998	30	1.4
13	Hays-Mitchell	Voices and visions from the streets: gender interests and political participation among women informal traders in Latin America	1995	30	1.3
14	Georges	Gender, Class, and Migration in the Dominican Republic: Women's Experiences in a Transnational Community.	1992	30	0.8
15	Stephen	Women's weaving cooperatives in Oaxaca: An indigenous response to neoliberalism	2005	28	2.0
16	Hays-Mitchell	Resisting austerity: A gendered perspective on neo-liberal restructuring in Peru	2002	26	1.5
17	Howes & Singh	Long-term trends in the world economy: the gender dimension	1995	26	1.1
18	Hite & Viterna	Gendering class in Latin America: How women effect and experience change in the class structure	2005	25	1.8
19	Wiig	Joint titling in rural Peru: Impact on women's participation in household decision-making	2013	24	4.0

in Latin America: Contextual and individual influences on gender and political participation by Desposato and Norrander (2009) with 231, 82, and 52 citations, respectively. These articles present an equitable participation in terms of their preparation, that is to say, 2 women and 2 men are counted as the authors who produced these three articles.

In terms of average number of citations per year, the three highest ranked articles are those by Molyneux (2002), Desposato and Norrander (2009), and Morgan and Buice (2013).

4.3   *Authors*

Turning to authorial trends, 169 individuals are registered as authors across the 111 articles in the sample, establishing an average productivity per author of 1.04 articles.

The productivity of the authors can be analyzed by different types of classification that contribute to the process of determining the roles played by each author within the subject of study. To fulfill this purpose, the classification put forward Crane (1977) will be used, in which authors' productivity can be explained through demarcating four groups: (1) large producers, those with an output of more than 10 articles; (2) moderate producers, authors who have produced between 5 and 9 papers; (3) applicants, comprising authors who have penned between 2 and 4 studies, and (4) transients comprising authors who have produced only one paper.

The data presented in Table 4.3 show the existence of two groups of authors. On the one hand, transient authors constitute 96.4% of the total registered authors; this type of author is characterized by contributing only one paper within the line of evolution of the topic. On the other hand, aspiring authors constitute 3.0% of the sample; these authors exhibit greater participation, but still limited. The very high dominance of transient authors in the sample could

TABLE 4.3   Classification of authors according to the Crane system

No. of articles per author	No. of authors	%	PI	Crane Classification	Authors
1	163	96.4	0.000	Passers-by	Other authors Radcliffe, S.A.; Espino, A.;
2	5	3.0	0.301	Applicants	Laurie, N.; Lawson, V.A.; Brown, L.A.
3	1	0.6	0.477		Hays-Mitchell, M.
Total	169	100			

Note: PI = Productivity Index

TABLE 4.4   Ranking of the most productive authors

Rank	Authors	Country	University	f	TC	C/f	h-index
1	Hays-Mitchell, M.	United States	Colgate University	3	151	0.02	6
2	Lawson, V.A.	United States	Ohio State University	2	2083	0.00	24
3	Radcliffe, S.A.	United Kingdom	University of Cambridge	2	1568	0.00	24
4	Brown, L.A.	United States	Ohio State University	2	1201	0.00	19
5	Laurie, N.	United Kingdom	University of Newcastle upon Tyne	2	1056	0.00	18
6	Espino, A.	Uruguay	University of the Republic of Uruguay	2	3	0.67	1

Note: f = Number of published articles; TC = Total citations received for published articles;
C/f = Average citations received for published articles; h-index = Hirsch index.

suggest that individuals studying gender and economics in Latin America tend to do so sporadically.

The ranking of the most productive authors (Table 4.4) consists of those individuals who have developed more than one publication within the area. The most productive author is M. Hays-with a total of 3 articles and a h-index of 6; followed by V.A. Lawson with 2 articles and a h-index of 24; while in third place is S.A. Radcliffe with two articles and a h-index of 24. In addition, it is noteworthy that all six of these most productive authors are women, something consistent with the trend described by Söderlund and Madison (2015) and Caro and Guarinos (2017) who highlight the majority presence of women researching topics related to gender across different areas of knowledge.

With regard to co-authorship trends, it can be posited that the more varied and greater the collaboration recorded in the preparation of articles, the greater the maturity of study of the subject matter (López López 1996). Based on this, it is noted that 68.5% (76) of the articles in the sample were developed individually, with the remaining 31.5% (35) being the result of collaborative endeavors.

Within the sub-sample of papers produced collaboratively, 18.9% (21) were produced by two authors, followed by 9% (10) of works produced by three authors and only 3.6% (4) were the result of collaboration between four or more authors (Figure 4.4).

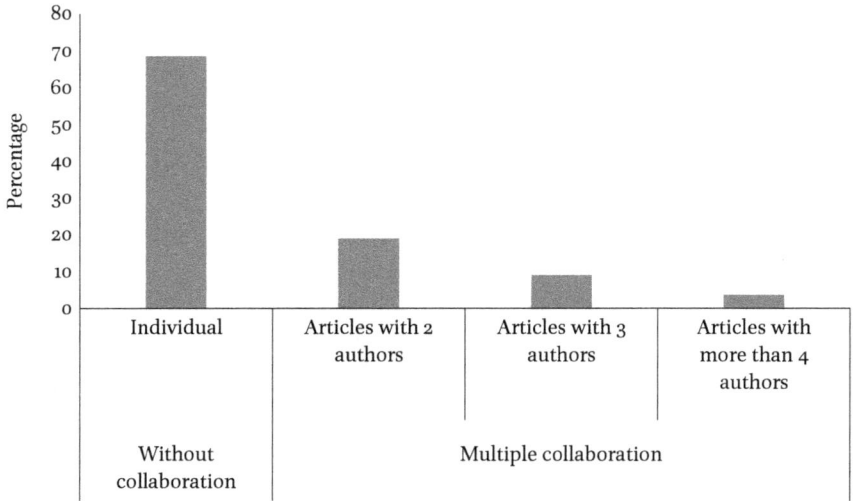

FIGURE 4.4   Co-authorship trends

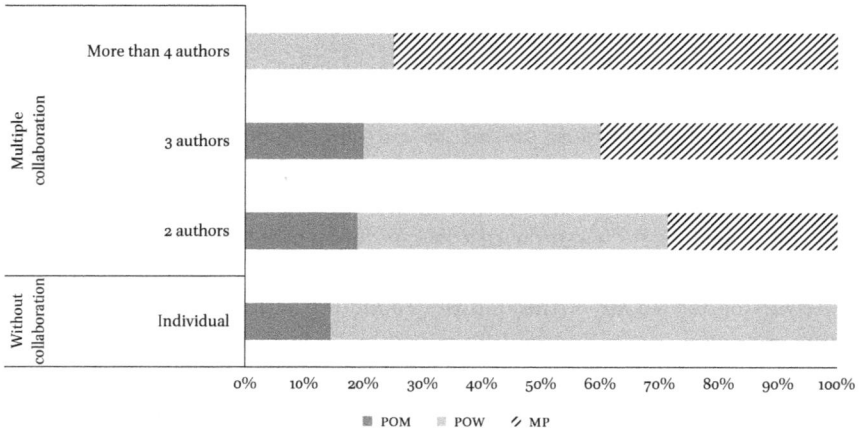

FIGURE 4.5   Co-authorship trends by gender
NOTE: POM = PARTICIPATION ONLY OF MEN; POW = PARTICIPATION
ONLY OF WOMEN; MP = MIXED PARTICIPATION.

Overall, on average there were 1.59 authors per article. Figure 4.5 explores these co-authorship trends in more detail by introducing gender as an additional variable. For papers produced in pairs, which is the predominant collaborative trend, 52.4% of these outputs were produced by two women, followed by 28.6% of documents produced in mixed collaboration (one man and one woman), while 19% were the work of two men.

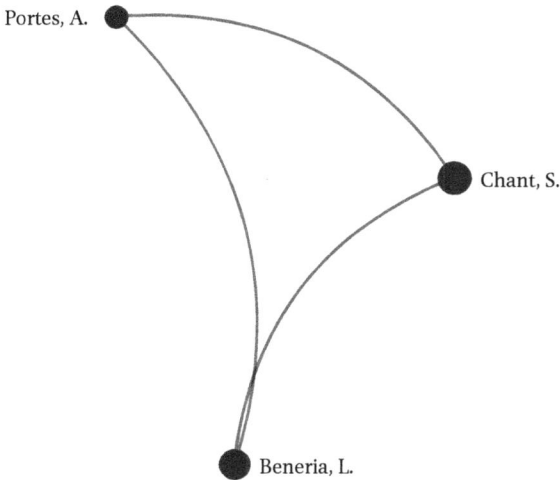

FIGURE 4.6 Co-citation of authors

In addition, a co-citation analysis of the authors in the sample revealed the presence of three individuals who are most prominent in this respect (Figure 4.6). In order of co-citation propensities these authors are S. Chant, I. Beneria, and A. Portes.

4.4   *Productivity by Country and Institution*
Productivity as a function of the affiliations registered by the authors allows evaluation and understanding of the salient information nodes which characterize this domain of research during the time period covered by the sample.

By means of a ranking of positions by geographical affiliation, it is clear that the United States is the main production node, registering 72 authors, 76 authorships, and 50 centers, followed by Chile with 13 authors, 13 authorships, and 12 centers.

In terms of international co-authorship trends, the top five most productive countries suggest the presence of two clusters. In Figure 4.7 Cluster 1 (light gray) presents the United States as the central construct, which has four country-level co-author relationships through 44 documents, the strongest relationship being with the United Kingdom with 11 papers produced. Cluster 2 (dark gray) places Chile as the central construct; three country-level co-author relationships are evident in this cluster through 9 articles, with the strongest relationship being with the United States through 4 publications.

In terms of productivity by institution, 127 different affiliations were recorded (universities, institutes, private companies, public institutions, international

TABLE 4.5   Authors, authorships, and centers by country of affiliation

Rank	Country	A	As	C
1	United States	72	76	50
2	Chile	13	13	12
3	United Kingdom	13	15	11
4	Argentina	4	4	7
5	Mexico	8	8	6
6	Brazil	5	5	5
7	Spain	6	6	5
8	Peru	4	4	4
9	Australia	5	5	3
10	Canada	3	3	3
11	Colombia	4	4	3
12	Ecuador	4	4	3
13	France	3	3	2
14	Netherlands	2	2	2
15	Uruguay	3	4	2
16	Austria	1	1	1
17	Bolivia	1	1	1
18	Costa Rica	2	2	1
19	Germany	1	1	1
20	Japan	1	1	1
21	New Zealand	1	1	1
22	Nicaragua	3	3	1
23	Norway	1	1	1
24	Paraguay	1	1	1
25	No affiliation	8	8	–

Note: A = Authors; As = Authorships; C = Centers

organizations, and so on). The majority of authors in the sample were affiliated to universities (77.3%; 99), followed by research institutes (10.9%; 14).

A ranking of the most productive institutions is presented in Table 4.6. Therein, Ohio State University, based in the United States, is the leader, with 6 affiliations; followed by The World Bank, whose headquarters are located in the United States, with 4 affiliations.

Two types of collaboration networks, institutional and geographic, can be established using the sub-sample of articles which were collaboratively

FIGURE 4.7   Co-authorships by country

TABLE 4.6   Most productive institutions by authorship and gender

R	Institution	Country	Men	Women	A	As
1	Ohio State University	United States	0	6	6	8
2	The World Bank	United States	2	2	4	4
3	Indiana University	United States	2	2	4	4
4	Griffith University	Australia	0	3	3	3
5	National Autonomous University of Nicaragua-León	Nicaragua	3	0	3	3
6	Development University	Chile	2	1	3	3
7	Federico Santa Maria Technical University	Chile	2	1	3	3
8	College of Mexico	Mexico	0	3	3	3
9	Colorado State University	United States	0	3	3	3
10	Tulane University	United States	2	1	3	3
11	University of California	United States	2	1	3	3
12	University of Oregon	United States	0	3	3	3

Note: R = Ranking; A = Authors; As = Authorships.

produced, which represents 31.53% (35) of the total outputs. Within this sub-sample, 60% (21) of the articles are written by authors with affiliations within the same country, and the remaining 40% (14) are works developed among authors from different countries. In the case of national collaborations, 57% (12) are articles are inter-institutional collaborations whilst 43% (9) involve authors who collaborate in the same country and within the same institution.

Analyzing this in more detail by introducing gender (Figure 4.8), 58.33% of the work carried out in national collaborative networks with authors in the same institution, involved exclusively women participants. This proportion is

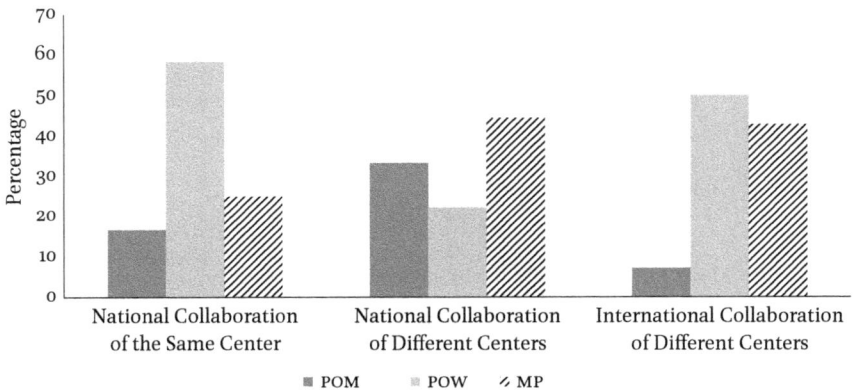

FIGURE 4.8 Collaborative networks by gender
Note: POM = Participation of men only; POW = Participation of women only; MP = Mixed
participation.

smaller if we turn to international collaborations (50%). Interestingly, with respect to national collaboration networks between different institutions, it is
noted that 44.44% of outputs were developed through the collaboration of authors of both sexes, while articles elaborated solely by women were only
22.22% of the total.

4.5   Journals

The 111 articles in the sample were published across 80 different journals. World
Development is the most productive journal with seven published articles, followed by Development in Practice with six publications. However, in relation
to the total number of citations, Development and Change leads with 243 cumulative citations to the published studies, while World Development is in
second position with 195 citations.

Regarding the geographical origin of the journals, they are mainly published
in the United Kingdom (40%; 32), followed by the United States (33.8%; 27). In
addition, in terms of externally ascribed quality metrics, 50% of the journals
are located in the first quartile of the SJR Index (Figure 4.9).

In addition, the Dispersion Index suggests a lack of nucleation in terms
of where articles in the sample are published; on average 1.39 articles are
published per journal with 80% of the journals having only published one
article on this subject. As a complement, it is possible to identify the concentration nuclei generated in relation to scientific outputs on this subject.

TABLE 4.7   Ranking of the most productive journals

Rank	Journal	Country	f	f%	TC	h-index	Q	SJR
1	World Development	UK	7	6.31	195	140	1	2.12
2	Development in Practice	UK	6	5.41	8	34	2	0.31
3	Gender, Place and Culture	UK	5	4.50	29	55	1	1.10
4	Gender and Development	UK	3	2.70	43	30	1	0.64
5	Development	UK	3	2.70	3	29	3	0.15
6	Latin American Research Review	US	3	2.70	77	39	2	0.31

Note: f = Number of published articles; f% = Relative frequency; TC = Number of citations for published articles; h-index = Hirsch index; Q = Quartile; SJR = Scimago Journal Rank Index.

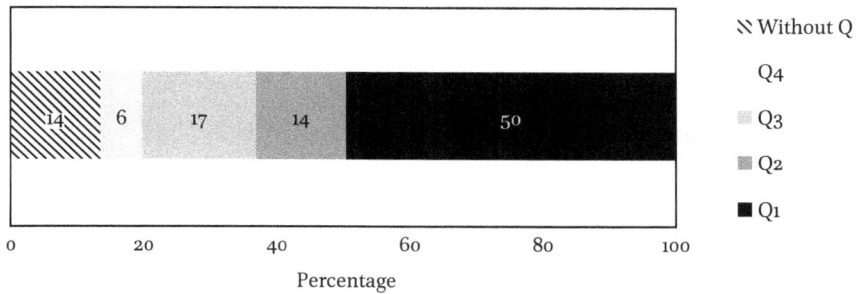

FIGURE 4.9 Distribution of journals according to SJR quartiles

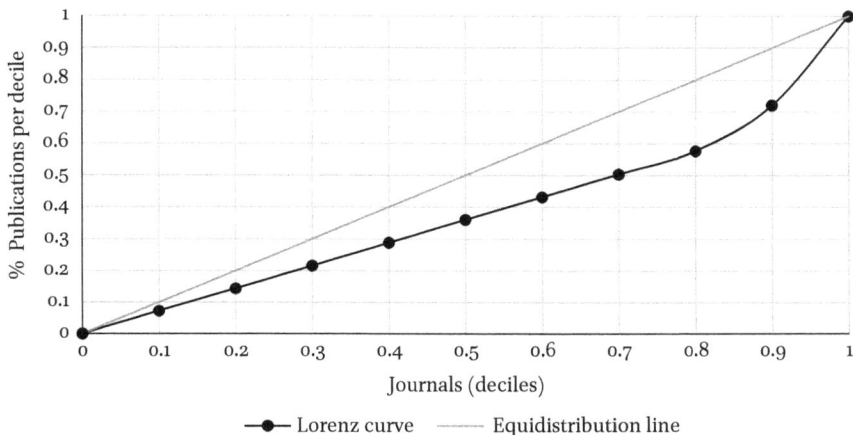

FIGURE 4.10 Lorenz curve—Bradford core of most productive journals

TABLE 4.8   Classification of articles by thematic area

Rank	Area	J	f	TC	C/f
1	Social Sciences	47	71	964	13.6
2	Arts and Humanities	9	13	108	8.3
3	Business, Management, and Accounting	6	6	25	4.2
4	Economics, Econometrics, and Finance	5	6	67	11.2
5	Medicine	4	4	10	2.5
6	Environmental Science	2	3	63	21.0
7	Biochemistry, Genetics, and Molecular Biology	2	2	38	19.0
8	Earth and Planetary Sciences	2	2	1	0.5
9	Health Professions	1	2	11	5.5
10	No information	2	2	43	21.5

Note: J = journals; f = number of published articles; TC = number of citations received for published articles; C/f = average number of citations received for published articles.

For this purpose, the Bradford law (Bradford 1934) is applied, which proposes that, when examining the production of any scientific field, it is possible to identify a high percentage of studies concentrated in a small number of journals. To test this, it is necessary to establish the minimum Bradford zone (MBZ) which takes a value of 32; in this way, by ordering the ranking of journals in descending order according to their productivity, it can be determined that the Bradford core corresponds to the group of journals whose productivity is equal to 32. With what has been established above, it can be seen that the Bradford core is made up of 33 journals as can be seen in Figure 4.10.

4.6   Thematic Areas

Moving on to the thematic areas through which the resources within Scopus are classified, most articles in the sample are classed as Social Sciences with 71 articles (64%) and a total of 964 accumulated citations, followed by Arts and Humanities with 13 articles (11.7%) and 108 citations.

At a higher resolution level, in relation to categories, Development stands out as the leader with 34 articles in 17 journals, followed by Geography, Planning, and Development, with 16 articles in 11 journals. The category exhibiting the highest number of citations (582) is also Development.

4.7   *Keywords*

Appropriate use of keywords by authors is important but the value of this is underrecognized. It can be seen that authors tend to use simple terms that allow them to reach the greatest audience in the general searches that are developed in the scientific community. However, unfortunately, the corollary of this is that keyword terms ascribed by authors may not duly represent the nature of their work. Hence, to maximize the chances of interested researchers locating studies which meet their objectives, it is necessary to expend a certain amount of effort to ensure appropriate study descriptors are used (Álvarez-García et al. 2019).

In recent years, keywords have become the most widely used mechanism for identifying documents by the scientific community. However, many articles lack keywords and this is often due to the format of disclosure pre-imposed by particular journals and publishers. Here, 46% (51) of the articles in the sample did not have this information.

From the remaining 60 documents, the presence of 230 keyword terms was identified and these were used a total of 354 times. The most often used keywords are presented in Table 4.9. The terms gender and Latin America lead in this respect because they appear as keyword terms in 24 articles.

TABLE 4.9   Keyword distribution

Rank	Keywords	Frequency	Rank	Keywords	Frequency
1	Gender	24	12	Entrepreneurship	3
2	Latin America	24	13	Gender and diversity	3
3	Men	9	14	Gender inequality	3
4	Working women	7	15	Globalization	3
5	Gender roles	6	16	Informality	3
6	Economic development	5	17	Labor and livelihoods	3
7	Ecuador	5	18	Latin America and the Caribbean	3
8	Gender equality	5	19	Mexico	3
9	Poverty	5	20	Neoliberalism	3
10	Employment	4	21	Women's rights	3
11	Women	4			

5   Conclusions

In recent years, bibliometric analysis has become a valuable reference tool for researchers, since it presents a detailed panorama of the evolution and current state of an academic subject. In this way, salient information is made available such as the most prominent and productive authors based on citations and outputs, the main journals interested in publishing topics related to the subject, countries and institutions focused on the development of research in a particular domain, among others.

Bibliometric analysis reveals that the publication of scientific articles dealing explicitly with *gender* and *economics* in Latin America, and which are indexed in Scopus, began in 1985. This coincides with the statement previously made by Caulfield (2001) which identified the mid-1980s as the point of emergence of scientific articles that place gender as a central category of analysis in the region.

The sample analyzed herein consists of 111 articles published over a 34-year period. The year of greatest production is 1998; and of the 13 articles published that year, 8 of them were developed individually. The year with the highest number of citations to articles in the sample is 2002 with 258 citations.

The evolution of the subject shows a period of exponential growth that corresponds to the second phase of behavior of scientific production indicated by López López (1996).

In relation to production at the authorial level, a predominance of transitory researchers is noted. The absence of a significant number of major producers could indicate the youthfulness of the subject. There is evidence for the emergence of a small group of aspiring authors who present between 2 and 3 studies, although 90% of these registered their affiliation in powers for the development of research at an international level such as the United States and the United Kingdom; only one author in this group emanates from elsewhere, namely Uruguay. This group represents 3% of the total number of authors and accounts for 10% of the articles in the sample.

With regard to the gender of authors, there was a greater presence of women (69.8%) compared to men (30.2%); further, over time, although more male researchers participated in the studies, the participation of women was observed to increase in proportional terms compared to men.

The three most-cited articles present equitable authorial participation (2 women and 2 men); the overall leader here in terms of citations is the work of Molyneux (2002) a female author. Moreover, it was revealed that all of the most productive authors in the sample were women.

In terms of collaboration trends, 85.5% of documents produced non-collaboratively were penned by women compared to 52.4% of documents produced in pairs. For papers with three authors, 40% exhibited a mix of genders and then moving up to four authors, mixed participation was shown to predominate. Overall these findings accord with Söderlund and Madison (2015) and Caro and Guarinos (2017) who noted a trend towards greater female presence in research on gender-related issues in a wide range of disciplines.

With regard to institutional affiliation, universities are the most predominant entities (77.3%), with *Ohio State University* leading in the sample in this respect. In terms of geographical affiliation, the United States tops the rankings with 72 authors, 76 authorships, and 50 institutions. With respect to international co-authorship trends, collaborative networks in two clusters can be identified, in which the main node is the United States and its strongest relationship being with the United Kingdom; the secondary node centers on Chile. This confirms observations by Wöhrer (2016) and Tsay and Li (2017) that most research on gender issues emanates from traditional Western centers of knowledge. This may seem somewhat paradoxical here given that the sample is framed in terms of research conducted in Latin American case-studies but of course this simply reflects the fact that national research and development expenditures are strongly correlated with economic development.

The journals with the highest concentration of articles *are World Development and Development in Practice*, which together account for 12% of articles and a total of 203 citations. However, it is another journal, *Development and Change*, which registers the highest number of citations (243).

Finally, in terms of classification, 59% of the articles in the sample are identified within the Social Sciences. Also, it is observed that 50% of the outputs are indexed in the first quartile according to the Scimago Journal Rank.

6   Limitations

This study has endeavored to express in a descriptive and quantitative way how the study of gender and economy in Latin American contexts has evolved. None of the indicators used sought to assess the quality of articles directly, although citation-based indicators are regularly used as proxies for quality.

It should also be emphasized that within this study only English terms were considered in a Spanish and Portuguese speaking region, since most of the articles published in high impact scientific journals are produced in that language or have, at least, titles, abstracts, and keywords translated into English. However, we recognize that this may lead to underestimating the amount of scientific production that was identified within the subject matter.

In addition, there is also a considerable amount of scientific research indexed in regional or lesser impact databases that has not been considered for the reasons given above, but whose future study could increase understanding of this issue.

Finally, in common with bibliometric research more generally, the analytical sample depends critically on the keywords used for the search query. Along this line, use of the term women may have been relevant to the topic as well, especially when considering the differential terminology used in studies prior to the mid-1980s.

References

Abbassi, J., and Lutjens, S. (2002). *Rereading Women in Latin America and the Caribbean. The Political Economy of Gender.* Rowman & Littlefield.

Abramo, L. (1998). "The sociology of work in Latin America: A complex development and current challenges." *Work and Occupations* 25(3): 305–332. https://doi.org/10.11 77/0730888498025003003.

Alonso, S., Cabrerizo, F.J., Herrera-Viedma, E., and Herrera, F. (2009). "H-Index: A review focused in its variants, computation and standardization for different scientific fields." *Journal of Informetrics* 3(4): 273–289. https://doi.org/10.1016/j.joi.2009.04.001.

Álvarez-García, J., Durán-Sánchez, A., and del Río-Rama, M.C. (2018). "Scientific Coverage in Community-Based Tourism: Sustainable Tourism and Strategy for Social Development." *Sustainability* 10(4): 1158. https://doi.org/10.3390/su10041158.

Álvarez-García, J., Maldonado-Erazo, C.P., Del Río-Rama, D.M., and Castellano-Álvarez, J.F. (2019). "Cultural Heritage and Tourism Basis for Regional Development: Mapping of Scientific Coverage." *Sustainability* 11(21). https://doi.org/10.3390/su11216034.

Andrés, A. (2009). *Measuring academic research: How to undertake a bibliometric study.* Elsevier.

Aslanbeigui, N., Pressman, S., and Summerfield, G. (1994). *Women in the age of economic transformation: gender impact of reforms in post-socialist and developing countries.* Routledge.

Balan, J. (1990). "Household economy and gender differences in international migration: a case study of Bolivians in Argentina." *Estudios Migratorios Latinamericanos* 5(15–16): 269–294.

Benería, L., and Roldán, M. (1992). *Las encrucijadas de clase y género* (Issues 04; HD9940, B4.). Fondo de Cultura Económica.

Blau, F., Ferber, M., and Winkler, A. (2002). *The Economics of Women, Men and Work.* Prentice Hall.

Blay, E.A. (1978). *Trabalho domesticado: a mulher na indústria paulista.* Editora Átiica.

Bonilla, C.A., Merigó, J.M., and Torres-Abad, C. (2015). "Economics in Latin America: A bibliometric analysis." *Scientometrics* 105(2): 1239–1252. https://doi.org/10.1007/s11192-015-1747-7.

Bradford, S.C. (1934). "Sources of information on specific subjects." *Engineering* 137: 85–86. https://ci.nii.ac.jp/naid/10016754267/en/.

Brockman, C.T. (1985). "Women and development in northern Belize." *Journal of Developing Areas* 19(4): 501–514.

Cabral, E. (1994). "No going back. Mexican women find opportunity and obstacles in a changing economy." *Ford Foundation Report (New York, N.Y.: 1992)* 25(3): 11–17.

Caro, F.J., and Guarinos, V. (2017). "Male presence in gender research networks in the communication field in Spain." *Masculinities and Social Change* 6(1): 62–90. https://doi.org/10.17583/MCS.2017.2452.

Carrasco, C. (2003). *Tiempos, trabajos y organización social: reflexiones en torno al mercado laboral femenino, Mujeres y economía.* Icaria.

Castaño, C. (1999). "Economía y género." *Política y Sociedad* 32: 23–42.

Caulfield, S. (2001). "The history of gender in the historiography of Latin America." *The Hispanic American Historical Review* 81(3): 449–490. https://doi.org/10.1215/00182168-81-3-4-449.

Chant, S. (1991). "Gender, migration and urban development in Costa Rica: the case of Guanacaste." *Geoforum* 22(3): 237–253. https://doi.org/10.1016/0016-7185(91)90010-N.

Cislak, A., Formanowicz, M., and Saguy, T. (2018). "Bias against research on gender bias." *Scientometrics* 115(1): 189–200. https://doi.org/10.1007/s11192-018-2667-0.

Corral, J.A., and Cànoves, G. (2013). "La investigación turística publicada en revistas turísticas y no turísticas: análisis bibliométrico de la producción de las universidades catalanas." *Cuadernos de Turismo* 31: 55–81. https://revistas.um.es/turismo/article/view/170741.

Crane, D. (1977). "Social structure in a group of scientists: a test of the "invisible college" hypothesis." In S. Leinhardt (Ed.), *Social Networks* (pp. 161–178). Academic Press. https://doi.org/10.1016/B978-0-12-442450-0.50017-1.

Cravey, A.J. (1997). "The politics of reproduction: Households in the Mexican industrial transition." *Economic Geography* 73(2): 166–186.

Cvencek, D., Meltzoff, A.N., and Greenwald, A.G. (2011). "Math-gender stereotypes in elementary school children." *Child Dev* 82(3): 766–779. https://doi.org/10.1111/j.1467-8624.2010.01529.x.

De Barbieri, T. (2004). "Más de tres décadas de los estudios de género en América Latina." *Revista Mexicana de Sociología* 66: 197–214. https://doi.org/10.2307/3541450.

de Lattes, Z.R., Sautu, R.A., and Wainerman, C.H. (1977). *Participación de las mujeres en la actividad económica de la Argentina, Bolivia y Paraguay: El caso argentino* (Vols. 1–2). CENEP.

Deere, C.D., and León, M. (2000). *Género, propiedad y empoderamiento: Tierra, Estado y mercado en América Latina.* Universidad Nacional de Colombia.

Desposato, S., and Norrander, B. (2009). "The Gender Gap in Latin America: Contextual and individual influences on gender and political participation." *British Journal of Political Science* 39(1): 141–162. https://doi.org/10.1017/S0007123408000458.

Durán-Sánchez, A., Álvarez-García, J., Del Río-Rama, M.C., and Sarango-Lalangui, P. (2018). "Analysis of the Scientific Literature Published on Smart Learning." *ESPACIOS* 39(10): 7–24.

Ellemers, N. (2018). "Gender Stereotypes." *Annual Review of Psychology* 69: 275–298. https://doi.org/10.1146/annurev-psych-122216-011719.

Ellis, M., Conway, D., and Bailey, A.J. (1996). "The circular migration of Puerto Rican women: Towards a gendered explanation." *International Migration* 34(1): 31–58.

Escorcia-Otálora, T.A., and Poutou-Piñales, R.A. (2008). "Análisis bibliométrico de los artículos originales publicados en la revista Universitas Scientiarum (1987–2007)." *Universitas Scientiarum* 13(3): 236–244.

Esquivel, V. (2011). *La economía del cuidado en América Latina.* PNUD.

European Commision. (2019). *She figures 2018.* European Union.

Fernández, M.T., Bordons, M., Sancho, I., and Gómez, I. (1999). "El sistema de incentivos y recompensas en la ciencia pública española." In J. Sebastián and E. Muñoz (Eds.), *Radiografía de la investigación pública en España.* Biblioteca Nueva.

Frank, M. (2006). "Access to the Scientific Literature—A Difficult Balance." *New England Journal of Medicine* 354(15): 1552–1555. https://doi.org/10.1056/NEJMp068004.

Fuwa, N. (2000). "The poverty and heterogeneity among female-headed households revisited: The case of Panama." *World Development* 28(8): 1515–1542. https://doi.org/10.1016/S0305-750X(00)00036-X.

Georges, E. (1992). "Gender, Class, and Migration in the Dominican Republic: Women's Experiences in a Transnational Community: GENDER, CLASS, AND MIGRATION." *Annals of the New York Academy of Sciences* 645(1): 81–99. https://doi.org/10.1111/j.1749-6632.1992.tb33487.x.

Goldschmidt, P.G. (1986). "Information synthesis: a practical guide." *Health Services Research* 21(2 Pt. 1): 215–237. http://www.ncbi.nlm.nih.gov/pmc/articles/PMC1068946/.

Guendelman, S. (1987). "The Incorporation of Mexican Women in Seasonal Migration: A Study of Gender Differences." *Hispanic Journal of Behavioral Sciences* 9(3): 245–264. https://doi.org/10.1177/07399863870093002.

Handley, I.M., Brown, E.R., Moss-Racusin, C.A., and Smith, J.L. (2015). "Quality of evidence revealing subtle gender biases in science is in the eye of the beholder." *Proceedings of the National Academy of Sciences* 112(43): 13201–13206. https://doi.org/10.1073/pnas.1510649112.

Harzing, A.-W., and Alakangas, S. (2016). "Google Scholar, Scopus and the Web of Science: a longitudinal and cross-disciplinary comparison." *Scientometrics* 106(2): 787–804. https://doi.org/10.1007/s11192-015-1798-9.

Hays-Mitchell, M. (1995). "Voices and visions from the streets: gender interests and political participation among women informal traders in Latin America." *Environment & Planning D: Society & Space* 13(4): 445–469. https://doi.org/10.1068/d13 0445.

Hays-Mitchell, M. (1997). "Development vs empowerment: the gendered legacy of economic restructuring in Latin America." *Yearbook—Conference of Latin Americanist Geographers* 23: 119–131. https://www.scopus.com/inward/record. uri?eid=2-s2.0-0031422672&partnerID=40&md5=b722a8b8343fa54e5d377ef185bc59 fa.

Hays-Mitchell, M. (2002). "Resisting austerity: A gendered perspective on neoliberal restructing in Peru." *Gender and Development* 10(3): 71–81. https://doi. org/10.1080/13552070215920.

Hernández-González, V., Sans-Rosell, N., Jové-Deltell, M.C., and Reverter-Masia, J. (2016). "Comparación entre Web of Science y Scopus, Estudio Bibliométrico de las Revistas de Anatomía y Morfología." *International Journal of Morphology* 34(4): 1369–1377.

Hite, A.B., and Viterna, J.S. (2005). "Gendering class in Latin America: How women effect and experience change in the class structure." *Latin American Research Review* 40(2): 50–82.

Holman, L., Stuart-Fox, D., and Hauser, C.E. (2018). "The gender gap in science: How long until women are equally represented?" *PLoS Biology* 16(4). https://doi. org/10.1371/journal.pbio.2004956.

Howes, C., and Singh, A. (1995). "Long-term trends in the World economy: The gender dimension." *World Development* 23(11): 1895–1911. https://doi.org/10.1016/ 0305-750X(95)00096-U.

Hubert, J.J. (1981). *General bibliometric models*. Libr Trends.

Jackson, S. (1998). "Feminist social theory." In S. Jackson and S. Jones (Eds.), *Contemporary Feminist Theories* (pp. 12–33). New York University Press.

Jelin, E. (1974). "Formas de organización de la actividad económica y estructura ocupacional: El caso de Salvador, Brasil." *Desarrollo Económico* 14(53): 181–203. https:// doi.org/10.2307/3466052.

Kidder, T. (1999). "Alternative financial institutions? Sustainability, development, social reproduction, and gender analysis." *Development in Practice* 9(4): 482–487.

Laurie, N. (1997). "From work to welfare: The response of the Peruvian state to the feminization of emergency work." *Political Geography* 16(8): 691–714. https://doi. org/10.1016/S0962-6298(96)00078-9.

Laurie, N. (1999). "State-backed work programmes and the regendering of work in Peru: Negotiating femininity in 'the provinces.'" *Environment and Planning A* 31(2): 229–250. https://doi.org/10.1068/a310229.

León de Leal, M. (1977). *Mujer y el desarrollo en Colombia*. ACEP.

López López, P. (1996). *Introducción a la bibliometría*. Promolibro.

Lovell, P.A. (2006). "Race, gender, and work in São Paulo, Brazil, 1960–2000." *Latin American Research Review* 41(3): 63–87.

Lustig, N., Rendon, T., and Bunster, X. (1979). "Female Employment, Occupational Status, and Socioeconomic Characteristics of the Family in Mexico." *Signs: Journal of Women in Culture and Society* 5(1): 143–153. https://doi.org/10.1086/493690.

Machado Neto, Z. (1978). "As meninas: Sobre o trabalho da crianca e da adolescente na familia de populac6es faveladas." In *Seminar on Women in the Labor Force in Latin America*.

Madeira, F.R. (1978). "El trabajo de la mujer en fortaleza." *Demografía y Economía* 12(1): 46–74. http://www.jstor.org/stable/40602165.

Merigó, J.M., Mas-Tur, A., Roig-Tierno, N., and Ribeiro-Soriano, D. (2015). "A bibliometric overview of the Journal of Business Research between 1973 and 2014." *Journal of Business Research* 68(12): 2645–2653. https://doi.org/10.1016/j.jbusres.2015.04.006.

Molinas, J.R. (1998). "The impact of inequality, gender, external assistance and social capital on local-level cooperation." *World Development* 26(3): 413–431. https://doi.org/10.1016/S0305-750X(97)10066-3.

Molyneux, M. (2002). "Gender and the silences of social capital: Lessons from Latin America." *Development and Change* 33(2): 167–188. https://doi.org/10.1111/1467-7660.00246.

Morales i Perez, S. (1999). "Agribusiness, rural development and gender in Latin America: Work and daily life of working women in Santa Rosa (Mendoza, Argentina)." *Documents d'Analisi Geografica* 35: 121–145.

Moreno, C. (1996). "An experience of women's participation in strengthening community management." *Habitat Debate / UNCHS (Habitat), the United Nations Centre for Human Settlements* 2(1): 11.

Morgan, J., and Buice, M. (2013). "Latin American attitudes toward women in politics: The influence of elite cues, female advancement, and individual characteristics." *American Political Science Review* 107(4): 644–662. https://doi.org/10.1017/S0003055413000385.

Nash, J., and Safa, H. (1976). *Sex and Class in Latin America*. Praeger Publishers.

Navarro, M. (1979). "Research on Latin American Women." *Signs: Journal of Women in Culture and Society* 5(1): 111–120. http://www.jstor.org/stable/3173538.

Pacheco, E., and Blanco, M. (1998). "Three modes of analysis in the incorporation of a gender perspective in socio-demographic studies of urban labor in Mexico." *Papeles de Población / Centro de Investigación y Estudios Avanzados de La Población, Universidad Autónoma Del Estado de México* 4(15): 73–94.

Pescatello, A. (1972). "The female in Ibero-America: an essay on research bibliography and research directions." *Latin American Research Review* 7(2): 125–141.

Podsakoff, P.M., MacKenzie, S.B., Podsakoff, N.P., and Bachrach, D.G. (2008). "Scholarly influence in the field of management: A bibliometric analysis of the determinants of university and author impact in the management literature in the past quarter century." *Journal of Management* 34(4): 641–720. https://doi.org/10.1177/0149206308319533.

Price, D.J. (1956). "The exponential curve of science." *Discovery* 17(6): 240–243.

Psacharopoulos, G., and Tzannatos, Z. (1993). "Economic and demographic effects on working women in Latin America." *Journal of Population Economics* 6(4): 293–315. https://doi.org/10.1007/BF00599040.

Radcliffe, S.A. (1990). "Between hearth and labor market: the recruitment of peasant women in the Andes." *International Migration Review* 24(2): 229–249. https://doi.org/10.2307/2546550.

Raynolds, L.T. (1998). "Harnessing women's work: restructuring agricultural and industrial labor forces in the Dominican Republic." *Economic Geography* 74(2): 149–169.

Reyes, G. (2011). "Centros urbanos de América Latina 1997, 2006: Disparidades salariales según género y crecimiento económico." *Revista de Ciencias Sociales*: 131–132. https://doi.org/10.15517/rcs.v0i131-132.3899.

Rico, M.N. (1998). "Women in water-related processes in Latin America: Current situation and research and policy proposals." *International Journal of Water Resources Development* 14(4): 461–471. https://doi.org/10.1080/07900629849097.

Roberts, J.T., and Dodoo, F.N.A. (1995). "Population growth, sex ratios, and women's work on the contemporary Amazon frontier." *Yearbook—Conference of Latin Americanist Geographers* 21: 91–105.

Rodriguez Enriquez, C. (2015). "Economía feminista y economía del cuidado: Aportes conceptuales para el estudio de la desigualdad." *Nueva Sociedad* 256(3): 1–15.

Rodríguez Enríquez, C. (2007). "Economía del cuidado, equidad de género y nuevo orden económico internacional." In A. Giron and E. Correa (Eds.), *Del Sur hacia el Norte: Economía política del orden económico internacional emergente*. CLACSO, Consejo Latinoamericano de Ciencias Sociales.

Rowlands, J. (1992). "Women, empowerment and development in Honduras." *Graduate Discussion Paper—University of Durham, Department of Geography*, 92–2.

Saffioti, H. (1969). *Women in Class Society*. Monthly Review Press.

Salvador, S. (2007). *Comercio, género y equidad en América Latina: Generando conocimiento para la Acción Política: Estudio comparativo de la "economía del cuidado" en Argentina, Brasil, Chile, Colombia, México y Uruguay*. Red Internacional de Género y Comercio, Capítulo Latinoamericano.

Schmukler, B. (1978). "La mujer en empresas familiares como trabajadora familiar no remunerada y trabajadora por cuenta propia dentro del sector comercio de alimentos en Argentina." In *Seminar on Women in the Labor Force in Latin America*.

Scott, A.M. (1986). "Women in Latin America: stereotypes and social science." *Bulletin of Latin American Research* 5(2): 21–27. https://doi.org/10.2307/3338649.

Shen, H. (2013). "Inequality quantified: Mind the gender gap." *Nature News* 495: 22–24. https://doi.org/10.1038/495022a.

Söderlund, T., and Madison, G. (2015). "Characteristics of gender studies publications: a bibliometric analysis based on a Swedish population database." *Scientometrics* 105(3): 1347–1387. https://doi.org/10.1007/s11192-015-1702-7.

Spinak, E. (1996). *Diccionario enciclopédico de bibliometría, cienciometría e informetría*. UNESCO CII/II.

Steinke, J., Lapinski, M.K., Crocker, N., Zietsman-Thomas, A., Williams, Y., Evergreen, S., and Kuchibhotla, S. (2007). "Assessing media influences on middle school aged children's perceptions of women in science using the Draw-A-Scientist Test (DAST)." *Science Communication* 29(1): 35–64. https://doi.org/10.1177/1075547007306508.

Stephen, L. (2005). "Women's weaving cooperatives in Oaxaca: An indigenous response to neoliberalism." *Critique of Anthropology* 25(3): 253–278. https://doi.org/10.1177/0308275X05055215.

Teele, D.L., and Thelen, K. (2017). "Gender in the Journals: Publication Patterns in Political Science." *PS—Political Science and Politics* 50(2): 433–447. https://doi.org/10.1017/S1049096516002985.

Teissedre, S. (1997). "First Mayan Women's Congress." *UN Chronicle* 34(4): 57.

Terjesen, S., and Amorós, J.E. (2010). "Female entrepreneurship in Latin America and the caribbean: Characteristics, drivers and relationship to economic development." *European Journal of Development Research* 22(3): 313–330. https://doi.org/10.1057/ejdr.2010.13.

Tsay, M.Y., and Li, C.N. (2017). "Bibliometric analysis of the journal literature on women's studies." *Scientometrics* 113(2): 705–734. https://doi.org/10.1007/s11192-017-2493-9.

Van der Lee, R., and Ellemers, N. (2018). "Perceptions of gender inequality in academia: Reluctance to let go of individual merit ideology." In B.T. Rutjens and M.J. Brandt (Eds.), *Belief Systems and the Perception of Reality* (pp. 63–78). Taylor and Francis Inc. https://doi.org/10.4324/9781315114903.

Vásconez, A. (2017). "Crecimiento económico y desigualdad de género: análisis de panel para cinco países de América Latina." *Revista CEPAL* 122: 85–113.

Wiig, H. (2013). "Joint titling in rural Peru: Impact on women's participation in household decision-making." *World Development* 52: 104–119. https://doi.org/10.1016/j.worlddev.2013.06.005.

Wöhrer, V. (2016). "Gender studies as a multi-centred field? Centres and peripheries in academic gender research." *Feminist Theory* 17(3): 323–343. https://doi.org/10.1177/1464700116652840.

PART 2

Ecuador

∵

CHAPTER 5

Gender Imaginary in Ecuador

A Literature Review

Esteban Arévalo

1   Introduction

Latin America is a relatively happy region (Helliwell et al. 2018; Latinobaró-metro 2018). This seems to contrast with a reality in which most of its countries are still struggling to achieve social justice so that all its inhabitants can exercise their rights as citizens. One of the main challenges in this regard is reducing gender inequality, which relegates women to second place behind men. The United Nations, through its development agenda, defined the gender inequality index based on four types of inequalities affecting women in the areas of reproductive health, education, political representation and labor market (United Nations Development Programme 2018). Despite the progress that has been made in Ecuador according to this index, it still describes a picture of substantial gender inequality, even greater than other countries in the region such as Chile, Peru, Mexico, and Cuba.

Hence it is particularly pertinent to analyze the causes of this inequality and how it has been naturalized in Ecuador's social imaginary. There is an extensive literature on the causes of inequality, framed in terms of social, economic, and racial differences, as well as gender (Camou and Maubrigades 2017; DeVerteuil 2009; Hunter 2013; Layton and Smith 2017; Schwindt-Bayer 2018; Sheahan and Iglesias 1998; Stepan 1996; Wade 1997). For this reason, gender studies are a fundamental axis to understand the problems of Ecuador and additionally to propose solutions to help build a more equitable society.

Gender roles, that is to say, acceptable behaviors for people according to their sex, are a social construction, a cultural element that varies with time and depends not only on biological sex but also on factors such as social position, race, and place of residence (Colebrook 2004). This is why it is important to analyze the factors that, throughout history, have shaped the ideal expected of women and the role imposed by society. Since Ecuador shares diverse historical and cultural elements with other countries in Latin America, the situations of Ecuadorian women and their role in the economy can be understood from two perspectives: regionally, as part of this Latin American context and from a national vision that, with its particularities, renders the Ecuadorian case worthy of a more detailed analysis.

The construction of gender over time in what is now Ecuador within Latin America has developed with a clear disadvantage for women (Galeano 1980; Socolow 2015). From pre-Columbian times women were separated from power and decision making, being relegated to domestic and reproductive tasks, considered as secondary to men (Silverblatt 1978). For women, the period of colonial conquest was characterized by sexual abuse and cultural destruction. Subsequently, colonial oppression through the Catholic Church imposed a morality based on the culture of Spain in the fifteenth century, organized according to race and with a role of permanent subordination to men (Chaves 2000; Clayton et al. 2017; Meade 2010; Socolow 2015)

This role was maintained during the Republican period (Clayton et al. 2017; French and Bliss 2006) throughout Latin America, where the secularization of the State resulted in it replacing the Church as the institution that legitimized the supremacy of men over women and dictated the norms of acceptable behavior (Dore 2000).

It was not until the twentieth century that feminist movements began to make organized demands for greater participation, although this did not translate into greater equity (Guy 2012; Schwindt-Bayer 2018). In the second half of the twentieth century, military regimes bloodily repressed popular associations, including feminists, who resisted, longing for substantive change and participation with subsequent democratic regimes. However, the representative democracy that emerged applied neoliberal policies on a large-scale generating poverty and migration, in which women faced a new type of structural violence.

All these adversities led to a greater participation of women in social movements and stimulated academic studies focused on gender and Feminism (De Barbieri 2004; Barrig 2016; Chant and Craske 2003; Chinchilla Stoltz 1993; Noonan 1995; Radcliffe and Westwood 1993; Tompkins 2008; Vargas 1992; Wade 2010) as well as on development (Bose and Acosta-Belén 1995; Buvinić et al. 2004; Lugones and Spelman 1983; Scarborough et al. 2019) oriented to the problem of gender inequality in Latin America. Despite these advances, much remains to be done concerning a problem that falls most acutely on rural indigenous women. While Ecuador has witnessed more progress in public policy compared to other Latin American countries, it is clear that requisite changes cannot come solely from the law. It is necessary for women to be able to express their problems in spaces of social participation. Only from an understanding of their realities can others be made aware of the daily exclusion that women face, a problem that must become the concern of society as a whole.

In this context, this chapter presents a historical review of the gender imaginary in the territory of what is now Ecuador. The hypothesis put forward is that in the area currently covered by Ecuador, women have historically been excluded and that this exclusion has been naturalized by society and the State. Beginning with gender segregation in pre-Hispanic societies, the situation worsened after the European conquest by the creation of a new social order based on race. Finally, the transition to a republican and democratic regime has not necessarily reduced exclusion but rather normalized it under a legal framework designed from a conservative perspective. Therefore, it will not be until society is organized around race and gender claims that definite progress will be made towards effective gender equality.

Through reviewing the literature related to the historical development of the region and the country, an attempt is made to describe the process that has shaped Ecuadorian society. In particular, emphasis is placed on the gender imaginary that dominated each period. At each stage, reference is made to key individuals who exemplify the evolution of this imaginary. Finally, the contemporary period is illustrated by a review of how social movements and gender studies have enabled changes in the situations of women in society, proposing innovations to the gender vision created over time. Based on this review, a series of conclusions are drawn regarding the gender problem in Ecuador and its current status.

Covering such a long chronological period presents challenges due to the number of events, elements, processes, and facts involved. An effort is made to appropriately synthesize prevailing knowledge and information so as to introduce the reader to the historical factors that have led to gender inequality in Ecuador. Additionally, where limitations in terms of historical records and studies present barriers, the case of Ecuador is explored from a Latin American perspective, on the understanding that there are important commonalities between the country on the one hand and the wider region on the other hand.

Finally, the objective is to emphasize the fact that inequality is not a casual phenomenon but responds to diverse historical causes that must be understood as a first step towards its confrontation. In addition, this review seeks to emphasize that inequality has historically been seen as natural and it has not been until recent times that it has been possible to denounce and combat it. As a result, the aim is to give an idea of the long process that the fight for gender equality has involved and thus to situate the academic work related to this subject as an important element in understanding its past and predicting its future.

2   America before the Conquest

At the time of the arrival of the European invaders, the territory that today corresponds to Latin America was inhabited by diverse cultures. At the organizational level, they ranged from a state of development similar to that of the Stone Age, such as the tribes of the Amazon basin, to true empires that incorporated a diversity of peoples and regions under central administration (Clayton et al. 2017). In this latter group were three civilizations that concentrated the majority of the population. The Mayas and Aztecs occupied regions that nowadays correspond to Mexico and Central America while the Incas spread to regions of South America.

Diverse local cultures also inhabited the territory of contemporary Ecuador. In the first chronicle of the history of Ecuador, González Suárez (1890) points out that in the 15th century the most notable tribes in the Andes were the *Shyris*, the *Puruhaes*, and the *Cañaris*. Meanwhile, the *Chonos, Huancavilcas*, and *Punaes* stood out on the coast. Additionally, Ayala Mora (2008) lists other mountain peoples such as the *Quillacingas, Pastos, Caranquis, Cochasquís, Otavalos*, and *Cayambes* to the north of Quito and the *Panzaleos, Píllaros, Sigchos, Puruháes*, and *Yumbos* to the south. At the southern end of the mountain range were the *Paltas* while the *Manteño* group was in the current Manabí province. Finally, the Amazon was populated by *Quijos* and *Jíbaros*.

Villages were organized internally in family clans, where their members had particular kinship as well as shared housing and means of production, including land. In addition, members had an obligation to work to support their family group and in turn benefited from such work regardless of gender. Silverblatt (1978) asserts that in these kinship-based communities, organizing power within the home occurred on the basis of age rather than gender. Similarly, access to land depended on belonging to the family clan and ensuring its cultivation. In addition, other community work could be requested from members by the group leader, regardless of gender. Finally, there was a ruling class that organized all the inhabitants. This group included the ethnic lords or *caciques*, whose position was hereditary, administrators, and the military—all these positions were reserved for men.

During the first half of the sixteenth century these peoples were subdued by the Incas. While organization into family clans and assignment of land to communities were maintained, the Inca conquest meant the payment of a tax, the surrender of land to the imperial administrative and religious system, and the surrender of women to serve in religious institutions. Regarding these changes, Silverblatt (1978) points out that the handing over of land to local or military administrators implied the introduction of private property into the economic system. However, this new form of individual land appropriation was a novelty that had only men as beneficiaries due to the exclusion of women from these key positions.

Women's expectations varied according to their class. The women of ruling and noble families had a high status with respect to the other women in the group to which they belonged. However, they could not exercise power on their own and did not have access to public office. Instead they were destined to marry men of the same social class at the convenience of their families. Regarding the daughters of rulers, it was common for their marriages to serve to establish alliances with other peoples (Socolow 2015). This was the case with Princess Toa whose marriage unified *Shyris* and *Puruháes* (González Suárez 1890). These women could then access power by advising or influencing their husbands, but never independent of a man. The women of families of the popular class were expected to marry and produce numerous children. It is noteworthy that among the Incas, virginity was not seen as something virtuous and couples were even allowed to live together before marriage to ensure their future success (Silverblatt 1987).

In terms of work, there was a social division of labor established according to gender. The woman was assigned childcare, housework, food acquisition, and preparation. Among the Incas, women could spin and weave, prepare farmland, plant, and harvest (Silverblatt 1978), and in some cases could act as midwives or healers using medicinal herbs. In general, women could not own property, which in practical terms mainly meant land which was the source of livelihood in a predominantly agricultural region. However, they could claim the use of their community's land (Socolow 2015) so that if they became widowed they had the support of their family group and their means of subsistence was secured.

It can thus be discerned that the women of the territory of the present Ecuador were integrated as much in the tasks of the home as in the productive system. Far from being able to act as individuals, their lives depended on their belonging to the family clan, within which they had some autonomy. Outside of the home, in the public sphere, both the State and religious apparatus which were closely linked in the ordering of society, excluded women from decision-making and participation.

3   The Conquest

The formation of what came to be known as Spain is widely attributed to the marriage of King Ferdinand of Aragon and Queen Isabella of Castile. They had subjected the Muslim territories in the Iberian Peninsula to war and finally united their own kingdoms by marriage. Various elements from this period of war and conquests remained in the imaginary of the Iberian genre. From Islam there was the perception that women should be protected from the outside world by confinement to their homes or by placing a woman's virginity as a token of her virtue and the honor of her family. In Christian Spain both the Church, the intellectual world, and the popular imaginary converged on the idea of the inferiority of women. It was believed that women were less intelligent than men and therefore incapable of acting with appropriate consciousness, guided only by carnal desires and emotions (Socolow 2015). The ideal for man was that of a knight, a conquering warrior in search of fame and fortune (Clayton et al. 2017). This was the prototype of the Spanish man who would arrive in America at the end of the 15th century.

The number of inhabitants of the continent at that time is still the subject of debate among scholars. Galeano (1980) puts the figure at no less than seventy million, situating between twenty five and thirty million in the Andean region while Clayton et al. (2017) estimate the total at fifty million with between ten and twelve million in the region of the Incas. Even with the uncertainties in these data, it is clear that America was widely populated and that the arrival of the first Spaniards to America did not constitute a discovery of the continent.

Nor was it a meeting of two cultures. The subsequent European expeditions did not have a cultural rapprochement objective. They were focused on immediate conquest and subsequent exploitation of the Indians they encountered in their path. For this they first used weapons but in the long term they used the imposition of a cultural, economic, and religious framework that lasted more than three hundred years. Within this imposed culture came a new vision of gender, which imposed a double oppression on indigenous women, both because of their gender and their race. In this system, deplorable as it was, women took an essential role with their work.

The Spanish social structure considered women to be weak, so access to the army, including the expeditionary forces, was reserved exclusively for men. For this army of Europeans with the image of the conquest of Spain still fresh, the objective was clear: a systematic occupation of the territories and a looting of those who lived there. The spoils very often included women who could be abused and abandoned or who were later taken as concubines by soldiers. Some of the upper class were given as an alliance between the Indians and the conquerors, but the majority were subjected to force. During this stage of abuse, the mestizaje process begins in America (Socolow 2015).

Many of the indigenous groups fiercely resisted the invasion and in some cases it was women who led resistance efforts. Examples are the *Guaraní* Juliana in Paraguay, Gaitana of the *Yalcon* tribe in Colombia and the *Taína* Anacona in the Dominican Republic, which in the 16th century commanded armed fighters (Kohan 2013). However, these were exceptions which can be viewed as women taking the lead in struggles only in extreme situations. Most women had to exercise their resistance silently, surviving and supporting their families, many widows or victims of abuse, persevering in the task of keeping their culture alive and a resistance that continues to this day.

Notwithstanding the violence, the highest mortality was caused by epidemics. This was a true demographic disaster in which, in certain areas such as the Caribbean, up to 90% of the original population perished (Socolow 2015). Galeano (1980) estimates that in one hundred and fifty years the total number of indigenous people in America had been reduced to only three million.

4   The Colonial Era

During the colonial era, women continued to suffer a double exploitation: labor and sexual. The Indians were despised as beings without culture and the Church still doubted whether they possessed a soul. Subdued and with their populations decimated, the survivors were enslaved with violence. Of women, it is surely nigh on impossible to imagine the immense suffering that meant the destruction of their social order and, for many, the separation of their communities given that their union with the tribe would have taken clear precedence over individual interest. For centuries, this was compounded by the double suffering of daily violence expressed through exploitative work regimes and continuous sexual abuse.

After the violent European appearance in the indigenous world, the Spaniards dedicated themselves to strengthening their control. Those who came later were no longer soldiers but settlers who were motivated to migrate so as to make a fortune. They could take one or more Indians as concubines especially if they were of noble classes and this gave them legitimacy before the Indians as leaders (Socolow 2015). From these unions began the crossbreeding.

In addition, a tribute to the crown was imposed on all Indians and abusive mechanisms were created to obtain it. Among these were the *encomiendas*, derived from an old feudal institution, in which a group of indigenous people were handed over to a Spaniard whom they served. A similar system was that of the *mitas* in which indigenous people worked for the Viceroyalty in the construction of public works, but also in mines, where the dangers and extreme work decimated the population. Where Indians were in short supply, the Spaniards began to bring slaves from Africa, who suffered the same or worse treatment as the Indians. In these systems, in addition to labor exploitation, women were very often sexually exploited by those with power such as the *encomenderos* or the foremen.

These institutions became a system of exploitation for the exclusive benefit of their commissioner or *encomendero*. In an attempt to create an alternative system and seeking to integrate the indigenous peoples who lived scattered over extensive areas, the Spanish Crown concentrated them in smaller areas called *reducciones* (Saito and Rosas Lauro 2017). This was intended to improve the management of the workforce pursuant of optimizing economic benefits. In addition, this approach also facilitated indoctrination in Christianity.

To better control agricultural production and ensure that it benefited the Spanish settlers, *haciendas* were also created. From the end of the 16th century, the Spaniards were given land which could be easily augmented with indigenous land by virtue of local chiefs willing to sell, or simply through expropriation (Kennedy and Troya 1987). Such expropriation was facilitated by the creation of *reducciones*. The *haciendas* were thus large extensions of arable land, *latifundios* (large estates) assigned to a single owner. Therein indigenous people were permitted to cultivate the land to meet their subsistence needs in return for paying the indigenous tribute. In this way, the land, a key element for the agri-oriented economy and a symbol of indigenous peoples' identity passed to monopoly control by the Spaniards. Entire families worked in the *haciendas*, thus women and men toiled to contribute to the payment of the tribute and for their subsistence.

Despite these interventions, in the countryside much of the indigenous culture remained, such as power relations and the division of labor according to gender (Clayton et al. 2017). Moreover, in many cases indigenous people were able to remain in communities, as they were necessary for agriculture. In these spaces, where the use of Spanish as a language was sometimes not accepted, women continued to be part of family clans subordinated to their husbands and communities. The situation of the mestizos was different since they were not subject to the tribute, being able also to form part of the haciendas or to dedicate themselves to agriculture or cattle raising in an independent way and without the tax burden imposed on indigenous people. Since they were not considered indigenous, they were able to integrate better into the *criollos* culture (Kalmanovitz 2008).

In addition, there was an institution that allowed for the pacification of populations through ideological control: The Catholic Church. Neither the army nor the colonial administrators were able to extend to the level of clergy and missionaries. These, however, were not only dedicated to evangelization since many had concubines, slaves, and great fortunes. The Church imposed the vision of the European family on the Indians: a couple with their children. This replaced the family clan and the concept of community work, with the woman taking care of all domestic tasks, but at the same time achieving greater autonomy within it (Núñez Sánchez 2015). In addition, a new conception of morality was imposed on women, including, for example, the requirement of virginity before marriage. This imaginary was incarnated by the Virgin Mary, who represented submission, sacrifice, motherhood, and devotion (Clayton et al. 2017). However, the ideal is a contradiction in itself. Virgin and mother at the same time, of European factions, and incompatible with the traits of indigenous women, being as a whole, an unattainable model source of frustration and guilt.

The cities became a destination for the Spaniards who tried to promote a sort of European culture with local characteristics. Initially permeable to mestizo descendants of indigenous nobles, the *criollo* society gradually associated mestizos with negative values and the inclusion of mestizo declined. However, the percentage of mestizos in America continued to increase throughout the colonial period. There were also Indians who were forced to migrate to the city in search of work. There, the indigenous women who married men from the same community maintained their traditional customs and appearance. Those who chose men of another origin ended up adopting elements of Spanish culture (Socolow 2015).

Unlike Peru or Bolivia, in the territory of the present Ecuador there was less mining activity. Instead, agriculture, including cattle rearing, pre-dominated. However, other areas of production boosted the economy. Hunefeldt (2003) recounts that, during the sixteenth century, because of textile production inside the *haciendas*, Quito became a center of exports to Lima (Peru), Bogotá (Colombia), and Chile. In the eighteenth century, when the production of the *haciendas* fell, this activity developed even more in the Ecuadorian area of Cuenca, exporting cotton textiles to the Ecuadorian coast, Peru, and Chile; this time attributable to work in the homes. This articulated trade networks for the sale and purchase of cotton that came from Lima. At the same time, Guayaquil turned its attention to timber and cocoa which by virtue of commercial developments at the end of the colonial era, began to be exported by sea. Unlike large estates, cocoa production occurred in small plots through family work. This increased the income and importance of the coastal region which, in turn, stimulated substantial migration from the Andean region.

This review of the colonial era makes it possible to outline a social system clearly structured around race. It defined people's status, rights, and quality of life. In addition, the ideological system imposed by religion kept women in the background. Despite this discrimination, the relevance of indigenous and mestizo women in the colonial economy can be seen through these productive processes. In the *encomiendas* and the *mitas*, the men left the communities to work. The women were in charge of caring for the home, the children, and the elderly, producing and preparing food and in many cases paying the indigenous tribute. They were also subjected to intense work in the textile industry and then in the family spinning workshops, an activity that although it could be shared with men to a certain degree, was considered eminently feminine. The large productive capacity of textiles for export could only ever have been the result of high female participation in the process.

5   Independence

The Spanish colonial system went into decline long before the wars of independence. Reforms initiated by Spain stimulated the discontent of the inhabitants of the colonies. When the metropolis entered a crisis, the conditions for independence had already been created.

During the 18th century, Spain endeavored to modernize the administration of America with measures that altered the balance that existed in the region. A decision was taken to expand the army, creating militias which involved all ethnic groups, attracting many because of the possibility of a salary or prestige. Evidently the women did not have a direct benefit since they were not part of the military corps. McFarlane (2008) noted how the very creation of a military set the scene for enshrining a new *criollo* male elite that would continue to influence the political future of the republics. Additionally, with the reform, military personnel from Spain occupied positions in the public administration. Although many wealthy families managed to have their daughters marry these military men to increase their status, the *criollos* saw with discontent their exclusion from positions of power (Marchena Fernández 2003).

To finance the army reforms, the tribute imposed on the Indians was increased. At the end of the 18th century, this resulted in indigenous uprisings in Peru, which was the prelude to the struggles for independence. They were led by Tupac Amaru II and Tupac Catari who, among their most determined combatants and strategists, were their wives Micaela Bastidas and Bartolina Sisa. For Mires (1988) women were particularly engaged in the struggle, desiring an end to not only the oppression by forced labor, but also sexual exploitation.

However, the reforms also led to the creation of universities, libraries, and access to knowledge in Europe. The enlightened thought and account of the revolution in France and in the English colonies in America reached small groups of *criollos*. The famous Quito doctor Eugenio Espejo and his sister Manuela, a nurse and journalist, were part of this group of enlightened people, even though they were mestizos. They were, however, exceptions since in the Spanish colonies only the *criollo* bourgeoisie had access to education and the rest of the population was not aware of or involved in political issues (McFarlane 2008). These enlightened groups proposed self-government but did not question religion or the social system organized by race and gender.

In 1808, France invaded Spain, and the *criollos* who were traditionally distanced from decisions in the public administration found in this vacuum of authority the opportunity to create self-governments. The first of these *criollo* rebellions was that of Quito in 1809, although it was soon deposed. An active member in the debates and planning of the governing board was the illustrious Manuela Cañizares, from Quito, again an exception in a group of men.

The independence process that ensued in the following years was a military confrontation, organized and decided by men. However, women suffered equally or more from the consequences of the conflict. In the Andean region, the Indians who had been incorporated into the army were fighting on both sides. Carrera Damas (2003) recounts that the Andean indigenous people in the Spanish army were accompanied to the campaigns by their women, who continued to be responsible for tasks such as looking for food and cooking for the men. In the cities the indigenous and mestizo women also collaborated with the independence troops by, for example, giving them supplies, clothes, lodging, and sending messages (García López 2011). In the military campaigns, the mestiza Juana Azurduy stood out: a Lieutenant Colonel who fought in the battles that liberated Bolivia and Argentina. The courage of Manuela Sáenz is also memorable, who, reaching the rank of Colonel, fought in the battles for Ecuador's independence while also being a sentimental companion of Bolívar and his advisor.

6   Republican Period

The process of independence went from being an uprising of the criollos in the cities, to being a mass movement that incorporated all ethnic groups and regions. However, the motivation was to achieve political independence from Spain and not to alter the established social structure. Thus, when independence was achieved, the new republics that emerged maintained stratification by race and gender. Similarly, religion, protected by the State, continued to dictate the norms of morality and behavior. Ecuador also did not alter the model of agricultural exploitation. Although the Indians were freed from paying the tribute, they remained dispossessed of their lands and the hacienda system remained in place.

The climate of repression that women still suffered is exemplified by a poet from Quito, Dolores Veintimilla de Galindo, who in 1857 publicly criticized the death penalty and the exclusion of indigenous people in Cuenca in her writing (Astudillo Figueroa 2015). Being a woman and having openly threatened the system, she was contested by literary and ecclesiastical sectors of Cuenca society with attacks on her personal honor which finally led to her suicide. In general, if there was an attempt to question established power, the Church, the bourgeoisie, and the military would respond, preserving the system.

This conservative society could exist both because of the social structure inherited from the colonial era and because of the model of democracy that Ecuador adopted as a republic. In terms of the latter, the vote was reserved only for the men of the bourgeoisie. Moreover, the model of democracy established in Latin America was based on that which created the United States, namely a system of representative democracy that presupposes the existence of a prepared, disinterested elite with high moral values that takes power to lead the nation. Citizens, occupied in productive tasks, leave the task of leading the State to this elite. Additionally, there is a division between the public space where the State acts and the private space, which represents the home and its intimacy, where the State does not enter.

The flaws in this design of representative democracy for Latin America are evident throughout the republican period of Latin America. At the state level, criollo or mestizo bourgeoisies and military powers ruled oppressively and for their own interests, reproducing the system of exclusion by race and gender. For Hernández Quiñones (2007) one of the main problems is the principle of differentiation which presupposes that the ruling elite, given its wisdom and superiority, does not need to take a mandate from its constituents, i.e., that they are not subject to their demands. At the household level, where much violence against women is practiced and cultural imaginaries are reproduced, women were left unprotected as the State did not interfere with this private space, leaving them far away from influencing public policies.

The turning point of the conservative state was undoubtedly the liberal revolution, commanded by Eloy Alfaro. This revolution arose from groups opposed to the conservative regime, mainly in coastal areas that did not depend on the traditional *latifundio* system as in the Andean region. Alfaro had a clear understanding of the modernization needs of the State when he became president in 1895. In his government, various initiatives allowed the separation of Church and State. Among these were the approval of civil marriage and divorce, the confiscation of Church lands and the end of its monopoly on education, which became public and secular.

With respect to women, the liberal revolution framed the origin of women's inferiority in an unnatural social process and sought to integrate them as citizens by encouraging their participation in the labor market. However, Sinardet (2000) clarifies that these reforms had their limitations because they were still based on a gender ideology that limited women to certain tasks and indissolubly associated them with the home. In the short-term the advances benefited only middle-class women and generated opposition from many groups, mainly and unsurprisingly from the Church. Finally, Alfaro himself would die a victim of his detractors.

Throughout the twentieth century, the States in the region made concessions to broader sectors of society and created conditions for improving their access to the consumer market, as they confronted the possibility of socialism as an alternative means of socioeconomic organization. This led to the establishment of welfare states (De Barbieri 2004). However, citizens continued to have no real participation in the direction of the State. In Ecuador, capitalism concealed many semi-feudal structures that survived mainly in the countryside and preserved the system of oppression of women. The only opposition to the State came from social movements, i.e., citizens groups that spontaneously organized to demand rights.

7   Indigenous Movements

Throughout the twentieth century, the situation of indigenous women could not be duly appreciated without mentioning the indigenous movements in Ecuador, which became the most representative phenomena in the prevailing social sector.

In the second half of that period, several countries with a majority indigenous presence experienced uprisings by armed groups against the central government. The main examples were Mexico with the *Ejército Zapatista de Liberación Nacional*, Guatemala with *Unidad Revolucionaria Nacional Guatemalteca*, and Peru with *Sendero Luminoso*. As Thorp et al. (2006) report, such conflicts were not ethnically but economically motivated, being in reality uprisings of the poorest and most excluded groups. Central governments, however, saw the indigenous component as a threat to the established social system. In Guatemala, where the conflict was most intense, repression had tragic results when the state carried out massacres in indigenous communities, solely because of their ethnic origin.

On the other hand, Ecuador had a different trajectory, partly by virtue of the existence of indigenous movements that channeled the longings of the communities. In the 1940s and with the support of the Communist Party, the *Federación Ecuatoriana de Indios* (Ecuadorian Federation of Indians) was created, a social movement that emerged as an opposition to the large estate structures of the haciendas that still monopolized the productive land in the Andean region. This organization did not have the tutelage of non-indigenous people in its leadership, but of indigenous activists, many of them having already experienced the problems of land governance (Becker 2013). Among its most active members were women such as Dolores Cacuango, Tránsito Amaguaña, and Angelita Andrango, who had long careers in indigenous activism.

Stemming from the continued struggles of indigenous organizations, during the 1960s and 1970s the long-awaited agrarian reform took place in Ecuador. Through successive processes, land was handed over to the indigenous people or their communities. However, this process should not simply be understood as an act of social justice since the landowners sought to get rid of excess labor that they no longer needed, while the political powers sought to neutralize the advance of indigenous groups and socialist movements through this concession (Pallares 2014). De La Torre (2000) reports that this change allowed the emergence of an indigenous middle class and the consolidation of a stronger movement. Moreover, among indigenous people it generated the desire to continue identifying themselves as such instead of changing their customs and appearance to be considered mestizos.

In the 1980s, the Confederation of Indigenous Nationalities (CONAIE) was created and in the 1990s played a major role in the creation of the indigenous political party *Pachakutik*. Starting in the 1990s, CONAIE's capacity to mobilize people and its policy of direct action gave it relevance as a major political actor. The organization played an active role in the defenestration of Presidents Bucaram in 1997 and Mahuad in 2000. Pachakutik has achieved political significance with the election of local representatives and legislators. With its pressure measures it has been able to influence the creation of public policies aimed at the development of indigenous communities and to direct the process of bicultural education (Yashar 2005).

However, despite gaining spaces of power and being recognized for its nonviolent strategy, in comparison to other countries, the indigenous leadership has not been successful in creating a discourse that effectively attacks racism and discrimination (Beck et al. 2011; Hooker 2005). Among the demands of the indigenous organization, calls for gender equality are lacking. Thus, although indigenous women have obtained representation as part of an ethnicity, this has not impacted on the gender inequality they face.

8   Feminism and Gender Studies in the Country and the Region

At the end of the 19th century, the first feminist movements appeared in Europe within what came to be known as the first wave of Feminism, where the main demand was the right of women to vote. In Latin America, movements of this kind also became manifest and the province of San Juan in Argentina pioneered this for municipal elections as early as 1862. Subsequently, there was a debate about extending that right to national elections with conservative groups opposed, arguing that women's participation in politics would take them away from their household duties and lead to the eventual collapse of society. By way of defense, the suffragettes appealed to the moral quality of women as mothers and wives, with the issue of women's equality itself not under discussion at the time. The debate was eventually inclined towards reformists, as the successive municipal elections did not translate into the feared social breakdown (Hammond 2009). Women's suffrage in that province was achieved in 1927.

In Ecuador the first female suffrage was that of Matilde Hidalgo de Procel as early as 1924, taking advantage of the fact that the constitution did not explicitly limit the right to vote by gender. This case opened the debate on the adequacy of universal suffrage, a right being explicitly enshrined in the constitution in 1929. Thus, Ecuador became the first country in South America to enfranchise women (Rivera Berruz 2018). This differs from other countries in the region such as Mexico, Colombia, and Peru where women's suffrage had to wait until the 1950s.

Hidalgo de Procel was an extraordinary feminist. She was also the first woman to obtain a medical degree and following her election as a representative for a local council, she remained popular among her constituents throughout her time in office. Another forerunner in politics was Nela Martínez, who became a leader of the Ecuadorian Communist Party and the first woman to be elected to the National Congress. While these women set a precedent for greater female participation, they were exceptions in a system and society dominated by men.

In general, although women's right to vote was a triumph for the activists and movements that promoted this, it did not bring about immediate changes in the situation of women. Neither the presence of women in spaces of power nor the creation of laws in favor of equity guaranteed real changes.

In Argentina, Eva Duarte, wife of President Juan Domingo Perón, was instrumental in obtaining universal suffrage for the entire country. However, Duarte was militant in support of her husband's party and aligned with its objectives which, although had positive social impacts, were not directly feminist. Similarly, Costa Rica, which as early as 1949 enshrined equal rights for men and women in its constitution, saw no change in practice until many years later. It was only in the mid-1980s that government agencies were created to address discrimination against women and promote their economic development (Chant 2009).

Even in the case of Cuba, where the 1959 socialist revolution emphasized the importance of women in its triumph, gender roles still carried weight in daily life. The revolution regarded Feminism as a bourgeois tendency that threatened the sanctity of those spaces where man and woman should unite (Molyneux 2000). Chase (2010) relates that even those who were feminists decided not to hinder the revolutionary process with their demands. Cuba stands out positively in the region on issues related to women such as mortality reduction, education, labor inclusion, and legal rights (Molyneux 2000). However, when analyzing the situation of women in Cuba, several authors from outside the island (Center for Democracy in the Americas 2013; Hernandez Truyol 1998; Meade 2010; Pertierra 2008) emphasize that although women began to have broad participation in the country's labor force, they did not lose their relationship with household chores. This was evident with the economic crisis that emerged on the island during the 1990s and after the fall of the Soviet Union, as women continued to play the traditional role of caring for the home while, at the same time, many also financially supported their families, thus with more responsibility than men. The national survey on gender equality published in Cuba by the National Statistics and Information Office (Oficina Nacional de Estadística e Información 2018) shows that women still devote more hours per week to unpaid domestic work and care work.

Back to the region, a new wave of Feminism began in the 1960s; the vote for women had been won in more and more countries and the respective constitutions enshrined equal rights for both sexes (Chinchilla Stoltz 1993). This influenced feminist activism in Ecuador. First, through social organizations, women began to come together to discuss their problems. Then, in the 1980s, the first social movements of and for women began to take shape in Ecuador (Lind 2005), although their demands were based on their experiences in daily life and not on a theory that articulated their claims.

At a global level, since, in practice, women could not exercise all their rights, Feminism then began to study the inequalities they experienced, the causes that generated them, and the gender violence that they produced, through so-called gender studies. The aim was to delegitimize the patriarchal ideology, to empower women to achieve their autonomy from men, and to promote the changes required in society to finally promote gender equality.

However, outside of the industrialized world many of these studies were criticized for being authored by and focused on the experiences of white Anglo-Saxon women from developed countries. For several authors, this led to theories of Feminism that did not adjust to the realities of women in other contexts, including women of other ethnic groups in those same countries (Aguilar, 2000; Lugones and Spelman 1983).

Starting in the 1970s, Latin America became an area of interest for gender studies. Again, the focus on women's realities was limited, for several reasons. First, the research was initially framed only in terms of the material living conditions of mestizo women in urban areas (Chant and Craske 2003). In addition, research tended to be pursued by Anglo-Saxon authors who, by definition, failed to understand the nuances and complexities of the situations faced by the women they studied (Chant and Craske 2003; Lugones and Spelman 1983). Finally, working from the United States or the United Kingdom, researchers commonly sought to have an impact on the world of knowledge, unlike researchers residing in Latin America who sought to generate changes in society (Mu and Pereyra-Rojas 2015).

Gender researchers in Latin America have had to face the difficulties of opening space to a new area in institutions with limited resources, in addition to facing rejection by a socio-political system based on the inequality they denounced. In spite of this, today we can find in academic journals a wide repertoire of publications on Latin America, many by local authors. Studies in Feminism have also become more diversified, encompassing psychology, philosophy, political science, and economics (De Barbieri 2004).

In addition, since the 1990s gender studies have gone beyond analysis of the material conditions in which women live to incorporate cultural aspects related to their daily lives such as their self-representations or symbolisms (Chant and Craske 2003). The cultural aspects that surround women are indispensable aspects in understanding their realities. For example, the ideology of Marianism, or idealization of the Virgin Mary as a female model, confines women to a role of submission to men but also to the violence to which their gender exposes them (Rondon 2003; Stevens 1979).

However, with the expansion of analytical perspectives, priorities can sometimes be lost sight of. For example, Aguilar (2000) warned of the creation of a postmodernist Feminism that, in its attempt to renew itself, analyses women's problems exclusively from the point of view of symbolism. As an example, she cites studies that from a symbolic point of view concluded that women engaged in prostitution enjoy power and autonomy. However, this analysis left aside the relationships of inferiority that inequality and economic fragility impose on women. Hence the imperative to include in gender studies essential areas such as political economy and class analysis/social division of labor. The latter addresses problems such as wage inequality and labor exploitation, economic fragility, and the impossibility of accessing subsistence resources, which are central to the realities of many women and the key to their inequality with respect to men.

In the same vein, Uribe López (2007) emphasizes that efforts pursuant of gender equity must start from macroeconomic policies. Macroeconomics in Latin America has been handled in neoliberal systems trying to homogenize the poor, that is, reducing them to a single category ignoring the complexities of the particular circumstances that generate and maintain their status and condition, as in the case of women, the constant inequality and exclusion to which they are subjected. Based on these assumptions, national economies have been managed via supposedly prioritizing economic growth, without addressing the real causes of poverty and inequality.

International organizations have been fundamental in putting the theory of Feminism into practice. The United Nations, within the framework of the protection of human rights, worked to establish an agreement that recognizes the inherent rights of women and to create mechanisms for their fulfillment. In 1979, the Convention on the Elimination of All Forms of Discrimination against Women was signed. A similar step was taken by the Organization of American States in 1994 with the Inter-American Convention on the Prevention, Punishment and Eradication of Violence against Women, also known as the Convention of Belém do Pará. Both are the basis for the generation of objectives for public policies for gender equality in the region.

The Economic Commission for Latin America and the Caribbean (ECLAC), which purpose is to contribute to sustainable development with equality in the region, recognizes the important theoretical contribution that Feminism has in the construction of women's personal autonomy, creating more equal conditions between the two genders and ultimately allowing the development not only of women but of society as a whole. Based on the contributions of Feminism, ECLAC highlights five points that are prerequisites for achieving this equality (ECLAC 2014). First, inclusion policies must take into account the historical subordination of women and neutralize male privileges, to guarantee such inclusion. Second, in response to the previous point, affirmative policies are required in which the entry of women into disputed spaces is actively promoted. Third, a politicization of private life is necessary that allows public policies to be applied also in the home, where a large part of the violence towards women is perpetrated. Fourth, in the public domain, it is necessary to guarantee women's access to the political sphere, through inclusion laws that guarantee their participation. Fifth, in the private domain, public policies should promote issues such as equality within the family, access to free time, and understandings of work in terms of time and labor rather than simple money, i.e., between paid (occupational) and unpaid (domestic) work.

From these points it can be understood that, on the road to gender equality, a new approach to masculinity must be discussed, confronting the patriarchal discourse that equates masculinity with superiority over women (Greig 2009). In this task men must necessarily be involved and committed.

In addition to a greater understanding of the historical causes of inequality and the generation of new gender approaches, a greater inclusion of women in political representation has also ocurred. Since universal suffrage was obtained, women's participation in politics has increased not only as voters but also as political representatives, with their presence in national parliaments, public administration positions, and even with six female presidents in the region throughout the twentieth and twenty-first centuries. However, Schwindt-Bayer (2018) notes that participation has been mixed in the region. First, women must face a system of elections that renders it difficult for them to run for office, so that despite progress in women's participation, equality in politics is far from being the norm. Therefore, in the exercise of political power, there is little space to promote an agenda towards gender equality. It is through representation in parliaments and not through the executive that more can be done to create a legal framework to promote equality.

In spite of the efforts that through legislation and regulations seek to correct the conditions that generate gender inequality, these can be evaded if there are no explicit mechanisms to guarantee compliance. The path towards gender equality necessarily implies reversing the mechanisms of privilege enjoyed by men and, therefore, men at the risk of losing historically maintained privileges, or women themselves rejecting the possibility of assuming new responsibilities or risks, may hinder this process (De Barbieri 2004). For example, starting in Europe in the 1970s and then around the world, laws were enacted to impose gender quotas in national parliaments to ensure women's participation. An initiative in this sense was implemented in the Brazilian parliament where the number of candidates allowed per list was increased on the condition that the additional candidacies were exclusively for women. The political parties, however, demonstrated disinterest in achieving gender equity by not completing candidacies exclusively for women and maintaining the prevalence of men. Since the law did not contemplate sanctions, this omission could not be realistically reprimanded (Araújo et al. 2018; Miguel 2008)

Moreover, conservative governments can capture the issue of gender inequality to create *façades* of inclusion and participation. Such was the case in Chile, where the National Service for Women and Gender Equity, created to imply a concern for equality, allowed instead a conservative agenda centered on notions of the traditional family (Chinchilla Stoltz 1993).

Outside of political representation, feminist movements continue to face the challenge of generating strategies against violence and gender inequality. Many of them have grouped together as non-governmental organizations (NGOs) to articulate their work. However, this has presented new challenges. In some cases the structuring into more complex organizations has led to the loss of the sense of popular participation that the movements embodied. Alvarez (1999) denounces an abundance of these organizations and at the same time warns of the risk they run of supplanting the women they supposedly represent as interlocutors of the State when they consider themselves experts on their situation. In addition, they can become mere executors of policies, becoming dependent on the State and not on the people they represent. For example, Barrig (2016) relates the case of many NGOs representing women in Peru, who became servile to the authoritarian and repressive government of Alberto Fujimori.

In contrast, Motta (2017) points to an alternative route between social movements in Latin America: radical education for emancipation. This implies that the movements create spaces for participation, close to women, in their communities, and in their homes. In these spaces and through dialogue, reflection, theorization, and finally a return to practice, the discourse of oppression is dismantled and a new vision is generated in which new Feminisms are created, arising not only from academic postulations, but as a shared process where the subjects of exclusion become creators of a new discourse. This proposal can finally be a path to a participatory democracy, from which a collective consciousness of the real problems of society can be created and from which governments committed to social interests can emerge.

9   Concluding Remarks

Contemporary Ecuador is characterized as unequal and exclusive based on—among others—race and gender criteria. This reality has been built over centuries, from colonial through to oligarchic domination. As a result of this context, gender inequality permeates all sectors of society and the public and private spheres.

Gender inequality is a type of injustice that attacks half the population and harms the whole society. Moreover, investments in technical education, infrastructure, or modernization of the State will not be entirely successful if a climate of equality and social justice does not become manifest. The scope of this problem ranges from the loss of talent and experience in the labor pool, which is still restrictive for women, to the family nuclei where women are prey to domestic work, care, and other unpaid tasks that are trivialized and minimized by society.

Despite much remains to be done, gender studies in the region and the country have shed light on this problem and enabled the creation of a theoretical basis for a new Feminism, which seeks to combat the causes of gender inequality, promote policies that increase equality, and empower women to become part of the process.

As noted at the onset of this chapter, Latin America has a high perception of happiness amongst its peoples, despite being the most unequal region in the world. Regarding gender disparities, its population demonstrates to be aware of the violence and disadvantages that women suffer (as shown by Latinobarómetro 2018), even considering violence against women as the most damaging form of violence to the country and one of the most frequent. However, although violence is considered negative, it is not seen as one of the main problems by its inhabitants. Similarly, inequality in other forms such as access to the labor market or unpaid work are not considered a major problem (Anglade, Useche and Deere 2017).

As documented throughout the chapter, discrimination and exclusion that women suffer emanates from a definition of gender roles that leaves them at a disadvantage and that has been naturalized throughout history, being reinforced by religious precepts (Barredo 2017; Goicolea et al. 2010; Muñoa Fernández and Luzuriaga Uribe 2018; O'Neill 2016), therefore explaining why it may not be seen as a major problem, despite actually being one. Added to this is the fact that in Ecuador there is discrimination on the basis of race, which in part is not even perceived by the population because it has historically been seen as natural (Beck et al. 2011).

Combined, these two aspects lead to a continuous discrimination of women both by gender and by race that affects them in areas such as health and economic autonomy as well as in their access to education and spaces of power. Although academic publications and government studies have explored and synthesized this problem and although various advances have been made from the public administration (Camacho 2014), there are numerous challenges that still remain before the population as a whole is made aware of the real dimensions of this problem.

Latin America, generally speaking, is a society based on an appreciation of family ties and a sense of belonging to the place of birth. It is also conservative, tending towards a morality more attached to religious interpretations than to law or academic perspectives on gender. The high perception of happiness could be interpreted as ignoring the dramatic problems affecting women in the region. This is why greater progress towards ending gender inequities and inequalities will require a broad discussion of this issue within society and increasing awareness of the negative effects that this problem brings to the lives not only of women but of all citizens.

From academia, through the study of gender and inequality, scholars can contribute with formal descriptions of women's realities from multiple perspectives and expose the unfair situations in which they live, giving voice to a historically excluded group. However, generating real change remains a work of popular action expressed both through social organizations and progressive governments. Ultimately, the interlocutors in any attempt at change must be the women themselves, for whom society's historic debt is far from being paid.

References

Aguilar, D.D. (2000). "Questionable Claims: Colonialism Redux, Feminist Style." *Race & Class* 41(3): 1–12. https://doi.org/10.1177/030639680041300i.

Alvarez, S.E. (1999). "Advocating feminism: The Latin American Feminist NGO 'Boom.'" *International Feminist Journal of Politics* 1(2): 181–209. https://doi.org/10.1080/146167499359880.

Anglade, B., Useche, P., and Deere, C.D. (2017). "Decomposing the Gender Wealth Gap in Ecuador." *World Development* 96: 19–31. https://doi.org/10.1016/J.WORLDDEV.2017.02.003.

Araújo, C., Calasanti, A., and Htun, M. (2018) . "Women, Power, and Policy in Brazil." In L.A. Schwindt-Bayer (Ed.), *Gender and Representation in Latin America*. Oxford University Press. https://doi.org/10.1093/oso/9780190851224.003.0012.

Astudillo Figueroa, A. (2015). "Dolores Veintimilla De Galindo y la descolonización del ser femenino." *Locas, Escritoras y Personajes Femeninos Cuestionando Las Normas: XII Congreso Internacional Del Grupo de Investigación Escritoras y Escrituras.* https://idus.us.es/xmlui/handle/11441/54679?locale-attribute=es.

Ayala Mora, E. (2008). *Resumen de historia del Ecuador* (3rd ed.). Corporación Editora Nacional.

Barredo, D. (2017). "La violencia de género en Ecuador: un estudio sobre los universitarios." *Revista Estudos Feministas* 25(3): 1313–1327. https://doi.org/10.1590/1806-9584.2017v25n3p1313.

Barrig, M. (2016). "Latin American Feminism Gains, Losses and Hard Times." *NACLA Report on the Americas* 34(5): 29–35. https://doi.org/10.1080/10714839.2001.11724593.

Beck, S.H., Mijeski, K.J., and Stark, M.M. (2011). "¿Qué es racismo? Awareness of Racism and Discrimination in Ecuador." *American Sociological Review* 46(1): 102–125. https://www.jstor.org/stable/41261372.

Becker, M. (2013). "Comunistas, indigenistas e indígenas en la formación de la Federación Ecuatoriana de Indios y el Instituto Indigenista Ecuatoriano." *Íconos—Revista de Ciencias Sociales* 0(27): 135. https://doi.org/10.17141/iconos.27.2007.193.

Bose, C.E., and Acosta-Belén, E. (1995). *Women in the Latin American development process*. Temple University Press.

Camou, M.M., and Maubrigades, S. (2017). "The Lingering Face of Gender Inequality in Latin America." In L. Bértola and J. Williamson (Eds.), *Has Latin American Inequality Changed Direction?* (pp. 219–241). Springer International Publishing. https://doi.org/10.1007/978-3-319-44621-9_10.

Center for Democracy in the Americas. (2013). *Women's Work: Gender Equality in Cuba and the Role of Women Building Cuba's Future*.

Buvinić, M., Mazza, J., and Deutsch, R. (Eds.). (2004). *Social inclusion and economic development in Latin America*. Inter-American Development Bank.

Camacho Z., G. (2014). *La violencia de género contra las mujeres en el Ecuador: análisis de los resultados de la encuesta nacional sobre relaciones familiares y violencia de género contra las mujeres*. Consejo Nacional para la Igualdad de Género.

Chant, S.H. (2009). "The 'Feminisation of Poverty in Costa Rica: To What Extent a Conundrum?" *Bulletin of Latin American Research* 28(1): 19–43. https://doi.org/10.1111/j.1470-9856.2008.00288.x.

Chant, S.H., and Craske, N. (2003). *Gender in Latin America*. Rutgers University Press.

Chase, M. (2010). "Women's Organisations and the Politics of Gender in Cuba's Urban Insurrection (1952–1958)." *Bulletin of Latin American Research* 29(4): 440–458. https://doi.org/10.1111/j.1470-9856.2010.00382.x.

Chaves, M.E. (2000). "Slave Women's Strategies for Freedom and the Late Spanish Colonial State." In E. Dore, M. Molyneux, E. Rodríguez, and M.E. Chaves (Eds.), *Hidden Histories of Gender and the State in Latin America* (pp. 109–126). Duke University Press.

Chinchilla Stoltz, N. (1993). "Women's Movements in the Americas: Feminism's Second Wave." *NACLA Report on the Americas* 27(1): 17–23. https://doi.org/10.1080/10714839.1993.11724645.

Clayton, L.A., Conniff, M.L., and Gauss, S.M. (2017). *A new history of modern Latin America* (3rd ed.). University of California Press.

Colebrook, C. (2004). *Gender*. Palgrave Macmillan.

De Barbieri, T. (2004). "Mas de tres décadas de los estudios de género en América Latina." *Revista Mexicana de Sociología* 66: 197. https://doi.org/10.2307/3541450.

De La Torre, C. (2000). "Racism in Education and the Construction of Citizenship in Ecuador." *Race & Class* 42(2): 33–45. https://doi.org/10.1177/0306396800422004.

DeVerteuil, G. (2009). "Inequality." *International Encyclopedia of Human Geography* (pp. 433–445). https://doi.org/10.1016/B978-008044910-4.00963-9.

Dore, E. (2000). "One Step Forward, Two Steps Back: Gender and the State in the Long Nineteenth Century." In E. Dore, M. Molyneux, E. Rodríguez, and M.E. Chaves (Eds.), *Hidden histories of gender and the State in Latin America*. Duke University Press.

Economic Commission for Latin America and the Caribbean. (2014). *Compacts for equality: towards a sustainable future: thirty-fifth session of ECLAC, Lima, 5–9 May, 2014*. https://www.cepal.org/en/publications/36693-compacts-equality-towards-sustainable-future.

French, W.E., and Bliss, K.E. (2006). "Introduction." In W.E. French, and K.E. Bliss (Eds.), *Gender, Sexuality, and Power in Latin America since Independence*. Rowman & Littlefield Publishers.

Galeano, E. (1980). *Las venas abiertas de América Latina*. Siglo XXI Editores.

García López, A.B. (2011). "La participación de la mujer en la independencia hispano-americana a través de los medios de comunicación." *Historia y Comunicación Social* 16(0): 33–49. https://doi.org/10.5209/rev_HICS.2011.v16.37148.

Goicolea, I., Wulff, M., Sebastian, M.S., and Öhman, A. (2010). "Adolescent pregnancies and girls' sexual and reproductive rights in the amazon basin of Ecuador: an analysis of providers' and policy makers' discourses." *BMC International Health and Human Rights* 10(1): 12. https://doi.org/10.1186/1472-698X-10-12.

González Suárez, F. (1890). *Historia general de la República del Ecuador. Tomo primero*. Imprenta del Clero.

Greig, A. (2009). "Troublesome Masculinities: Masculinity in Trouble." *IDS Bulletin* 40(1): 69–76. https://doi.org/10.1111/j.1759-5436.2009.00011.x.

Guy, D.J. (2012). "Gender and Sexuality in Latin America." In J.C. Moya (Ed.), *The Oxford Handbook of Latin American History* (Vol. 1). Oxford University Press. https://doi.org/10.1093/oxfordhb/9780195166217.013.0013.

Hammond, G. (2009). "Suffrage in San Juan: The Test of Women's Rights in Argentina." *Bulletin of Latin American Research* 28(1): 1–18. https://doi.org/10.1111/j.1470-9856.2008.00287.x.

Helliwell, J.F., Layard, R., and Sachs, J. (2018). *World happiness report 2018*. https://worldhappiness.report/ed/2018/.

Hernández Quiñones, A. (2007). "Las promesas incumplidas de la democracia liberal y los desafíos de la gobernabilidad democrática." In C. Zorro Sánchez (Ed.), *El desarrollo: perspectivas y dimensiones. Aportes interdisciplinarios*. Ediciones Uniandes.

Hernandez Truyol, B.E. (1998). "Women in contemporary Cuba." In N.P. Stromquist (Ed.), *Women in the Third World: an encyclopedia of contemporary issues* (pp. 618–625). Routledge.

Hooker, J. (2005). "Indigenous Inclusion/Black Exclusion: Race, Ethnicity and Multicultural Citizenship in Latin America." *Journal of Latin American Studies* 37(2): 285–310. https://doi.org/10.1017/S0022216X05009016.

Hunefeldt, C. (2003). "Transfondo socioeconómico: un análisis sobre los albores de la independencia y las particularidades económicas y sociales andinas de fines del siglo XVIII y principios del XIX." In G. Carrera Damas (Ed.), *Historia de América Andina, Volumen 4—Crisis del régimen colonial e Independencia*. Universidad Andina Simón Bolívar / Libresa.

Hunter, M.L. (2013). *Race, Gender, and the Politics of Skin Tone*. Routledge. https://doi.org/10.4324/9780203620342.

Kalmanovitz, S. (2008). *La economía de la Nueva Granada*. UTADEO. Facultad de Ciencias Económicas y Administrativas.

Kennedy, A., and Troya, C.F. (1987). "Obrajes en la audiencia de Quito. Un caso estudio: Tilipulo." *Boletín Americanista* 37: 143–202. http://revistes.ub.edu/index.php/BoletinAmericanista/article/view/12774.

Kohan, N. (2013). *Simón Bolívar y nuestra independencia. Una lectura latinoamericana*. Editorial Yulca.

Latinobarómetro. (2018). *Informe Latinobarómetro 2018*. http://www.latinobarometro.org.

Layton, M.L., and Smith, A.E. (2017). "Is It Race, Class, or Gender? The Sources of Perceived Discrimination in Brazil." *Latin American Politics and Society* 59(1): 52–73. https://doi.org/10.1111/laps.12010.

Lind, A. (2005). *Gendered paradoxes: women's movements, state restructuring, and global development in Ecuador*. Pennsylvania State University Press. https://www.jstor.org/stable/10.5325/j.ctt7v1hz.

Lugones, M.C., and Spelman, E.V. (1983). "Have we got a theory for you! Feminist theory, cultural imperialism and the demand for 'the woman's voice.'" *Women's Studies International Forum* 6(6): 573–581. https://doi.org/10.1016/0277-5395(83)90019-5.

Marchena Fernández, J. (2003). "La expresión de la guerra, el poder colonial, el ejército y la crisis del régimen colonial." In G. Carrera Damas (Ed.), *Historia de América Andina, Volumen 4—Crisis del régimen colonial e Independencia*. Universidad Andina Simón Bolívar / Libresa.

McFarlane, A. (2008). "Los ejércitos coloniales y la crisis del imperio español, 1808–1810." *Historia Mexicana* 58(1): 229–285. https://historiamexicana.colmex.mx/index.php/RHM/article/view/3362.

Meade, T.A. (2010). *A history of modern Latin America: 1800 to the present*. Wiley-Blackwell.

Miguel, L.F. (2008). "Political Representation and Gender in Brazil: Quotas for Women and their Impact." *Bulletin of Latin American Research* 27(2): 197–214. https://doi.org/10.1111/j.1470-9856.2008.00263.x.

Mires, F. (1988). *La rebelión permanente: las revoluciones sociales en América Latina*. Siglo Veintiuno Editores.

Molyneux, M. (2000). "State, Gender, and Institutional Change: The Federación de Mujeres Cubanas." In E. Dore, M. Molyneux, E. Rodríguez, and M.E. Chaves (Eds.), *Hidden histories of gender and the State in Latin America* (pp. 291–321). Duke University Press.

Motta, S.C. (2017). "Emancipation in Latin America: On the Pedagogical Turn." *Bulletin of Latin American Research* 36(1): 5–20. https://doi.org/10.1111/blar.12526.

Mu, E., and Pereyra-Rojas, M. (2015). "Impact on Society versus Impact on Knowledge: Why Latin American Scholars Do Not Participate in Latin American Studies." *Latin American Research Review* 50(2): 216–238. https://doi.org/10.1353/lar.2015.0021.

Muñoa Fernández, E., and Luzuriaga Uribe, E. (2018). "El macho guayaco: de la calle a las figuras mediáticas. Una primera mirada." *La Ventana* VI(48): 139–167. http://www.redalyc.org/articulo.oa?id=88455796004.

Noonan, R.K. (1995). "Women against the state: Political opportunities and collective action frames in Chile's transition to democracy." *Sociological Forum* 10(1): 81–111. https://link.springer.com/article/10.1007/BF02098565.

Núñez Sánchez, J. (2015). *Los fenómenos naturales en la historia del Ecuador y el sur de Colombia*. CCE Benjamín Carrión.

Oficina Nacional de Estadística e Información. (2018). *Encuesta Nacional sobre Igualdad de Género*. http://www.one.cu/enig2016.htm.

O'neill, K.L. (2016). "Religion and Gender in Latin America." In V. Garrard-Burnett, P. Freston, and S.C. Dove (Eds.), *The Cambridge History of Religions in Latin America* (pp. 525–546). Cambridge University Press. https://doi.org/10.1017/CHO9781139032698.034.

Pallares, M. (2014). "50 años del gran cambio en el campo." *Ideas: El Comercio*.

Pertierra, A.C. (2008). "En Casa: Women and Households in Post-Soviet Cuba." *Journal of Latin American Studies* 40(04): 743. https://doi.org/10.1017/S0022216X08004744.

Rivera Berruz, S. (2018). "Latin American Feminism." In E. Zalta (Ed.), *The Stanford Encyclopedia of Philosophy* (Winter 2018). Metaphysics Research Lab, Stanford University. https://plato.stanford.edu/archives/win2018/entries/feminism-latin-america/.

United Nations Development Programme (2018). *Human Development Report 2019. Beyond income, beyond averages, beyond today: Inequalities in human development in the 21st century*. http://hdr.undp.org/en/2018-update.

Uribe López, M. (2007). "Tres Falacias sobre la Relación entre Macroeconomía y Pobreza." In C. Zorro Sánchez (Ed.), *El desarrollo: perspectivas y dimensiones. Aportes interdisciplinarios*. Ediciones Uniandes.

Radcliffe, S.A., and Westwood, S. (Eds.). (1993). *Viva: Women and popular protest in Latin America*. Routledge. https://doi.org/10.4324/9781315832265.

Rondon, M.B. (2003). "From Marianism to terrorism: the many faces of violence against women in Latin America." *Archives of Women's Mental Health* 6(3): 157–163. https://doi.org/10.1007/s00737-003-0169-3.

Saito, A., and Rosas Lauro, C. (Eds.). (2017). *Reducciones: la concentración forzada de las poblaciones indígenas en el Virreinato del Perú*. Fondo Editorial, Pontificia Universidad Católica del Perú.

Scarborough, W.J., Lambouths, D.L., and Holbrook, A.L. (2019). "Support of workplace diversity policies: The role of race, gender, and beliefs about inequality." *Social Science Research* 79: 194–210. https://doi.org/10.1016/J.SSRESEARCH.2019.01.002.

Schwindt-Bayer, L.A. (2018). "Conclusion. The Gendered Nature of Democratic Representation in Latin America." In L.A. Schwindt-Bayer (Ed.), *Gender and Representation in Latin America* (Vol. 1). Oxford University Press. https://doi.org/10.1093/oso/9780190851224.003.0014.

Sheahan, J., and Iglesias, E. (1998). "Kinds and causes of inequality in Latin America." In N. Birdsall, C. Graham, and R.H. Sabot (Eds.), *Beyond tradeoffs: market reforms and equitable growth in Latin America*. Brookings Institution Press.

Silverblatt, I. (1978). "Andean Women in the Inca Empire." *Feminist Studies* 4(3): 36. https://doi.org/10.2307/3177537.

Silverblatt, I. (1987). *Moon, sun, and witches: gender ideologies and class in Inca and colonial Peru*. Princeton University Press.

Sinardet, E. (2000). "La mujer en el proyecto nacional de la revolución liberal ecuatoriana (1895–1925): ¿qué representación de la mujer?" In F. Morales Padrón (Ed.), *XIII Coloquio de Historia Canario-Americana; VIII Congreso Internacional de Historia de America (AEA)* (pp. 1441–1457). Ediciones del Cabildo de Gran Canaria. https://dialnet.unirioja.es/servlet/articulo?codigo=2198613.

Socolow, S.M. (2015). *The Women of Colonial Latin America*. Cambridge University Press. https://doi.org/10.1017/CBO9781139031189.

Stepan, N. (1996). *The hour of eugenics: race, gender, and nation in Latin America*. Cornell University Press. https://www.jstor.org/stable/10.7591/j.ctv75d682.

Stevens, E.P. (1979). "Marianismo: the other face of Machismo." In A. Pescatello (Ed.), *Female and male in Latin America* (pp. 90–101). University of Pittsburgh Press.

Thorp, R., Caumartin, C., and Gray-Molina, G. (2006). "Inequality, Ethnicity, Political Mobilisation and Political Violence in Latin America: The Cases of Bolivia, Guatemala and Peru." *Bulletin of Latin American Research* 25(4): 453–480. https://doi.org/10.1111/j.1470-9856.2006.00207.x.

Tompkins, C. (2008). "Imagining new identities and communities for feminisms in the Americas." *Hispanic Issues On Line* 2: 1–33. https://conservancy.umn.edu/handle/11299/202459.

Uribe López, M. (2007). "Tres Falacias sobre la Relación entre Macroeconomía y Pobreza." In C. Zorro Sánchez (Ed.), *El desarrollo: perspectivas y dimensiones. Aportes
interdisciplinarios*. Ediciones Uniandes.

Vargas, V. (1992). *Como cambiar el mundo sin perdernos: El movimiento de mujeres en el
Perú y América Latina* (1st ed.). Ediciones F. Tristán.

Wade, P. (2010). *Race and Ethnicity in Latin America*. Pluto Press. https://doi.org/
10.2307/j.ctt183p73f.11.

Wade, P. (1997). *Race and ethnicity in Latin America*. Pluto Press.

Yashar, D.J. (2005). "Ecuador: Latin America's strongest indigenous movement." In
Contesting Citizenship in Latin America (pp. 85–151). Cambridge University Press.
https://doi.org/10.1017/CBO9780511790966.004.

CHAPTER 6

Gender Wage Gaps in Ecuador

Ximena Songor-Jaramillo and Carlos Moreno-Hurtado

1 Introduction

Socioeconomic characteristics have traditionally been associated with wage differences between groups. In this context, endogenous factors such as education and specialization of the labor force are expected to generate advantages for human capital resulting in better wages being received in the labor market (Becker 1957; Mincer and Polachek 1974). However, identifying similarities in the endogenous characteristics of individuals leads to confusion when explaining the origin of wage disparities. A question then arises as to whether individuals' exogenous characteristics explain wage gaps or not. A number of studies have been developed around this issue by breaking down the wage differential to determine causative factors and contextualize it between groups, mainly in terms of gender and ethnicity (e.g., Alvarado and Cortés 2012; Ayala-Jaramillo 2017; Benítez and Espinoza 2018; Botello-Peñaloza 2015; Canelas and Salazar 2014; Cóndor-Pumisacho 2010; Di Paola and Berges 2000; Espinoza and Sánchez 2009; Gallardo and Ñopo 2009; Galvis 2010; García-Aracil and Winter 2006; Martínez-Tamayo 2009; Rivera 2013; Sarmiento-Moscoso 2017; Tenjo et al. 2005).

A comprehensive analysis of wage disparities must consider barriers to labor market access. In this context, this chapter focuses on the issue of women's access to the labor market in Ecuador; women being the group that, from the assignment of productive and reproductive roles, has traditionally experienced labor segregation. This, in turn, leads us to consider other particular characteristics that condition participation in the labor market such as area of residence, age, marital status, and level of education.

Although statistically significant barriers to labor market access for women are identified in this study, the analysis of wage differentials also reveals gaps against men. These results could lead the reader to assume the existence of a favorable scenario for women; however, by breaking down the identified wage gap, a persistent factor of discrimination against female wage earners is observed. Although this identified discriminatory component became noticeably smaller in 2017 compared to 2007, it nevertheless denotes the persistence of a differential explained by exogenous factors such as gender, which harms women.

The next section presents a review of the salient literature before detailing the methodological process applied herein. The results of inferential analysis are then presented. Finally, in last section, discussion and conclusions are offered.

2   Literature Review

One of the mechanisms by which gender discrimination is manifested—traditionally against women—is through differences in salary. In methodological terms, a standard method used to assess gender wage gaps is that developed by Oaxaca (1973) and Blinder (1973). The utility of this methodology lies in the fact that it allows the average wage gap to be broken down into two components: the first revealing explicit differences presented by the model, those explained by differences in the characteristics of individuals (in the endowment of attributes); the second component presents structural disparities, those that are not explained, since they are presented in a context of equality of preliminary conditions. This latter differential not explained by the model can be considered as a proxy for discrimination in the labor market.

Blinder (1973) explored wage disparities in an American context and segmented groups on the basis of the race of individuals, referring specifically to white and black men. The analysis is then expanded to the gender level with a comparison of salaries between white men and white women. The author concludes that 70% of the race differential and 100% of the sex differential are attributable to discrimination.

On the other hand, the work carried out in the same year by Oaxaca considered the salary of urban workers in the United States as a function of their years of education, type of worker (public, private, or self-employed), industry, occupational category, health conditions, migration, marital status, size of urban area, and region. The author then explored how the magnitude of the estimated discrimination coefficient depends on the selection of control variables in the wage regression (Oaxaca 1973).

The work developed by these two scholars provided the framework for several authors working in this domain. Subsequent studies have suggested methodological improvements which, in turn, led to generating quantile decompositions of wage gaps (Blau and Kahn 1992; DiNardo et al. 1996; Firpo et al. 2007; Fortin and Lemieux 1998; Gosling et al. 2000; Jones 1983; Koenker and Hallock 2001; Machado and Mata 2005; Madden 2000; Rosenzweig and Morgan 1976).

In what follows, various empirical studies that analyze gender inequalities in specific contexts are introduced. In the first instance, Di Paola and Berges (2000) focus on discrimination by gender in Mar de Plata based on data taken from the Permanent Household Survey; the authors estimate Mincerian[1] income functions for men and women. To identify the reasons for the existing wage gap, they consider the methodology proposed by Blinder (1973) and Oaxaca (1973). This study by Di Paola and Berges (2000) corrects the sample selection bias invoked by the estimation of simple Mincerian equations by applying the two-step procedure suggested by Heckman (1979).

The results presented by Di Paola and Berges (2000) highlight the relevance of the division of labor, specifically the reproductive roles in the household. This is evident in the equation for women's participation in the labor force, when considering variables related to the structure of the household (stratum to which the household belongs, income of the head of the family, number of family members) as explanations for this probability. The results of the differentials of the estimated Mincerian equations specify that a proportion of the wage gap (28% specifically) is due to differences in the human capital endowments of men and women (in relation to work experience); the remaining 72% of the gap corresponds to residual discrimination against women. The authors highlight the relevance of the inclusion of the inverse of the Mills reason— relative to the procedure suggested by Heckman (1979) in the wage equations— because it permits robust decomposition of the gap without over- or underestimation.

Tenjo et al. (2005) estimate wage gaps between men and women in particular Latin American countries, specifically in Argentina, Brazil, Colombia, Costa Rica, Honduras, and Uruguay. For this purpose, the authors use Oaxaca's methodology. A particularity of this study is the presentation of results that contemplate the correction of sample selection bias and those that do not. The data used emanate from household surveys in each country; the analysis is performed for employed and unemployed individuals, and hourly wages are predicted by estimating Mincerian equations.

The results reveal considerable levels of segregation identified by employment sector and by occupation in all sampled countries, excepting Honduras. However, wage disparities diminish with the passage of time in favor of women, which is largely explained by women's access to economic sectors with

---

1 The so-called Mincerian income equation refers to the uni-equational model proposed by Mincer (1974, Chapter 3), in which salary is a function of education (linear) and experience (non-linear). For a detailed analysis, see also Mincer (1974, Chapter 4).

higher wages. But it must be taken into account that despite this increased access to sectors with higher wages, women remain earning less income than men. One of the reasons for this is the number of hours worked by female members of the labor force, which, no doubt, due to the assignment of reproductive roles, is geared towards working fewer hours than men.

Similar results are identified in the study carried out by Galvis (2010) in which, in the metropolitan areas of Colombia, gender segregation in terms of employment sector and occupational position is identified. In applying Oaxaca's decomposition method, the author revealed that an important part of the identified salary gap is explained by discriminatory effects. A key conclusion of this study concerns individuals' qualifications: if wages depended on this factor alone, the wage gap would favor women in Colombian metropolitan areas.

The available literature for Ecuador reveals different studies focused on wage gaps based on individual characteristics such as ethnicity and gender. Canelas and Salazar (2014), Cóndor-Pumisacho (2010), Gallardo and Ñopo (2009), and García-Aracil and Winter (2006), suggest that wage gaps are explained more by ethnicity than by gender. Gallardo and Ñopo (2009) analyzed along the distribution curve, and gaps by gender and ethnicity were notably evidenced at the lowest points of the wage distribution.

Among other research that analyzes gender wage gaps (e.g., Alvarado and Cortés 2012; Ayala-Jaramillo 2017; Benítez and Espinoza 2018; Botello-Peñaloza 2015; Cóndor-Pumisacho 2010; Espinoza and Sánchez 2009; Martínez-Tamayo 2009; Rivera 2013; and Sarmiento-Moscoso 2017), human capital is identified as one of the determining factors, highlighting the fact that returns from academic training are greater at the highest points of the distribution (Espinoza and Sánchez 2009).

Decomposing the wage differential between men and women, Sarmiento-Moscoso (2017) identifies significant differences in the income received by both groups, in favor of men. However, if this difference were due solely to the endowment of socioeconomic characteristics, women should be the ones with the highest income. The discrimination coefficient that the study identifies is against women; however, the disparities and this discriminating factor have decreased over time.

By contrast, Benítez and Espinoza (2018) identify wage gaps against men in Ecuador in terms of socioeconomic characteristics at the gender level. In other words, women benefit from better conditions than men, which would justify higher wages. However, when the gaps are broken down, a factor of discrimination against women is identified.

3   Data

To carry out this research, data from the National Survey of Employment, Unemployment and Underemployment (ENEMDU) of Ecuador, corresponding to the fourth quarters of 2007 and 2017 and gathered by the National Institute of Statistics and Censuses (Instituto Nacional de Estadística y Censos, INEC) was used (INEC 2007; 2017). This survey seeks to gather information about the sociodemographic and occupational characteristics of individuals in urban and rural areas. Only information from public and private wage earners between 15 and 64 years of age is considered. The analysis excludes employers and self-employed people because their declared income is a combination of factors such as work and fixed capital and, therefore, is not comparable with the income (wages) of other employees. Salaried workers registered as day laborers or domestic workers were also excluded because these groups were too homogenous in terms of gender with the former being predominantly men and the latter predominantly women.[2] Finally, outliers were excluded to converge more closely with parametric assumptions. The final sample sizes in 2007 and 2017 were 9,904 and 16,897 observations, respectively.

To analyze wages, an hourly earnings variable is considered, adjusted to the consumer price index (CPI) for each of the regions for which data are available for this indicator. The hourly wage variable is constructed from the monthly income recorded by the individuals and a proxy of monthly hours. With regard to work in the informal sector, political decision-makers tend to frame this in terms of legality, not productivity as per the ENEMDU.[3] According to Perry et al. (2007) there are at least two basic concepts: the first considers informal workers as those individuals who lack social security; meanwhile, the concept of productivity refers to individuals in precarious, low productivity jobs in small enterprises, normally based on family activities.

For a regional analysis, according to the comparison of center and periphery zones (Prebisch 1981), a variable is available which, based on the horizontal regionalization project of the National Secretariat for Planning and Development of Ecuador, distinguishes between central zones (the metropolitan

---

2   In the group of workers classified as day laborers, participation of men varied between 87 and 89% in the two years of study (2007 and 2017). In the case of domestic workers, the participation of women in this group ranges from 94 to 96%.

3   The National Institute of Statistics and Censuses (INEC) of Ecuador defines an informal worker as an individual who works in economic establishments that have up to 10 workers and do not have complete accounting records or do not have RUC, that is Unique Registry of Taxpayers (INEC 2016).

TABLE 6.1   Hourly wages, education, and formal employment for men and women in 2007 and 2017

	2007			2017		
Sex	Adjusted hourly wage ($ USD)	Education (years)	Formal employment (%)	Adjusted hourly wage ($ USD)	Education (years)	Formal employment (%)
Male	2.63 (3.00)	11.73 (4.58)	49.28	3.05 (2.44)	12.44 (4.05)	74.88
Female	2.59 (2.61)	13.62 (4.32)	57.64	3.16 (2.47)	14.28 (4.07)	75.31
Total	2.61 (2.86)	12.43 (4.58)	52.37	3.09 (2.45)	13.13 (4.15)	75.04

Note: Standard errors in parentheses.

districts of Guayaquil and Quito, zones 8 and 9 respectively) and between peripheral areas (zones 1 to 7).

Table 6.1 presents initial observations concerning gender pay differentials through descriptive statistics of the main variables under study. It is generally observed that, in 2007, despite the fact that women had better individual characteristics (e.g., greater accumulation of human capital, more education, less likely to be working in the informal sector), there is a wage difference in favor of men. However, in 2017, the difference in salaries is in favor of women, which, in a general way, could be explained by women's individual characteristics.

As can be seen in Table 6.2, focusing on individuals living in metropolitan areas, such as Quito and Guayaquil, it is evident that hourly wages diverged between men and women in 2007 (the salary of the control group, men, is higher), but not in peripheral areas where they seem to converge (the salary of the treatment group, women, is slightly higher). By 2017, the opposite is true because in metropolitan areas, there are wage disparities between men and women in favor of the treatment group, but in the periphery, although the difference is very small, it is against women.

In the informal sector, both in 2007 and 2017, there are gender wage gaps against women. In the formal sector, there is a wage difference in favor of men of a similar magnitude to what was observed in the informal sector in that year. However, in 2017 average wages are higher for women compared to men.

Finally, public sector workers evidently receive higher wages than workers in the private sector. Within sectors, differences persist between the control and treatment group in terms of income, except in 2017 in the public sector,

TABLE 6.2 Hourly wage and education for men and women in 2007 and 2017, by group

Group	Sex	2007 Adjusted hourly wage ($ USD)	2007 Education (years)	2017 Adjusted hourly wage ($ USD)	2017 Education (years)
Center	Male	3.02 (3.62)	12.57 (4.38)	3.18 (2.74)	12.87 (3.63)
	Female	2.89 (2.90)	14.07 (3.98)	3.49 (3.08)	14.53 (3.73)
	Total	2.97 (3.36)	13.14 (4.29)	3.30 (2.88)	13.50 (3.76)
Periphery	Male	2.30 (2.31)	11.05 (4.64)	2.96 (2.21)	12.16 (4.27)
	Female	2.32 (2.29)	13.21 (4.57)	2.93 (1.90)	14.11 (4.28)
	Total	2.31 (2.31)	11.82 (4.73)	2.95 (2.10)	12.89 (4.38)
Informal sector	Male	1.77 (1.93)	10.04 (3.98)	1.99 (1.18)	10.79 (3.55)
	Female	1.54 (1.57)	11.71 (4.23)	1.76 (0.91)	11.26 (3.68)
	Total	1.70 (1.82)	10.59 (4.13)	1.91 (1.09)	10.96 (3.61)
Formal sector	Male	3.50 (3.59)	13.47 (4.52)	3.40 (2.64)	13.00 (4.05)
	Female	3.37 (2.94)	15.03 (3.81)	3.61 (2.64)	15.27 (3.69)
	Total	3.45 (3.34)	14.10 (4.31)	3.48 (2.64)	13.86 (4.07)
Public sector	Male	4.21 (3.13)	14.82 (4.22)	4.64 (2.94)	14.94 (3.72)
	Female	3.98 (2.9)	16.21 (3.24)	4.63 (2.7)	17.08 (2.57)
	Total	4.11 (3.03)	15.42 (3.89)	4.63 (2.83)	15.9 (3.42)

TABLE 6.2   Hourly wage and education for men and women in 2007 and 2017, by group *(cont.)*

		2007		2017	
Group	Sex	Adjusted hourly wage ($ USD)	Education (years)	Adjusted hourly wage ($ USD)	Education (years)
	Male	2.26	11.02	2.60	11.75
		(2.84)	(4.36)	(2.07)	(3.85)
Private sector	Female	2.15	12.80	2.55	13.12
		(2.35)	(4.29)	(2.08)	(4.02)
	Total	2.22	11.65	2.58	12.23
		(2.68)	(4.42)	(2.07)	(3.97)

Note: Standard errors in parentheses.

where the difference is small. It should be noted that, whether by area or by sector, women spend longer in education on average compared to men; a characteristic that, *a priori*, could explain the reasons why in some cases gender wage disparities occur against men.

From a quantile analysis, Table 6.3 provides descriptive statistics by percentiles. For expository purposes, only data corresponding to the 10th, 25th, 50th, 75th, and 90th percentiles are shown. Table 6.3 identifies not only gender wage disparities, but also differences within the wage distributions of men and women in metropolitan areas (centers), the periphery, the formal and informal sector, and the public and private sectors.

In the first (overall) row of Table 6.3, for 2007 and 2017 in the lowest percentiles, wage inequalities against women can be observed; although this trend reverses at higher percentiles. In 2007, wages between men and women converge towards the median, while in 2017, this happens from the first quartile.

A similar pattern is apparent for metropolitan and peripheral areas, both for 2007 and 2017. In the informal economy, men's wages are always higher than women's, but, by contrast, women's wages tend to be higher than men's in the formal economy. Labor formalization allows wages convergence between men and women.

It should also be noted that there are also differences in the participation of men and women in different employment sectors, usually rooted in stereotypes created by differences in roles and behaviors. In Ecuador, the five sectors with the highest share of jobs in the public and private sectors, for both 2007

TABLE 6.3 Hourly wages (USD) for 10th, 25th, 50th, 75th, and 90th percentiles in 2007 and 2017, by group

Group	Sex	2007					2017				
		[p10]	[p25]	[p50]	[p75]	[p90]	[p10]	[p25]	[p50]	[p75]	[p90]
Overall	Male	0.85	1.20	1.76	2.98	5.02	1.39	1.86	2.38	3.50	5.26
	Female	0.71	1.10	1.75	3.26	5.10	1.28	1.86	2.38	3.88	5.49
	Total	0.82	1.15	1.76	3.06	5.05	1.36	1.86	2.38	3.58	5.37
Center	Male	0.90	1.29	2.01	3.40	5.69	1.49	1.91	2.39	3.57	5.26
	Female	0.84	1.26	1.92	3.40	5.86	1.43	2.02	2.39	4.16	5.96
Periphery	Male	0.81	1.14	1.71	2.62	4.28	1.31	1.79	2.27	3.45	5.22
	Female	0.69	1.02	1.70	3.00	4.46	1.19	1.77	2.36	3.70	5.07
Informal	Male	0.73	1.02	1.40	2.01	2.79	0.95	1.36	1.82	2.38	2.98
	Female	0.57	0.82	1.17	1.71	2.67	0.89	1.19	1.62	2.21	2.48
Formal	Male	1.10	1.59	2.53	4.18	6.70	1.66	2.03	2.50	3.88	5.93
	Female	1.12	1.68	2.57	4.18	6.06	1.74	2.14	2.96	4.31	5.96
Public sector	Male	1.57	2.40	3.43	5.05	7.58	2.12	2.85	4.16	5.37	7.72
	Female	1.34	2.25	3.40	4.84	6.86	2.29	3.08	4.22	5.36	7.16
Private sector	Male	0.82	1.11	1.62	2.39	4.02	1.30	1.77	2.20	2.82	3.96
	Female	0.69	1.00	1.52	2.50	4.11	1.19	1.61	2.15	2.69	4.16

and 2017, are shown in the first column of Table 6.4. These five sectors account for 63.3% and 61.7% of workers in 2007 and 2017, respectively. Therein, the jobs with the highest average hourly wages in 2007 and 2017 occur in the domains of public administration/defense and social security ($3.98 and $4.77) and education ($3.46 and $3.99).

TABLE 6.4   Workers (% at the country level) by sex in the five main branches of activity in 2007 and 2017

| Branch of activity | 2007 | | | |
	Total % of workers	Adjusted hourly wage ($ USD)	Men (%)	Women (%)
Vehicle trade and repair	18.0	2.02	18.1	17.7
Manufacturing Industries	16.1	2.11	17.0	14.4
Education	13.0	3.46	8.3	21.0
Public administration/ defense and social security	8.4	3.98	10.2	5.3
Transport, storage, and communications	7.9	2.31	9.5	5.2

| Branch of activity | 2017 | | | |
	Total % of workers	Adjusted hourly wage ($ USD)	Men (%)	Women (%)
Vehicle trade and repair	16.8	2.33	16.9	16.7
Manufacturing Industries	16.1	2.49	18.7	11.8
Public Administration/ Defense, and Social Security	11.3	4.77	12.8	8.8
Education	10.1	3.99	6.1	16.7
Accommodation and Food Service activities	7.5	1.89	4.6	12.3

In 2007, the three sectors in which men have the greatest participation are trade and repair of vehicles (18.0%), manufacturing industries (17.1%), and public administration/defense and social security (10.2%). It should be noted that more men are employed in jobs with relatively low salaries (such as Agriculture, Livestock, Hunting, Forestry, and Fishing at 9.5% and Construction at 9.1%) than are employed in Education which, at the national level, is one of the five most important activities for public and private wage earners.

In 2017, the most important activities for men are the same; however, in this year, Manufacturing Industries (18.7%) registered a greater participation compared to Vehicle trade and repair (16.9%). As in 2007, Agriculture, Livestock, Hunting, Forestry, and Fishing (8.3%) and Construction (5.5%) stand out, above one of the five most important activities at the national level.

For women, in 2007, the most important activities are Education (21.0%), Trade and repair of Vehicles (17.7%), and Manufacturing Industries (14.4%). Among the principal activities at the national level, Accommodation and food services (7.1%) and Real Estate activities (5.8%) concentrate more women than Public Administration/Defense and Social Security and Transport, Storage, and Communications. By 2017, somewhat of a shift is apparent. For example, the percentage of the female labor force employed in Education and Vehicle trade and repair are both down compared to 2007 (both at 16.7%). Increased female participation is observed with respect to employment in Accommodation and food services (12.3%) which by 2017 had grown to represent the third most important category in terms of female employment. Indeed, at the aggregate level, i.e., not disaggregating by gender, this sector grew from accounting for 4.8% of the workforce in 2007 to 7.5% in 2017. It should also be noted that activities in social and health services concentrate a significant percentage of women (more than 'Public administration/defense and social security') in 2017.

Descriptive statistics in Table 6.4 explain some of the findings of previous tables. Between 2007 and 2017, there is a growth in labor participation of workers in Public Administration/Defense and Social Security, with a greater growth of female participation. This branch of activity is the one that receives the highest salaries. In addition, a relevant finding is the considerable labor participation of women in Education, another activity with high wages.

4   Methodology

Decomposing the observed wage differences between men and women in Ecuador, we start from the Mincerian equation (Mincer 1958) which is expressed as follows:

$$W_i^m = X_i^m \beta^m + u_i \tag{1}$$

$$W_i^f = X_i^f \beta^f + u_i \tag{2}$$

Where:

W_i = natural logarithm of hourly wage;

X_i = matrix of variables that determine the level of wages;

β_i = parameters to be estimated;

u_i = stochastic error term;

m = control group, male;

f = treatment group, female.

The following expression (3) corresponds to the Oaxaca-Blinder salary decomposition (Blinder 1973; Oaxaca 1973), a procedure that provides detailed information about the contribution of each explanatory variable in the determination of salary differentials (between a control group and a treatment group). In the detailed decomposition of wage gaps, this procedure highlights three effects: endowment, coefficient, and interaction. To identify these effects, the Oaxaca-Blinder salary decomposition considers a counterfactual element, such as with respect to $X_i^f \beta^m$:

$$W_i^m - W_i^f = X_i^m \beta^m - X_i^f \beta^f$$

$$W_i^m - W_i^f = X_i^m \beta^m - X_i^f \beta^f + X_i^f \beta^m - X_i^f \beta^m$$

$$W_i^m - W_i^f = \beta^m \left(X_i^m - X_i^f \right) + X_i^f \left(\beta^m - \beta^f \right) \tag{3}$$

Where:

$\beta^m \left(X_i^m - X_i^f \right)$, the gender dimension, expresses the endowment effect, i.e., wage disparities in terms of differences in characteristics between men and women.

$X_i^f \left(\beta^m - \beta^f \right)$ expresses the coefficient effect, i.e., wage disparities due to a component of discrimination, which is identified by considering that both men and women have the same characteristics (X_i).

The detailed Oaxaca-Blinder decomposition also considers an additional effect which accounts for simultaneous differences between groups in the characteristics of individuals and their wage yields. Equation (4) augments equation (3) to incorporate the interaction effect:

$$W_i^m - W_i^f = \beta^m \left(X_i^m - X_i^f \right) + X_i^f \left(\beta^m - \beta^f \right) + \left(X_i^m - X_i^f \right)\left(\beta^m - \beta^f \right) \quad (4)$$

In quantile terms, the procedure applied by Fortin et al. (2011) also provides a detailed salary breakdown similar to that of Oaxaca-Blinder. That methodology is based on the estimation of re-centered influence function (RIF) regressions for men and women, a procedure that allows the estimation of unconditional[4] regressions for each percentile of interest (Firpo et al. 2009). The detailed decomposition, using RIF regressions for each percentile, τ, can be expressed as follows:

$$\Delta^{q_\tau} = q_\tau \left(F_{W_m|g=m} \right) - q_\tau \left(F_{W_f|g=f} \right)$$

$$\Delta^{q_\tau} = \left[q_\tau \left(F_{W_m|g=m} \right) - q_\tau \left(F_{W_f|g=m} \right) \right] + \left[q_\tau \left(F_{W_f|g=m} \right) - q_\tau \left(F_{W_f|g=f} \right) \right]$$

$$\Delta^{q_\tau} = \Delta_S^{q_\tau} + \Delta_X^{q_\tau} \quad (5)$$

In equation (5), $q_\tau \left(F_{W_{m,l}|g=m,l} \right)$ refers to the logarithm of the salary of the quantile (percentile) of study of individuals, whether male or female; $q_\tau \left(F_{W_f|g=m} \right)$ is the counterfactual term. Finally, $\Delta_S^{q_\tau}$ and $\Delta_X^{q_\tau}$ refer to the endowment and coefficient effects, respectively.

The main objective herein, given the gender characteristics of the labor market, is to identify and study the effect of the coefficient described above, which explains the component of discrimination that exists between men and women in Ecuador. Note that there are other methods of wage decomposition, by percentiles, that use the procedure of conditional quantile regression estimates (Koenker 2005; Koenker and Basset 1978). The advantages of using the unconditional methodology of quantile regressions lies in the fact that it marginalizes the effect on the wage distribution of covariances in the model (Borah and Basu 2013).

---

4   Unconditional regressions marginalize the effect of individual characteristics throughout the distribution of wages.

5   Results

The dynamic analysis of wage differentials allowed us to identify some find-ings not foreseen in the research hypothesis. Figures 6.1 and 6.2 show the wage gaps and their decomposition by effects: endowment, coefficient, and interac-tion; however, the detailed decomposition of the coefficient effect is shown in Tables 6.5 and 6.6. Overall, the results, both in salary differences and in effects, reveal disparities in favor of men. Figure 6.1, for example, shows that in the lower part of the wage distribution (up to the third decile), there are signifi-cant wage gaps against women that are mainly explained by discrimination.[5] Here, it is evident that the interaction effect is particularly important in wage decomposition, highlighting the simultaneous role of the characteristics of individuals and the wage structure in Ecuador. This same figure also shows that wage gaps become reduced in favor of women (decile 6) and the interac-tion effect negative (decile 7), thus expressing that, on average, women have higher incomes in this part of the distribution.

Overall, descriptive statistics suggest that wage differentials against wom-en are attenuated due to their individual characteristics, especially as a consequence of the accumulation of knowledge acquired by virtue of a greater number of years in education. Women's wages are on average higher when the endowment component is analyzed (e.g., better educated, less informal).[6] In 2007, with the exception of the lower part of the wage distribution, the interac-tion effect does not represent a significant determinant of wages and, moreover, is only significant in those percentiles where wage differentials were found to be significant (and this is not the case for the entire distribution).

Figure 6.1 illustrates the effect of the coefficient measuring gender wage dis-crimination. As shown therein, in 2007 discrimination occurred against wom-en and tended to be worse from the intermediate percentiles of the wage dis-tribution, where the effect is close to 40%.

The abovementioned information shows that there is discrimination against women due to the structure of the labor market. This implies that men with the same characteristics as women receive higher wages throughout the distri-bution. The wage gaps identified are not greater because they are attenuat-ed by the characteristics of women in the labor market and, therefore, the

---

5   As can be seen graphically, the wage discrimination against women is greater than the en-dowment effect which, by contrast, favors women; this explains the gap.

6   Descriptive statistics in this section have already given us an idea of the characteristics of women in the Ecuadorian labor market and, with that, an argument as to why they could receive better salaries than men.

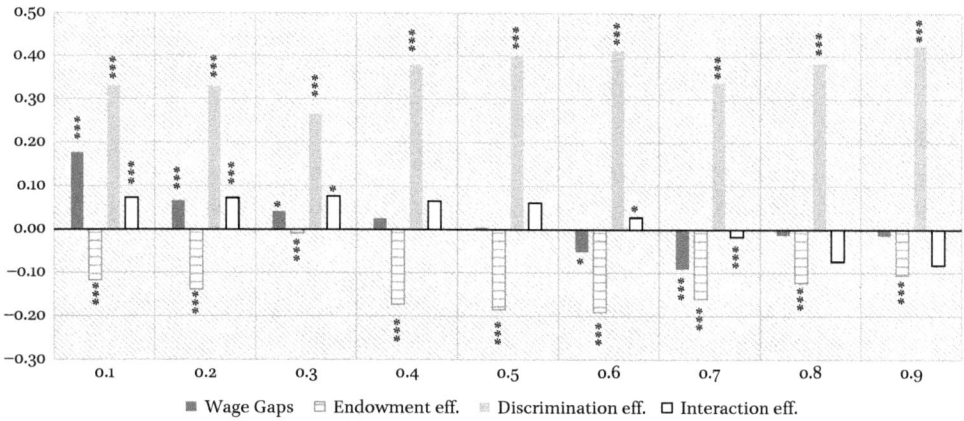

FIGURE 6.1 Gender pay gaps and their decomposition into three effects: endowment, discrimination, and interaction, 2007
NOTE: * P < 0.1, ** P < 0.05, *** P < 0.01

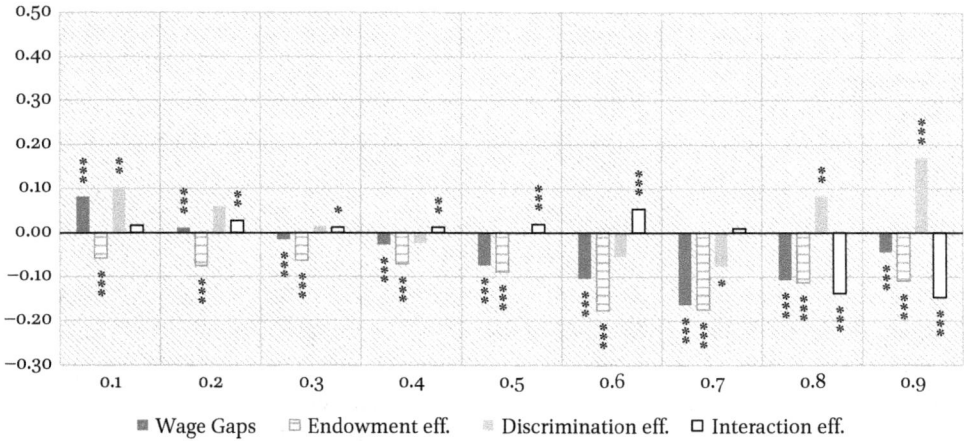

FIGURE 6.2 Gender pay gaps and their decomposition into three effects: endowment, discrimination and interaction, 2017
NOTE: * P < 0.1, ** P < 0.05, *** P < 0.01.

differentials can be insignificant or even negative. However, compared to 2007, the results for 2017 bring with them new conclusions. In 2017, these differences in income between men and women are even smaller;[7] they are considerably

---

7   This difference is very small in the first two deciles and insignificant in the following three deciles.

TABLE 6.5   Oaxaca-Blinder and Unconditional Wage Decompositions, 2007[a]

	(O-B)	(p10)	(p25)	(p50)	(p75)	(p90)
Differential						
Wage estimate (m)	0.6570***	−0.1543***	0.1803***	0.5677***	1.0930***	1.6170***
	(0.0112)	(0.0146)	(0.0127)	(0.0126)	(0.0186)	(0.0263)
Wage estimate (f)	0.6367***	−0.3302***	0.0976***	0.5636***	1.1856***	1.6310***
	(0.0156)	(0.0233)	(0.0195)	(0.0200)	(0.0225)	(0.0308)
Wage gap	0.0203	0.1759***	0.0827***	0.0041	−0.0926***	−0.0140
	(0.0192)	(0.0275)	(0.0233)	(0.0237)	(0.0292)	(0.0405)
Adjustment (selection bias)	0.2322***	0.2860***	0.2609***	0.2758***	0.1144**	0.2361***
	(0.0391)	(0.0705)	(0.0519)	(0.0488)	(0.0570)	(0.0830)
Endowment effect						
Total	−0.1446***	−0.1176***	−0.1549***	−0.1847***	−0.1363***	−0.1053***
	(0.0124)	(0.0175)	(0.0153)	(0.0153)	(0.0155)	(0.0176)
Coefficient effect						
Formal sector	−0.0959***	−0.1358***	−0.1459***	−0.1513***	−0.0050	0.0121
	(0.0221)	(0.0365)	(0.0315)	(0.0310)	(0.0342)	(0.0452)
Periphery	0.0154	0.0451	0.0370	−0.0083	0.0011	0.0474
	(0.0176)	(0.0304)	(0.0244)	(0.0228)	(0.0279)	(0.0421)
Secondary education	−0.0595***	−0.1260***	−0.1335***	−0.1149***	0.0506*	0.0286
	(0.0186)	(0.0395)	(0.0313)	(0.0262)	(0.0259)	(0.0311)
Bachelor's degree	0.0229*	−0.0660***	−0.0690***	−0.0484***	0.1306***	0.2130***
	(0.0121)	(0.0154)	(0.0129)	(0.0136)	(0.0203)	(0.0367)
Had a partner	0.0356***	0.0255	0.0386***	0.0376***	0.0231	0.0596**
	(0.0109)	(0.0179)	(0.0140)	(0.0129)	(0.0163)	(0.0257)
Has a partner	0.0579***	0.0477	0.0703***	0.0504**	0.0243	0.0907**
	(0.0174)	(0.0293)	(0.0235)	(0.0228)	(0.0280)	(0.0394)
Private sector	−0.0099	−0.0562	−0.0498	0.0055	−0.0578	0.0300
	(0.0346)	(0.0385)	(0.0312)	(0.0392)	(0.0661)	(0.1073)
Constant	0.3911***	0.5963***	0.5912***	0.6288***	0.1499	−0.0578
	(0.0744)	(0.1341)	(0.0986)	(0.0902)	(0.1234)	(0.1883)
Total	0.3576***	0.3305***	0.3391***	0.3994***	0.3169***	0.4236***
	(0.0388)	(0.0705)	(0.0516)	(0.0482)	(0.0575)	(0.0864)

TABLE 6.5 Oaxaca-Blinder and Unconditional Wage Decompositions, 2007[a] (cont.)

	(O-B)	(p10)	(p25)	(p50)	(p75)	(p90)
Interaction effect						
Total	0.0191*	0.0731***	0.0768***	0.0611***	−0.0662***	−0.0821***
	(0.0102)	(0.0189)	(0.0148)	(0.0129)	(0.0158)	(0.0243)

a For brevity, the same percentiles shown in Figure 1 are not considered, but only the first and last decile and the three quartiles.
Notes: * p <0.1, ** p <0.05, *** p <0.01; standard errors are in parentheses; Informal sector = 0; education approved (pre-baccalaureate = 0); marital status (single = 0, in the "had a partner" category divorced, separated and widowed individuals are grouped; in "has a partner" individuals in free union and married individuals are grouped); public sector = 0. For brevity, details of the decomposition of the endowment and interaction effects are not shown.

TABLE 6.6 Oaxaca-Blinder and Unconditional Wage Decompositions, 2017[a]

	(O–B)	(p10)	(p25)	(p50)	(p75)	(p90)
Differential						
Wage estimate (m)	0.9303***	0.3280***	0.6216***	0.8675***	1.2532***	1.6605***
	(0.0076)	(0.0140)	(0.0076)	(0.0068)	(0.0129)	(0.0179)
Wage estimate (f)	0.9577***	0.2469***	0.6203***	0.8690***	1.3571***	1.7036***
	(0.0099)	(0.0181)	(0.0116)	(0.0095)	(0.0163)	(0.0192)
Wage gap	−0.0275**	0.0811***	0.0013	−0.0015	−0.1039***	−0.0431
	(0.0125)	(0.0229)	(0.0138)	(0.0117)	(0.0208)	(0.0262)
Adjustment (selection bias)	−0.0777***	0.0618	−0.0348	−0.0732***	−0.1510***	−0.0853*
	(0.0227)	(0.0471)	(0.0296)	(0.0245)	(0.0395)	(0.0452)
Endowment effect						
Total	−0.1008***	−0.0579***	−0.0681***	−0.0889***	−0.1563***	−0.1095***
	(0.0077)	(0.0123)	(0.0086)	(0.0069)	(0.0115)	(0.0127)
Coefficient effect						
Formal sector	−0.0647***	−0.1177**	−0.1376***	−0.0608***	−0.0057	−0.0260
	(0.0207)	(0.0592)	(0.0320)	(0.0213)	(0.0267)	(0.0254)
Periphery	0.0573***	0.0903***	0.0536***	0.0181	0.0704***	0.1156***
	(0.0148)	(0.0288)	(0.0173)	(0.0143)	(0.0255)	(0.0342)
Secondary education	−0.0122	−0.0320	−0.0763***	−0.0262*	0.0683***	0.0626***
	(0.0130)	(0.0373)	(0.0215)	(0.0139)	(0.0179)	(0.0178)
Bachelor's degree	0.0606***	0.0004	−0.0415***	−0.0187**	0.1230***	0.2807***
	(0.0116)	(0.0202)	(0.0127)	(0.0095)	(0.0188)	(0.0299)

TABLE 6.6   Oaxaca-Blinder and Unconditional Wage Decompositions, 2017[a] *(cont.)*

	(O–B)	(p10)	(p25)	(p50)	(p75)	(p90)
Had a partner	0.0265***	0.0305**	0.0344***	0.0247***	0.0235*	0.0121
	(0.0073)	(0.0154)	(0.0083)	(0.0070)	(0.0130)	(0.0164)
Has a partner	0.0610***	0.0919***	0.0505***	0.0564***	0.0702***	0.0575**
	(0.0126)	(0.0273)	(0.0154)	(0.0125)	(0.0217)	(0.0275)
Private sector	0.0447**	0.0533**	0.0426***	0.0702***	0.0362	−0.1294**
	(0.0208)	(0.0236)	(0.0163)	(0.0178)	(0.0426)	(0.0620)
Constant	−0.1263**	−0.0138	0.0889	−0.0673	−0.3315***	−0.2024*
	(0.0552)	(0.1264)	(0.0691)	(0.0517)	(0.0937)	(0.1208)
Total	0.0469**	0.1028**	0.0147	−0.0037	0.0544	0.1708***
	(0.0230)	(0.0469)	(0.0293)	(0.0242)	(0.0399)	(0.0496)
Interaction effect						
Total	−0.0239***	0.0169	0.0186**	0.0194***	−0.0491***	−0.1466***
	(0.0077)	(0.0136)	(0.0084)	(0.0066)	(0.0124)	(0.0200)

a   For brevity, the same percentiles shown in Figure 6.1 are not considered, but only the first and last decile
    and the three quartiles.
Notes: * $p <0.1$, ** $p <0.05$, *** $p <0.01$; standard errors are in parentheses; Informal sector = 0; education
approved (pre–baccalaureate = 0); marital status (single = 0, in the "had a partner" category divorced,
separated and widowed individuals are grouped; in "has a partner" individuals in free union and married
individuals are grouped); public sector = 0. For brevity, details of the decomposition of the endowment and
interaction effects are not shown.

reduced and, in fact, in the high part of the wage distribution (except decile 9)
they are negative.

The first explanation for these results is again based on the endowment effect in favor of women, which is even lower than in 2007. However, the following question arises: what role does the coefficient now play in determining
wage differentials? The answer is almost nil; it is only marginally positive in the
low (decile 1) and high part of the wage distribution (deciles 8 and 9). Compared to the effects revealed in 2007, it can be concluded that there has been a
reduction in gender wage disparities caused by reduced discrimination against
women in the labor market.

Once the discrimination effect in the decomposition of gender wage inequality has been identified, the contribution of individual characteristics to
this effect can be analyzed. Tables 6.5 and 6.6 show in detail the effect of the
coefficient that is particularly interesting in this research, both in terms of the
linear salary decomposition methodology of Oaxaca (1973) and Blinder (1973),

and decomposition based on unconditional quantile regression,[8] after Fortin et al. (2011).

According to Table 6.5, in 2007 Oaxaca-Blinder decomposition suggests wage discrimination against men. Similarly, within the wage distribution, up to intermediate deciles (the median, for example), gender discrimination in the formal sector occurs against men. For the remainder of the distribution, the effect of working in the formal sector becomes insignificant. It is worth noting that that if the analysis focuses on the informal sector, the opposite is true; in this case, wage discrimination affects the treatment group, women.[9] On the other hand, as also shown in Table 6.5, no significant discrimination arises due to the zone (center or periphery) in which individuals work.

In terms of education as a proxy for human capital, income discrimination on the basis of having attained the baccalaureate (at least 13 years of schooling) is negative, implying that, in this group, men receive lower salaries than women.[10] This supposes that, between a man and a woman with a high school diploma, it will be the latter who receives the higher hourly wage. It should be noted that this effect is significant only up to the median distribution.[11] If one considers the category of having attained at least one professional title, in the linear analysis (Oaxaca-Blinder), the wage discrimination is reversed; that is, it is now reversed against women, although the effect is very small in percentage terms.

However, the quantile analysis shows that this does not happen throughout the distribution. For example, in the case of those individuals with lower wages (up to the second quartile), where the effect, by contrast, is negative (also relatively small, but discriminatory against men). After the median, the situation coincides with the linear description; that is to say, in the highest percentiles of the distribution of salaries, having a bachelor's degree is associated with strong income discrimination against women.

If the analysis is guided by the role of women in the family structure, those who cease to be single will find themselves in worse conditions with the exception of the lower part of the wage distribution and in the third quartile. The

---

8   It should be noted that unconditional quantile regressions (UQR) have an advantage over conditionals (CQR) ones. This happens because the effects estimated by UCR do not depend on the set of covariance or explanatory variables in the model.

9   If the analysis focuses on the informal sector, the effect is opposite (positive) and significant in linear wage decomposition and at the 10th, 25th, and 50th percentiles.

10   It should be noted that the data reveal the following relative distribution of men and women by level of education: 50% of men are pre-high school graduates, 36% are high school graduates and 14% are professionals. In terms of women, 29% are pre-high school graduates, 50% have a high school diploma and 21% are professionals.

11   Scarcely significant (at 10%), in the third quartile the effect coefficient is positive.

effect does not vary much throughout the distribution of salaries, but it is greater if the woman has a partner, which reveals the unequal assignment of roles in the household, with the social stereotype of a male breadwinner figure present. This evidence shows that the role of women in the family brings with it stigmas that place them at a disadvantage at work and, therefore, the possibility of being discriminated against.

Next, in 2007 the effect of discrimination against women is not anchored to the nature of the sector (public or private) in which they work; the effects are not significant. By 2017, the effect of this variable is similar in terms of significance as in 2007. However, instead of increasing income discrimination against men to quartile two, by contrast, it is reduced. This, from another perspective, provides evidence that in the informal sector, it is women who are discriminated against, but this effect is reduced to insignificance as one moves towards the middle of the wage distribution. On the other hand, unlike the first year of study, in peripheral areas, the effect coefficient is positive and, from a quantile perspective has a 'U' shape if wage discrimination is analyzed from the lowest to the highest percentiles. These results suggest that gender wage segmentation is lower in metropolitan districts.

The role of education is again relevant and transcendental in the analysis, not only because of the magnitude of its effect on wage discrimination, but also because of its ambiguity throughout the distribution. Thus, for example, where individuals have a bachelor's degree, according to the results of the Oaxaca-Blinder decomposition, there is no wage discrimination. However, within the wage distribution, from the first quartile, the effect is significant; up to the fifth decile, the coefficient effect is negative and is reduced as a monotonous function, until it becomes positive, which denotes discrimination against women. With respect to the possession of a professional title, the results are similar between 2007 and 2017. In the lower part of the distribution of salaries, the linear effect is discriminatory against women but ends up being positive in higher percentiles. The results from the covariance of education show the inequality effect (against women) of schooling and particularly of having a professional degree, in the upper part of wage distribution. However, this discrimination does not translate in wage disparities because of the endowment effect in favor of women (see Figures 6.1 and 6.2).

Regarding the civil status of individuals, which to some extent affects gender roles in the family, the results are similar between 2007 and 2017. Linearly, there is a reduction in wage discrimination for women who had a partner, but there is also an increase in this same discrimination when the woman has a partner. By 2017, the effects throughout the wage distribution (Table 6.6) are significant, similar in all percentiles for the 'had partner' category and decreasing, not monotonously in the 'has partner' category. Again, the effect is greater if the woman has a partner. Finally, with regard to sector of employment, women are discriminated against in the private sector but not the public sector, where they have primacy over men. It is noteworthy that this effect first grows, but then it is reduced considerably until becoming negative in the highest decile of the distribution of salaries.

As shown in Figures 6.1 and 6.2, the coefficient effect denoting income discrimination between men and women is significant only at the low and high part of the wage distribution. However, in a linear (general) way through the results of the Oaxaca-Blinder decomposition, the effect is significant and relies on the control variables considered in the analysis, both for 2007 and 2017 (with certain exceptions, depending on the period). In this way, the research shows that gender wage discrimination, particularly that which affects women, has been significantly reduced, from 35.8% to 4.7%, according to the covariances examined. Further, this reduction is similar between the poorest and richest deciles of the wage distribution; in the middle, gender discrimination because of salaries does not exist.

6   Discussion of Results and Conclusions

Although men's hourly wages were higher than those of women in 2007, this gap was reversed by 2017. However, there is a statistically significant and stable factor, considering the permanence of the sign, which explains the wage gaps in the two years; this factor denotes discrimination against women in 2007 and 2017. However, it should be noted that there has been a notable reduction in the coefficient between 2007 and 2017 which allows us to infer that, even though it is clear that discrimination against women in the Ecuadorian labor market is a factor that remains structurally, it has been reduced over the last years.

When analyzing individual and work characteristics—type of employment (formal/informal), area of residence, level of education, marital status, sector (public/private)—we observe that, in 2007, women who worked in the formal sector received higher salaries than men who worked in the same sector. This differential is significantly explained by a discriminatory component towards men from the first to the fifth decile. For the remainder of the distribution, employment sector is not a factor that generates gender discrimination. This pattern is maintained in 2017.

Although several studies identify considerable wage gaps against women, the results found herein coincide with those presented in the work developed by Benítez and Espinoza (2018), also for the Ecuadorian case. In 2007 and 2017, women who have a bachelor's degree,[12] linearly, in the third quartile and in the richest decile, receive lower salaries than men who also have a bachelor's degree. This differential is explained by a discriminatory factor towards women. In the poorest decile (only in 2007), in the median distribution, and in the third quartile (in 2007 and 2017), an opposite effect of education is observed—a significant discriminatory component against men. Thus, education does not explain the wage difference between men and women. This is contrary to what is expressed in neoclassical economic theory. Moreover, as Sarmiento-Moscoso (2017) states, based on the quality of the labor force (measured by their level of scholarity), women should receive a wage that is differentiated from that of men—as is the case in Ecuador in 2017.

With regard to living and working in peripheral areas—that is, those areas outside the metropolises of Quito and Guayaquil—in 2007, this is not a determining factor when analyzing gender gaps explained by a discriminatory component. However, by 2017 it is a significant factor, not only in statistical terms, but also because of the magnitude of the coefficient, which generates discrimination against women (Espinoza and Sánchez 2009; Sarmiento-Moscoso 2017; Petter-Pérez and Moreno-Hurtado 2019). Similarly, employment sector is an insignificant factor in the initial year but by 2017, this changes so that discrimination against women is observed, linearly and along the distribution curve, with the exception of the richest decile, where it is presented as a factor that generates discrimination against men.

On the other hand, if we start from an analysis of the productive and reproductive roles assumed and assigned based on the gender of the individual to analyze the gaps between men and women, it is important to highlight marital status as a relevant variable. In this regard, in the two reference years, a discriminatory factor is identified against women who shared and currently share their lives with a partner, in relation to men in the same situations. This result is seen linearly and approximately along the distribution curve (except in the case of the first decile and the third quartile in 2007, where civil status is not significant). In some percentiles, during the ten-year period, a considerable worsening of conditions is apparent in relation to single women, as Canelas and Salazar (2014) point out.

Finally, it is important to emphasize the relevance of wage decomposition by quantiles, since inferring conclusions from the central point of the

---

12   In this section, this variable is analyzed as a proxy for education, because of the objectivity it provides to measure the advantage that having completed higher or fourth level education represents in salary, in relation to the variable years of education (Songor-Jaramillo et al. 2019).

distribution could lead the researcher to underestimate or overestimate the real wage gap (for example, concluding that in 2007 there are no wage gaps, or stating that in 2017 they are against men). In 2007, there were wage differences in favor of men in the first three deciles. In the 6th and 7th deciles, the differences are also significant, but in favor of women. Although not the focus of this research, the endowment effect (better characteristics) in favor of women throughout the distribution curve is also noteworthy. However, a significant discrimination effect is also evident in all deciles of the population, particularly in the highest part of the distribution (among individuals with the highest wages).

In relation to the combined effect of the coefficient of endowment and discrimination, this is significant only in the lower part of the distribution, but not in intermediate and upper deciles. Although in certain deciles, women receive higher salaries than men, which is explained by the better characteristics they possess (better educational level, subjectively assumed by more years of schooling; greater participation in formal employment), the discriminatory factor against women is significant and considerable in all deciles of the distribution (between 30% and 40%). As can be seen, discrimination in Ecuador is attributed to structural aspects of the labor market.

By 2017, significant wage gaps are identified against women only in the first and second deciles. In other points of the distribution, the gaps are against men (4th, 6th, 7th, and 8th deciles) or they are insignificant (3rd, 5th, and 9th deciles). Unlike what was observed in 2007 in relation to the interaction effect, in 2017 this factor becomes relevant in most deciles. As in 2007, in the first, eighth, and ninth deciles, a significant discriminatory component against women is identified in 2017, although its impact is notably lower than that observed in the initial year. Nevertheless, one outstanding result is in the seventh decile, where the discrimination observed is significant against the wages received by men. With regard to the endowment effect, it remains significant in favor of women at all points in the distribution.

Similar to Gallardo and Ñopo (2009), whose work in the Ecuadorian context revealed different results in the low and high points of the distribution in relation to the average, exploring the effect of control variables (public and private sector; formal and informal work; marital status; area of residence) in the different points of the wage distribution curve, gives clear guidance vis-a-vis the direction that public policy should take to maximize the likelihood of narrowing wage gaps between men and women.

In sum, the results herein present evidence of the discrimination that persists against women in the Ecuadorian labor market. A purely descriptive analysis could lead to erroneous conclusions, since, between 2007 and 2017, the real hourly wage received by women was higher than that received by men. However, by identifying the determinants of the salaries received by the two groups, we can clearly identify that certain factors exacerbate gender discrimination against women (marital status and education) and against men (formal rather than informal work). Beyond conceiving it as mere evidence, this analysis aims to become a tool for policy makers, who should design labor market policies based on diagnosis beyond the descriptive.

The limitations of this study are that it does not differentiate between the endowment effect and the coefficient that the category of occupation generates in the wages that men and women receive in Ecuador. Further, this study does not include self-employed workers, and this could become increasingly important to investigate given prevailing tendencies towards decentralization of occupations and peer-to-peer economic relationships in the context of increasingly ubiquitous online work habits.

References

Alvarado, R., and Cortés, Y. (2012). *Wages differentials in Ecuador: A regional approach with sample selection of Heckman and Oaxaca-Blinder decomposition* (Paper No. 37470; MPRA). https://mpra.ub.uni-muenchen.de/37470.

Ayala-Jaramillo, V. (2017). *Análisis semiparamétrico de la brecha salarial de género en Ecuador* [Bachelor's thesis, Universidad San Francisco de Quito]. http://repositorio.usfq.edu.ec/handle/23000/6438.

Becker, G. (1957). *The Economics of Discrimination (1st ed.)*. University of Chicago Press.

Benítez, D., and Espinoza, B. (2018). *Discriminación salarial por género en el sector formal en Ecuador usando registros administrativos* (No. 6; Cuaderno de Trabajo). https://www.ecuadorencifras.gob.ec/documentos/web-inec/Bibliotecas/Libros/Discriminacion_salar_por_genero_sec_for_Ecu.pdf.

Blau, F., and Kahn, L. (1992). "The Gender Earning Gap: Learning from International Comparisons." *The American Economic Review* 82(2): 533–538. https://www.jstor.org/stable/2117457.

Blinder, A.S. (1973). "Wage Discrimination Reduced Form and Structural Estimates." *Journal of Human Resources* 8(4): 436–455. https://doi.org/10.2307/144855.

Borah, B., and Basu, A. (2013). "Highlighting differences between Conditional and Unconditional Quantile Regression Approaches through an Application to assess Medication Adherence." *Health Economics* 22(9): 1052–1070. https://doi.org/10.1002/hec.2927.

Botello-Peñaloza, H.A. (2015). "Determinantes de la discriminación racial en el mercado laboral en Ecuador, 2010–2012." *Equidad & Desarrollo* 24: 9–30. https://doi.org/10.19052/ed.3409.

Canelas, C., and Salazar, S. (2014). "Gender and ethnic inequalities in LAC countries." *IZA Journal of Labor & Development* 3(1): 1–15. https://doi.org/10.1186/2193-9020-3-18.

Cóndor-Pumisacho, J.E. (2010). *Discriminación salarial en el mercado laboral por etnia* [Master's tesis, Facultad Latinoamericana de Ciencias Sociales, Sede Ecuador]. https://repositorio.flacsoandes.edu.ec/handle/10469/3248.

DiNardo, J., Fortin, N., and Lemieux, T. (1996). "Labor market institutions and the distribution of wages, 1973–1992: A semiparametric approach." *Econometrica* 64(5): 1001–1044. https://doi.org/10.2307/2171954.

Di Paola, R., and Berges, M. (2000). "Sesgo de selección y estimación de la brecha por género para Mar del Plata." *xxxv Reunión Anual de La Asociación Argentina de Economía Política.* http://nulan.mdp.edu.ar/891/.

Espinoza, N., and Sánchez, L. (2009). *Estimación de la Brecha Salarial entre Hombres y Mujeres: Un Análisis por Cuantiles para el Ecuador.* Facultad de Ciencias Humanísticas y Económicas (ESPOL).

Firpo, S., Fortin, N., and Lemieux, T. (2007). *Decomposing Wage Distributions using Recentered Influence Functions Regressions* (June). University of British Columbia.

Firpo, S., Fortin, N., and Lemieux, T. (2009). "Unconditional Quantile Regressions." *Econometrica* 77(3): 953–973. https://doi.org/10.3982/ECTA6822.

Fortin, N., and Lemieux, T. (1998). "Rank regressions, wage distributions, and the gender gap." *The Journal of Human Resources* 33(3): 610–643. https://doi.org/10.2307/146335.

Fortin, N., Lemieux, T., and Firpo, S. (2011). "Decomposition Methods in Economics." In O. Ashenfelter and D. Card (Eds.), *Handbook of Labor Economics* (pp. 1–102). Elsevier. https://doi.org/10.1016/S0169-7218(11)00407-2.

Gallardo, L., and Ñopo, H. (2009). *Ethnic and Gender Wage Gaps in Ecuador* (Working Paper 679). Inter-American Development Bank. https://www.econstor.eu/handle/10419/51500.

Galvis, L. (2010). *Diferenciales salariales por género y región en Colombia: Una aproximación con regresión por cuantiles.* (No. 131; Documentos de Trabajo Sobre Economía Regional). https://doi.org/10.32468/dtseru.131.

García-Aracil, A., and Winter, C. (2006). "Gender and Ethnicity Differentials in School Attainment and Labor Market Earnings in Ecuador." *World Development* 34(2): 289–307. https://doi.org/10.1016/j.worlddev.2005.10.001.

Gosling, A., Machin, S., and Meghir, C. (2000). "The changing distribution of male wages in the U.K." *The Review of Economic Studies* 67(4): 635–666. https://doi.org/10.1111/1467-937X.00148.

Heckman, J. (1979). "Sample selection bias as a specification error." *Econometrica* 47(1): 153–162. https://doi.org/10.2307/1912352.

Instituto Nacional de Estadística y Censos. (2007). *Encuesta Nacional de Empleo, Desempleo y Subempleo.* INEC. https://www.ecuadorencifras.gob.ec/estadisticas/.

Instituto Nacional de Estadística y Censos. (2016). *Metodología para la medición del empleo del Ecuador*. INEC.

Instituto Nacional de Estadística y Censos. (2017). *Encuesta Nacional de Empleo, Desempleo y Subempleo*. INEC. https://www.ecuadorencifras.gob.ec/enemdu-2017/.

Jones, F.L. (1983). "On Decomposing the Wage Gap: A Critical Comment on Blinder's Method." *The Journal of Human Resources* 18(1): 126–130. https://doi.org/10.2307/145660.

Koenker, R. (2005). *Quantile Regression*. Cambridge University Press. https://doi.org/10.1017/CBO9780511754098.

Koenker, R., and Bassett, G. (1978). "Regression Quantiles." *Econometrica* 46(1): 33–50. https://doi.org/10.2307/1913643.

Koenker, R., and Hallock, K.F. (2001). "Quantile regression." *Journal of Economic Perspectives* 15(4): 143–156. https://doi.org/10.1257/jep.15.4.143.

Machado, J.F., and Mata, J. (2005). "Counterfactual decomposition of changes in wage distributions using quantile regression." *Journal of Applied Econometrics* 20(4): 445–465. https://doi.org/10.1002/jae.788.

Madden, D. (2000). "Towards a Broader Explanation of Male-Female Wage Differences." *Applied Economics Letters* 7(12): 765–770. https://doi.org/10.1080/135048500444769.

Martínez-Tamayo, S. (2009). *Estimación de la subestimación: brecha salarial por género entre profesionales en Ecuador. Año 2008* [Master's thesis, Facultad Latinoamericana de Ciencias Sociales Sede Ecuador]. https://repositorio.flacsoandes.edu.ec/handle/10469/2035.

Mincer, J. (1974). *Schooling, Experience, and Earnings*. NBER. http://www.nber.org/books/minc74-1.

Mincer, J. (1958). "Investment in Human Capital and Personal Income Distribution." *Journal of Political Economy* 66(4): 281–302. https://doi.org/10.1086/258055.

Mincer, J., and Polachek, S. (1974). "Family investments in human capital: Earnings of women." In T. Schultz (Ed.), *Marriage, Family, Human Capital, and Fertility* (pp. 76–110). National Bureau of Economic Research. http://www.nber.org/chapters/c3685.

Oaxaca, R. (1973). "Male-Female Wage Differentials in Urban Labor Markets." *International Economic Review* 14(3): 693–709. https://doi.org/10.2307/2525981.

Perry, G., Maloney, W., Arias, O., Fajnzylber, P., Mason, A., and Saavedra-Chanduvi, J. (2007). *Informality: Exit and Exclusion*. The World Bank. https://doi.org/10.1596/978-0-8213-7092-6.

Petter-Pérez, L., and Moreno-Hurtado, C. (2019). "Subempleo en el mercado laboral juvenil en Ecuador." *Revista NuestrAmérica* 7(13): 265–280. http://wsww.redalyc.org/articulo.oa?id=551957774014.

Prebisch, R. (1981). "La periferia latinoamericana en el sistema global del capitalismo." *Revista de La CEPAL* 13: 163–171. https://repositorio.cepal.org/handle/11362/11912.

Rivera, J. (2013). "Theory and Practice of Discrimination in the Ecuadorian Labor Market (2007–2012)." *Analítika: Revista de Análisis Estadístico* 5(1): 7–22. https://ideas .repec.org/a/inp/inpana/v5y2013i1p7-22.html.

Rosenzweig, M.R., and Morgan, J. (1976). "Wage Discrimination: A Comment." *The Journal of Human Resources* 11(1): 3–7. https://doi.org/10.2307/145069.

Sarmiento-Moscoso, S. (2017). "Evolución de la desigualdad de ingresos en Ecuador, periodo 2007–2015." *Analitika: Revista de Análisis Estadístico* 13(1): 49–79. https:// www.ecuadorencifras.gob.ec/documentos/web-inec/Revistas/Analitika/Anexos_ pdf/Analit_13/2.pdf.

Songor-Jaramillo, X., Moreno-Hurtado, C., and Petter-Pérez, L. (2019). "Youth labor precariousnes in Ecuador: what is the role of ICT?" *14th Iberian Conference on Information Systems and Technologies (CISTI)*. https://doi.org/10.23919/cisti.2019.8760698.

Tenjo, J., Ribero, R., and Bernat, L.F. (2005). *Evolución de las diferencias salariales por sexo en seis países de América Latina* (No. 2005–18; Documento CEDE). https://ideas .repec.org/p/col/000089/002656.html.

CHAPTER 7

The Cost of Femininity: Evidence for the City of Guayaquil

Diana Morán, Diana Cabrera and María Moreno

1   Introduction

The hierarchy between the feminine and the masculine in a world where power relations prevail results in gender inequality and inequity, a conception that is culturally rooted in gender roles as social constructs that are increasingly entrenched in heteropathic[1] economies. At the global level, different nations have attempted to enact rights for equality to prevail against gender discrimination, as well as to implement policies that allow for the creation of consumer ombudsmen and eliminate, or at least reduce, gender discrimination. For example, in Ecuador the Ombudsman's Office and the Organic Law for the Defense of Consumers, among others, serve these purposes as part of the development objectives of this country to achieve equity therein.

It goes without saying that all acts of discrimination against women are condemned under the Convention on the Elimination of All Forms of Discrimination against Women (United Nations 1981). This antecedent is related, within Agenda 2030, to the achievement of Gender Equity that prevails as one of the Sustainable Development Goals to be pursued by the countries that are part of, and that is sponsored by, the United Nations. Motivations and intentions to achieve this goal are fundamentally due to the commitment made by nations through the Universal Declaration of Human Rights which determines that the rights of all human beings are inalienable and equal (United Nations 1948). However, the reality is that, despite efforts, these are continually constrained either by cultural issues or by lax or non-existent enforcement of laws protecting women against discrimination, domestic violence, forced marriage, teenage pregnancies, unequal rights with respect to owning property and businesses, and overwork in a context of unpaid and unrecognized domestic work and care.

---

1   A socio-political system in which the male gender and heterosexuality take precedence over any other form of gender or sexual preference.

Thus, inequality, inequity, and gender discrimination are empirically reflected in the difficulties that women face in living with dignity due, among other things, to the receipt of a lower salary compared to the salary that a man receives for the same activity. Women also face difficulties in terms of access to education either because of constraints imposed by culture, poverty, or infrastructure, since in such contexts the same capacities and opportunities are not provided or developed for women as they are for men. Women also have to contend with a lack of freedom of determination over their bodies, such as when and with whom they decide to marry, when and how many children they decide to have, and whether they have access to and decision making control over the use of contraceptive methods; in other words, determination over their own reproductive health and sexual relations. Other forms of discrimination are observed in women's participation in the political environment, which is less than a quarter globally (World Bank 2018). This is explained by the difficulties women face in being able to break the 'glass ceilings' to ascend to the top, and which is much stronger the higher the executive position she holds, mainly due to social pressures.

When such data are analyzed globally, the results are overwhelming. Despite efforts to achieve the Sustainable Development Goals and comply with the Convention on the Elimination of All Forms of Discrimination against Women, inequality and gender discrimination still persist (World Bank 2018). In other words, women's rights are still being eroded and this suggests that the efforts of most states to eradicate gender discrimination have thus far been insufficient.

The problem focused on here is whether there is overpricing of products through gender-related price discrimination. The aim is to demonstrate gender overpricing manifested through personal consumer products, as well as to establish a link between these price differences and socially constructed gender roles and stereotypes. Drawing attention to this problem could reduce inequality and discrimination against consumers that are developed through market instruments, showing that there is a social construction of genders that is used by companies to impose surcharges, and could thus be used by policy makers to protect consumers.

In short, it is important to acknowledge discourses and frameworks beyond neoliberalism, that allow to understand how discrimination by gender has become structural to economies and, in that exercise, to be able to sustain a proposal of analysis that allows us to recognize and to eradicate new forms of discrimination that begin to gestate and to generalize inside capitalist economies.

Thus, the chapter is structured as follows. The second section contains the theoretical framework, which synthesizes an explanation of social constructions through body cult, gender roles, and consumption, leading to a new and novel form of discrimination. Section three delineates the methodology pursuant of contrasting product categories in terms of the gender of consumers. The fourth section takes us to the results that allow us to visualize how much more women pay compared to men, thus evidencing an overprice or pink tax. Finally, conclusions are offered in the final section.

2   Theoretical Framework

2.1   *Body Cult, Gender Roles, and Consumption as Social Constructions*
A characteristic of the capitalist system is a hierarchical form of gender where the masculine is put before the feminine. That is to say, it is based on a relation of power maintaining patriarchy as the norm (Federici 2010) where the figure of the father or the man is the regent of the system. The main intention of this section is to understand how this system socially constructs gender identities, the sexual division of labor, the symbolism of the body, and consumption patterns.

All of these points converge or are constituted as the prevalence of one gender over the other in that system. Serving as a basis for subsequent analysis, the following question is paramount. How do companies use gender hierarchies to generate greater profits? For D'Alessandro (2016) the body is the means by which the woman fulfills her expectations or frustrates them and to this we add an additional question as follows. Beauty, besides having social roles and attributes has color. In this sense, what color is beauty?

We will review how social constructions are created in terms of gender roles and consumption, which makes it clear that it is possible for equality to prevail by recognizing differences. Since the ultimate goal is not for the feminine to take precedence over the masculine or vice versa, but rather for there to be a correlation or symmetry of forces, participation, decision, and access it must be considered that equality requires recognition and inclusion of differences (Scott and Lamas 1992).

To this end, we will begin by synthesizing the most representative ideas based on both gender economics and feminist economics. In terms of the former, the object of study is the differences between men and women; it looks for the inclusion of women in contrast to androcentric discourses that position men at the center of everything. Thus, gender economics incorporates women in the analysis of realities. Meanwhile, feminist economics attempts to transform gender inequality. That is to say, being normative, it seeks to transform the decentralization of markets as well as labor discrimination specifically against women (Rodriguez Enriquez 2015). From this point of view, it is considered that economic functioning depends on the production of life more than on the production of capital. Thus, both gender economics and feminist economics provide us with important notions about women's participation both in society and in the economy in general. Such a distinction is perceptible through the gender category as a social phenomenon (Butler 2009) without which it would not be possible to establish a critique of the constitution of gender as the basis of oppression.

This gender category, adopted since the 1970s, distinguishes that characteristics considered to be feminine are acquired socially rather than naturally. Therefore, the idea or concept of the feminine is determined by society and it can be said that this represents creations or transformations that are cultural rather than biological. As such they do not obey some functional assignment. Society determines and grants differences based on sex and these can vary depending on the particular society in question and the particular time-period being considered.

In summary, to speak of gender could refer to women directly but also to the cultural construction of sexual difference or social relations of the sexes in a world where that of women is part of that of men (Lamas 2015).

This framework makes gender inequity visible when, in the societal model, roles are assigned according to sex; where, on the one hand, women only bear domestic and care responsibilities, while on the other hand, in the labor market, they are further disadvantaged due to labor instability and lack of social coverage, in addition to a lower salary compared to men.

This explains the existence of a sexual division that transcends even the labor sphere and that hierarchizes participation, performance, and the development of capacities between the feminine and masculine gender. Capitalism is an eminently patriarchal hierarchy.

Analysis through the gender category implies that cultural construction is manifested through the symbolization of sex as a male/female dichotomy. From this perspective, gender is a collective symbolic action on *bodies*, on what men and women should be or the role to be played in society. In this way relations between them are normalized, they maintain and reproduce specific institutions, orient action and give meaning to them, institutionalizing inequality and social stratification (De Barbieri 2004).

In short, gender marks the perception of the social, political, and religious as power and domination (Lamas, 2015) while the body is constructed culturally and symbolically but also, as we shall see later, determines consumption due to gender identities; the body, as we have seen, would have a certain position as a symbolic object.

From the distinction of gender as male and female, the body is established as a social representation. Based on this distinction or differentiation of genders, it is possible to assign them equally differentiated roles and build identities to each gender; which implies that once these divisions or roles are manifested in society, they will become difficult to overcome. Roles are manifested through the differential activities and responsibilities that men and women have in society, the behaviors that they assume and the spaces in which they govern (Gallego 2009). That is to say, the activities differentiated between men and women, even in terms of consumption, turn out to be a social construction that contrasts the masculine with the feminine.

Models of social behavior differentiate men from women. In this distinction of societal roles, women are associated with beauty, youth, seduction, and so on while in men values such as knowledge, strength, courage, and discovery prevail (Gallego 2009). Thus, understanding the role of the body as a symbolic construction and not as a reality in itself, allows us to understand the cult of the body as a starting point for the analysis of increasing consumerism, as the means for achieving the aspirations of well-being (Cuevas Barberousse 2009). This is because of the stereotype and the parameters that must be met, particularly by women, to achieve greater goals—including a job.

In other words, just as there is a social construction of gender, so too, society assigns a particular position to the body based on its own social representations, where consumption is articulated with the (re)production of gender relations, particularly domestic work (Pérez 2017) and the market as the means to achieve socially constructed identity objectives. From this perspective, we can infer that the cult of the body, together with the social construction of gender and the roles assigned to both men and women, determines the behavior of men and women in society, which in turn determines the type of consumption.

Relating the cult of the body and the woman's body as a symbol of eroticism, sensuality, and femininity, we can begin to distinguish a tyrannical relationship between consumption and gender discrimination (Cuevas Barberousse 2009) where the body is the symbolic representation of gender and, as the latter is represented through the body, the body then determines differences between the feminine and the masculine.

This link allows us to arrive at one of the most important conclusions of this work, which has been developed in similar research. To elaborate, capitalism permeates, determines, and reinforces gender identities by giving them qualities, roles, spaces, behaviors, and so on (Gallego 2009) and gender-based advertising and discrimination are the tools that help to build and maintain exacerbated gender identities. The sexual division of labor is perpetuated, thus aggravating inequalities, inequities, and discrimination against women.

Companies capture the female market resulting in the transfer of gender roles to the market as an economic burden for women. Thus, the satisfaction of human needs, which regularly occurs through the market, is taken advantage of by companies that provide goods or services, developing strategies such as differentiation between products and price discrimination based on income or price elasticity of product demand, to position themselves in target markets.

Differentiated behaviors, better known as gender roles or stereotypes, are used by marketing and advertising in the capitalist system. They take them to promote products according to the 'needs' of each gender, which, as discussed, are socially constructed. However, what was not clear until the New York Department of Consumer Affairs (DCA) conducted a gender price study in 2015, is that the market system uses these differences in needs to promote its products with an additional strategy: discriminating and differentiating prices according to the 'needs' of each gender (Department of Consumer Affairs 2015).

This price discrimination, based on consumption patterns, stereotyped in terms of gender, has led the Academy to coin the term *pink tax*, which is defined as the surcharge that women pay only for being women, a situation that will be explored in what follows.

2.2   A Novel Form of Discrimination

In a world where the body is worshipped, image and physical appearance determine what is or is not important, thus a Faustian relationship between femininity and being a woman prevails, driven through marketing. This has far-reaching results, as it means that it is women, rather than men, who become potential consumers of cosmetics, medicinal products, food, and fashion in general (Cuevas Barberousse 2009).

This pressure on women causes them to spend more of their income on products such as those mentioned above, which can be up to a $1400 pink tax per year due to a surcharge that can be up to 50% on similar products in California (U.S.) (Evia 2015) and, given that women's income is generally much lower in comparison to that of men, this results in even greater pressure on their purchasing power.

This is the origin of a particular type of price discrimination that is rarely discussed and debated, but which concerns us greatly and hence brought us together on this issue. This is price discrimination in terms of gender. This type of discrimination according to gender, this pink tax or *'impuesto rosa'* in Spanish, occurs in various economies and is continuously reproduced within the capitalist model as a strategic form that companies have adopted to obtain greater profits at the expense of women, as well as construction and social pressure on gender.

This situation prevails despite the fact that the *Convention on the Elimination of All Forms of Discrimination against Women* in Article 2, subparagraphs C and E, states that countries undertake:

> (c) To establish legal protection of the rights of women on an equal basis with men and to ensure through competent national tribunals and other public institutions the effective protection of women against any act of discrimination.
> (e) To take all appropriate measures to eliminate discrimination against women by any person, organization or enterprise.
>
> UNITED NATIONS 1981

Perhaps by involuntary omission or because there has been insufficient academic attention to this issue, in various economies, overpricing has been observed especially on female products. It is therefore necessary to first understand, from the perspective of neoclassical economic theory, what price discrimination is as a monopolistic strategy drawing on concepts of reserve price and consumer surplus, and then move on to examples of surcharges that are reproduced in both developed and developing countries before presenting our case-study focused on the city of Guayaquil in Ecuador. For this purpose, Varian (1989) and Parkin and Loría (2010) are used to understand, situate, and explore price discrimination.

In general terms, companies that sell differentiated products in the market can be catalogued as companies with market power if their products have no close substitutes or if there are barriers that prevent the entry of other companies to sell the same product. The difference between firms with market power and competitive firms is that the former, because of their market position, can participate in price formation, i.e., they are price setters; whereas the latter cannot influence prices and their production decisions depend on the quantity that maximizes their profit.

A competitive company, which is characterized as such because it sells a good with close substitutes, could not apply any strategy to capture more customers because it would involve higher costs (inputs to differentiate its product, advertising, and so on) that would be reflected in higher prices, which would result in consumers buying substitute goods. While a company with market power, being the only seller in some cases, can apply marketing strategies pursuant of increasing sales and expanding their market.

Although a company can achieve market power for different reasons, for expository purposes we focus on the use of two pricing strategies: it could sell at a single price or apply price discrimination and, given that its restriction is the market, to sell more it would have to charge a lower price. If you sell at a single price to all your customers, you are likely to do so at the highest price that consumers are willing to pay, so that the price would be equal to their reserve price to capture the highest possible profits.

Another important factor to analyze when setting prices in the market relates to the type of good or service that is offered and its relationship with the *elasticity of demand*. The price elasticity of demand can be elastic, inelastic, or unitary. When we speak of elastic demand, this implies that the elasticity of demand is greater than 1, i.e., if the price is reduced by 1%, the quantity demanded increases more than proportionately (> 1%); whereas when demand is inelastic when the price is reduced by 1%, the quantity demanded increases less than proportionately (< 1%). Finally, the price elasticity of demand can be unitary which means that a 1% price reduction results in a 1% increase in the quantity demanded.

In the first case, people respond to price variation and are willing to buy much more, resulting in an increase in total income as well as in profit for the company. In the second case, people are unwilling to buy substantially more despite declining prices, resulting in a decrease in total income and a reduction or loss of income; in this case, marginal income is negative. In the third case, total income does not vary, i.e., perfect compensation occurs between the income gain due to the amount sold and the price reduction, hence the marginal income is zero.

To maximize profits, the company with market power sets the highest price consumers are willing to pay; at the intersection point where both their income and marginal cost are equal, the price is higher for both income and marginal cost. The enterprise must establish the price and quantity of production at levels where its marginal revenue (MR = the income for each additional unit produced and sold) is equal to its marginal cost (MC = the cost of producing that additional unit) to achieve its profit maximization objective. If, instead, MR > MC, the company could increase its profits by increasing production; if MR < MC then profits increase if production decreases.

However, the strategy of placing a single price on the market for the goods a company produces, is no longer the most widely used because doing so does not guarantee profit maximization. On the other hand, if the same good is offered at two different prices, one high and one low, it is possible that the buyer who purchases the product at a lower price may resell it because of the nature of the good.

Hence, new strategies were developed that allow companies to obtain higher revenues by differentiating the market by heterogeneously pricing the same good or service; thus, price discrimination appears as the most recurrent way to segment the market.

Thus, price discrimination involves selling different units of a good or service at different prices and hence distinguishing between different types of buyers. An additional assumption of this strategy is that non-trivial resale would not occur. Examples of price discrimination can be observed with respect to cinemas or bus tickets which regularly institute differentiated prices for children, students, the elderly, and the general public. Another salient example pertains to flights where the norm is for airlines to differentiate between first, business, and economy classes. The objective of price discrimination is to capture consumer surplus[2] and convert it into profits for the business.

There are three degrees, forms, or levels of discrimination. Firstly, there is perfect price discrimination which consists of placing a price on each consumer, identifying what their reserve price is, that is, exactly how much they are willing to pay for the good and appropriating all consumer surplus. This first-degree discrimination is not applicable in this context and serves only as an illustration; however, it does have empirical salience in other domains such as with lawyers and private doctors or where the buyer is a company/organization rather than an individual.

The second degree consists of instituting non-linear prices, or not unique, by blocks of goods or by volumes but not by type of consumer, so we see that the greater the volume to be purchased by consumers, the lower the price.

To further introduce ourselves to the subject of this research, we will explore discrimination between groups of buyers. People differ in the value they place on a product and thus their willingness to pay; this difference is due to intrinsic characteristics such as age, employment status or, as in the case herein, gender.

This is third-degree price discrimination, which relates to the new wave of overpricing being pursued by companies, because different buyers are assigned different prices but each buyer pays a constant amount of money for all units of the same product. On this basis, what the company does is to identify two markets, the male and the female, and thus force the division within it. In this case, particular consideration is given to the elasticity of demand, i.e., the sensitivity of demand to a change in price. So, more elastic demand will be charged the lower price, since an increase in the price of the product will result in a disproportionately large decrease in demand; this would then be the case of the male market. Therefore, this market is said to have highly price-sensitive demand. Moving on, the most inelastic demand will be charged the highest possible price, because the quantity demanded will decrease less than in

---

2 Consumer surplus, in this sense, is formed by the difference between the maximum price a
   consumer is willing to pay for a good (this is their *reserve price*) minus what they actually pay
   (the market price).

proportion; this would be the case of prices allocated to the female market, due to social pressures to look beautiful and feminine, women will be willing to pay more for a product.

This is how gender price discrimination works, especially in the female market, leveraging and influencing gender stereotypes, through advertising, where women are linked to aesthetics, beauty, fashion, and so on.

In short, companies that differentiate demand vis-à-vis gender, use pressure and social construction around gender to their advantage, and maintain them, to influence price. Hence, various investigations point to the existence of this new sales modality that is expressed in the variation of the prices of shared products, or products of similar use, by both genders (Arias Paredes et al. 2017; CBC News 2016; Martínez Navarro et al. 2018; Medina 2016; Observatorio de Coyuntura Económica y Políticas Públicas 2017). To reiterate, this is known as the 'pink tax,' causing women to pay a surcharge for products similar to those used by men.

As noted, economic theory addresses the issue of price discrimination, which consists of segmentation of the consumer market to take advantage of different consumption patterns, and the subsequent setting of higher prices that allow producers to obtain greater benefits. The possibility of setting differentiated prices for the same product, or between close substitutes, can be explained by the willingness to pay expressed by different groups for the same good or service. In other words, the power to set differentiated prices lies in the price elasticity of demand of consumer groups into which the market as a whole can be segmented. Thus, a group whose price elasticity is lower, that is, a group that maintains a greater availability to pay, will end up paying a higher price for consumption of that good.

According to Bauman (2007), the transition towards a consumer society has changed us as individuals from seeking satisfaction of needs, to being agents with ostentatious consumption capacity. In this sense, the responsibility for household consumption has fallen on women, as caregivers of the family; that is to say, women as the main decision-makers and actors of consumption in society. In this way, the household has become the consumption unit of the new capitalism, whose agent is the housewife (Carosio, 2008). It is therefore a logical consequence that since women are the decision-makers in household consumption, they are the main targets of marketing and advertising strategies. Along this line, Carosio (2008) points out that women, as purchasing agents in determining household consumption decisions, are configured as four entities. First, purchases as a 'housewife' through the acquisition of products for the home; second, purchases by the 'mother woman,' who is responsible for providing the best goods and services for her family; third, the 'wife woman' provides the goods that her husband needs; and fourth and finally, the 'woman buyer for herself' who establishes herself as a plaintiff of beauty products and clothing, following the canon of beauty established by the patriarchal society.

According to the foregoing, consumption in terms of fashion or beauty objects refers almost exclusively to female consumption, particularly young women, impressionable by the images of glamour and perfection that are offered from the beauty industry (Soley-Beltran 2012). These requirements towards women start from the conception of 'the feminine,' from what is conceived as a set of natural and characteristic features of women. Lagarde (2005) defines femininity as a set of attributes that women must demonstrate during their lives through the realization of activities, behaviors, attitudes, feelings, beliefs, ways of thinking, mentalities, and languages; characteristics that are attributed to sex as a biological category, therefore, these characteristics are understood as natural for women.

Fashion and advertising through visual representations reveal the objectification that we women suffer in the process of building glamour, which as a category is unattainable, but is presented as real in advertising (Soley-Beltran 2012).

As a critique to this situation, Soley-Beltran (2012) argues that it is time to promote critical visual literacy in order to decode the values encrypted in the images, to develop a new 'way of seeing' more representative of diversity and to demand models of beauty that redirect the 'aesthetic,' from the mere possession of supposedly ideal bodies to the realm of the senses and the eroticization of the whole personality. One breathes the need for a new style: a more conscious and sovereign (aesthetic), alien to the incessant change of fashions, exempted from the mandate of possession and close to the joyful experience of being shared in freedom. In short, it is time to call for a more ethical aesthetic that is governed by new computer principles.

3   Methodology

To meet the objective of this research, the methodology in 'From Cradle to Cane: The Cost of Being a Female Consumer' carried out in 2015 by the New York Department of Consumer Affairs is used (Department of Consumer Affairs 2015). In that study, the prices of a total of 794 products were compared, divided into 5 different categories, covering 24 stores in New York City. In addition to recording the prices of the products to be compared, photographs were included for corroborative purposes. Inferential mean-difference tests (t tests) were carried out for all product categories, as well as for each subcategory.

Herein, information was collected between January and March 2018 and covered a sample of 45 stores[3] located in the city of Guayaquil, thus ensuring broad coverage of the market for personal consumer products. The products analyzed were divided into 5 categories: Personal care, children's clothing and accessories, adult clothing and accessories, toys, and technology. Within these 5 categories, 35 subcategories were demarcated. The sample comprised a total of 592 products, 296 for men and 296 for women (Table 7.1).

Unlike other studies (such as Martínez Navarro et al. 2018) where prices were evaluated for products with different degrees of similarity,[4] in this investigation reasonably homogeneous products are compared to eliminate possible biases in the investigation and in the subsequent analysis so as to ensure as best as possible that gender effects can be captured. In this sense, products were excluded which were for the exclusive use of one gender (e.g., high heels, dresses, and sanitary towels in the case of women and ties and briefcases in the case of men).

The adscription of products in terms of consumers' gender followed two criteria of a communicative nature. The first envisaged the inclusion of an explicit reference to men or women on product packaging. In the absence of an explicit reference, the second criterion considered the use of colors or designs that outlined the gender of the intended purchaser (e.g., pink or purple

TABLE 7.1   Number of products by category

Category	Male products	Female products	Total
Personal care	41	41	82
Adult clothing and accessories	70	70	140
Children's clothing and accessories	32	32	64
Toys	108	108	216
Technological products	45	45	90
Total products	**296**	**296**	**592**

3   This includes physical and online stores operating in the sample market.
4   Those authors identified 4 product groups: quasi identical products, similar products with non-functional differences, similar products with functional differences, and exclusive products for one gender.

colors, decorative designs displaying flowers or princesses, elements associated with 'the feminine').

To quantify the significance of price differences in the sample, t-tests are performed. However, it should be duly noted that this research faces some methodological limitations in terms of sample framing. To generalize the results to the population level it would be necessary to sample a wider spatial area, taking account of other cities and towns in Ecuador.

4   Results and Discussion

In this section, price comparison results are presented to demonstrate whether, for the Guayaquil market, there is overpricing of personal consumption products that harms women—a price difference that is not based on the characteristics of the products themselves, but rather responds to an artificial difference, based on notions of genders and their consumption patterns.

Table 7.2 summarizes the price differences with respect to the 592 products compared and grouped into the five categories defined in Table 7.1. In four of the five categories studied, female consumers pay a premium for the same type of products aimed at male consumers, i.e., evidence suggests that a pink tax does indeed exist in the Guayaquil personal consumption products market.

TABLE 7.2   Average prices by product category

Category	Female average	Male average	Difference	Percentage difference	t
Personal care	$15.14	$13.48	$1.66	10.9%	2.64 (0.005)
Adult clothing and accessories	$45.33	$44.11	$1.21	2.7%	0.97 (0.165)
Children's clothing and accessories	$22.11	$22.58	$0.47	2.1%	−1.07 (0.145)
Toys	$28.78	$27.86	$0.92	3.21%	1.90 (0.029)
Technological products	$677.53	$669.69	$7.84	1.2%	0.31 (0.376)

Note: Grey shading indicates that, on average, women pay a higher price than men. p-values are in parentheses.

A more detailed analysis suggests that gender roles are more intensified in the consumption of personal care products thus reaffirming the idea of the aesthetics of the feminine, so that in this category women in average percentage terms pay up to 10.9% more for the same products as their male counterparts, with price discrepancies ranging from $0 to $29.46. The results are statistically significant at the 1% level.

In the second category, overpricing of female products is again observed. On average, men pay 2.7% less than women.However, this is not a statistically significant difference. Moving on to children's clothing and accessories, and noting that children are not the buyers here but the consumers, the evidence suggests that there are no significant differences between the price paid by women and men.

In the toy market, the difference observed in the personal care category is repeated with a 3.21% gender-based price difference that negatively affects women. This is statistically significant at a 5% level. Finally, for technological products, the pink tax is around 1.2% but not statistically significant.

The differences in prices revealed in the foregoing resonate with the findings of other investigations. In New York City, there were indications of a pink tax in all analyzed product categories, ranging from 4% to 13%. It is duly noted that according to the findings of both this study and that in New York, the greatest surcharge is evident with respect to personal care products, a finding that testifies to the aesthetic division of consumption previously discussed.

TABLE 7.3   Average prices by product category: Guayaquil and New York

Category	Guayaquil		New York	
	Total products	Gendered price difference	Total products	Gendered price difference
Personal care	82	10.9%	122	13%
Adult clothing and accessories	140	2.7%	292	8%
Children's clothing and accessories	64	2.1%	168	4%
Toys	216	3.21%	106	7%
Technological products	90	1.2%		–
Adult health products	–	–	106	8%

Note: Grey shading indicates that, on average, women pay a higher price than men.

Thus, women are willing to pay a higher price for products related to beauty maintenance, such as shampoos, perfumes, lotions, deodorants, razors, and so on (Table 7.3).

Since the origins of humanity, men and women have always been sexually different. According to Lagarde (2005) the conformation of genders is the result of a process in which different social and cultural characteristics have been attributed to each sex and as a consequence of this division society imposes different ways of life on them, developing a whole 'culture of femininity.' The social demands on the feminine are translated, in aesthetic terms, into demands on the body. Therefore, personal care responds to the symbolic configuration of the representation of the feminine.

In this sense, consumption patterns are markedly differentiated between men and women, especially when it comes to personal care products. The evidence found is compatible with the preceding analysis, thus, it is observed that women pay approximately 10.9% more, on average, for articles that respond to the logic of the body cult, hence gender roles, and within these, the mystique of the feminine has implications in the economic sphere since not only the demand for this type of products is greater among female consumers but also women pay a higher price for this consumption. In this sense, for women, the body and its beauty have an extra price.

Table 7.4 shows the difference in prices for personal care products, in terms of 6 sub-groups. The positioning of pigeonholed products in the field of aesthetics has a greater prevalence among female consumers; advertisements emphasize the consumption of these items in the case of women, thus, advertising marketing strategies are directed towards this segment of consumers (Carosio 2008). Hence, the cult of aesthetics, and in a more concrete sense, the cult of beauty, finds in consumption one of the ways through which the idea of femininity and of being a woman is channeled (Cuevas Barberousse 2009).

The surcharge paid by women for personal care products ranges between 1% and 15%; the largest difference compared to its male equivalent is in the area of fragrances, followed by antiperspirants and razors, with 15.4%, 11.1%, and 6.1% respectively. However, only in the case of hair care and fragrance products the differences are statistically significant (at the 10% and 1% levels, respectively). The difference in prices found here is similar to the results of a study carried out by the Argentine Confederation of Medium-sized Enterprises (CAME), which through a survey in Buenos Aires, determined premiums of 18.5%, 8.8%, and 14.2% for the three product groups (CAME 2018). Likewise, a survey in the Brazilian city of Sao Paulo showed that in the case of deodorants and razors the pink tax was 2%, and 15%, respectively (Cunha 2015). Research carried out by Idealo Magazín (2016), a magazine specialized in online shopping for the

TABLE 7.4   Average prices by personal care sub-categories

Product	Total products	Female average	Male average	Gendered price difference	t
Razors	16	$4.63	$4.35	6.05%	1.60 (0.110)
Oral care	10	$4.11	$3.98	3.16%	1.43 (0.111)
Hair care	12	$5.97	$5.64	5.53%	1.61 (0.084)
Fragrances	20	$88.93	$75.19	15.45%	3.60 (0.002)
Antiperspi-rants	14	$4.41	$3.92	11.11%	1.16 (0.145)
Soaps	10	$3.53	$3.50	0.85%	0.18 (0.430)

Note: Grey shading indicates that, on average, women pay a higher price than men. p-values are in parentheses.

Spanish market, revealed that the pink tax ranges between 7% and 24% for the three categories analyzed: fragrances and perfumes, shoes, and wristwatches (the highest surcharge being with respect to fragrances and perfumes).

In another of the categories selected for analysis, the figures reflect similar results. In 4 of the 7 sub-categories within adult clothing and accessories, women pay a higher price for the same items, and in the remaining three the difference in prices is tilted to the detriment of male consumers. Importantly, as shown in Table 7.5, none of the differences are significant and thus there is no evidence for a pink tax in this category. However, for comparative reasons, the price evaluation did not consider exclusive clothing for women, such as high heels, dresses, skirts, and so on that exhibit high prices in the market.

The prevalence of differential prices to the detriment of the female public seems not to transfer to the case of children's clothing. Table 7.6 delineates 5 subcategories of products intended for children classified into bathroom accessories, footwear, shirts, outfits, and trousers. Only in the first category is there a disadvantageous overprice towards females, but this is not statistically significant. In the remaining subcategories, the price analysis shows that products for boys have a higher price than the counterpart products for girls. Although no significant gendered price difference was found for this category in the aggregate, the overprice to the detriment of males is statistically significant in two subcategories at the 10% level, namely footwear and shirts where male consumers are found to pay a premium of 0.76% and 5.55% respectively.

TABLE 7.5   Average prices by adult clothing and accessories sub-categories

Product	Total products	Female average	Male average	Difference in prices	t
Accesso-ries	38	$43.43	$40.08	7.71%	0.76 (0.220)
Shirts	32	$26.46	$27.48	3.85%	−0.69 (0.240)
Sweaters/ Blazers	18	$60.83	$62.54	2.82%	−0.30 (0.350)
Jeans	8	$57.99	$52.24	9.92%	0.84 (0.220)
Trousers	12	$48.32	$44.66	7.57%	0.90 (0.200)
Slippers	8	$9.58	$7.65	20.15%	1.20 (0.130)
Shoes	24	$70.69	$74.14	4.88%	1.02 (0.160)

Note: Grey shading indicates that, on average, women pay a higher price than men. p-values are in parentheses.

TABLE 7.6   Average prices by children's clothing and accessories sub-categories

Product	Total products	Female average	Male average	Difference in prices	t
Bathroom accessories	12	$19.28	$18.33	4.93%	1.27 (0.129)
Footwear	10	$18.38	$18.52	0.76%	−1.60 (0.091)
Shirts	18	$29.90	$31.56	5.55%	−1.55 (0.079)
Outfit sets	16	$19.02	$19.44	2.21%	−0.48 (0.320)
Pants and jeans	8	$31.60	$32.53	2.94%	−0.25 (0.408)

Note: Grey shading indicates that, on average, women pay a higher price than men. p-values are in parentheses.

Table 7.7 presents results for technological products in terms of 4 sub-categories; in one of them it was not possible to prove the existence of a pink tax, tactile equipment. In the remaining three the percentage difference in prices ranges from 0.01% to 27.7% but none of these differences are statistically significant.

TABLE 7.7   Average prices by technological products sub-categories

Product	Total products	Female average	Male average	Difference in prices	t
Touchscreen devices	12	$461.22	$461.22	0%	–
Accessories for touchscreen devices	26	$23.50	$16.99	27.7%	0.99 (0.170)
Computers and accessories	24	$125.28	$123.96	1.05%	0.50 (0.313)
Audio and video equipment	28	$67.53	$67.52	0.01%	0.012 (0.495)

Note: Grey shading area indicates that, on average, women pay a higher price than men.
p-values are in parentheses.

Finally, Table 7.8 focusses on the category of toys and accessories. In aggregate terms, as already discussed, the pink tax is close to 3.21% and statistically significant. A more detailed analysis shows that there are product groups where the difference in prices is not statistically significant, i.e., the first 5 subcategories. However, the average price of furniture aimed at women is $32.64, while for men this is significantly lower at $28.89, being this difference statistically significant at the 10% level. Musical and electronic toys also reflect a punishment for women, in which an overprice of 4.54% is observed, and again this difference is statistically significant at the 10% level. Gender roles and their influence on economic behavior are also reflected in the subcategory of soft toys. The price comparison here shows that the average price paid by women would be up to 6.78% above the price assumed by men, this difference being significant at the 1% level.

The Organic Law for the Defense of Consumers (2015), effective since 2000, prohibits unsubstantiated increases in the prices of goods and services distributed in Ecuadorian territory. Specifically, Article 51 states: "Speculation is absolutely prohibited.[5] Any other unfair practices that levies or causes indiscriminate rises in the prices of goods and / or services is also prohibited" (p. 32).

Moreover, Article 54 makes it explicit that in exceptional cases:

---

5   The same law defines speculation as an illicit commercial practice that consists of taking advantage of a market need to artificially raise prices, either through the concealment of goods or services, or sales restriction agreements among suppliers, or the reluctance of suppliers to meet consumer orders despite there being stocks that allow doing so, or the elevation of product prices above official inflation indices, producer prices, or consumer prices.

TABLE 7.8   Average prices by toys and accessories sub-categories

Product	Total products	Female average	Male average	Difference in prices	t
Bathroom accessories	28	$9.50	$9.82	3.37%	−0.79 (0.219)
School accessories	38	$21.88	$21.89	0.05%	−0.04 (0.483)
Sports and professions	10	$13.41	$12.97	3.28%	0.66 (0.271)
Transport	46	$83.50	$82.87	0.75%	0.53 (0.297)
Table games	32	$15.86	$15.88	0.13%	−0.03 (0.486)
Furniture	10	$32.64	$28.89	11.49%	1.77 (0.075)
Musical and electronic	34	$31.31	$29.89	4.54%	1.64 (0.059)
Soft toys	18	$22.14	$20.64	6.78%	3.45 (0.004)

Note: Grey shading indicates that, on average, women pay a higher price than men. p-values are in parentheses.

> ...the President of the Republic, duly substantiating the measure, may temporarily regulate the prices of goods and services. Such regulation may be exercised by the President of the Republic when the economic situation of the country has caused an unjustified escalation of prices. It shall be executed by means of an Executive Decree, which shall establish the expiration of the measure when the causes for the respective resolution have disappeared.
>
> p. 32 (translated by the authors)

In accordance with the two preceding articles, the State will seek mechanisms to avoid artificial price increases. Importantly, it is noted that this Law does not contemplate price discrimination on the basis of gender, which may be explained by the fact that in 2000, the year in which this law was enacted, gender had not been mainstreamed into Ecuadorian legal instruments. However, at present, the Law still does not prohibit the setting of differentiated prices according to the gender of the consumer. In this sense, and taking into account what is contained in the Constitution of Ecuador (2008) and in Article 340, it is essential to identify and evaluate unjustified increases in the prices of consumer products aimed at women.

5   Conclusions

This research has sought to identify and explore differences in prices for personal consumer products according to the gender of the consumer, as well as to establish the link between these price differences and the gender roles and stereotypes that have been constructed throughout history, and which, ultimately, are combined as a determining element of the consumption patterns evidenced by men and women. To this end, prices were compared in different retail stores in the city of Guayaquil, based on the division of products into 5 categories. t-tests were used to quantify the significance of the gendered differences on prices.

The results suggest the existence of price discrimination to the detriment of female consumers, a difference in prices that resonates with and justifies the term, *pink tax*. Overall, in 4 of the 5 categories analyzed, the products destined to the female public exhibited a surcharge of up to 10.9%, being the difference statistically significant for personal care products and for toys. A more detailed examination illustrates that within the category of personal care products, which is directly related to the aesthetics of 'the feminine,' the pink tax can be as high as 15.45%, as is the case with fragrances and perfumes.

There are some subcategories where men pay higher prices, although the price differences are significant only in the case of children footwear and shirts. In general terms, overpricing mostly affects women across most of the categories included in this study.

Finally, through price comparison in these 5 groups of products it has been possible to show that, overall, a pink tax exists in the form of overpriced products with the same characteristics and whose only differentiation is in terms of the color of packaging or, in some cases, other subtle differences. Thus, women respond to the current model of consumption, which according to Carosio (2008) is not only alienating, needs-generating, superfluous, but sustains and reinforces patriarchy based on the traditional model of femininity.

References

Arias Paredes, L.M., Mansilla Merlano, F., and Rincón Puche, L. (2017). "Impuestos y Desigualdad de Género en Colombia." *Revista Económica Supuestos*. http://revista-supuestos.com/otros/2017/4/17/impuestos-y-desigualdad-de-gnero-en-colombia.

Bauman, Z. (2007). *Vida de Consumo*. Fondo de Cultura Económica.

Butler, J. (2009). "Performatividad, precariedad y políticas sexuales." *Revista de Antropología Iberoamericana* 4(3): 321–336.

CAME. (2018). *Informe Impuesto Rosa*. Focus Market.

Carosio, A. (2008). "El género del consumo en la sociedad de consumo." *La Ventana* 27: 130–169.

CBC News. (2016). *"Pink tax" sees women pay 43% more than men for personal care products: report*. CBC. https://www.cbc.ca/news/business/pink-tax-1.3553524.

Constitution of Ecuador. (2008). https://www.asambleanacional.gob.ec/sites/default/files/documents/old/constitucion_de_bolsillo.pdf.

Cuevas Barberousse, T. (2009). "Cuerpo, feminidad y consumo: El caso de jóvenes universitarias." *Revista de Ciencias Sociales* II(123): 79–92.

Cunha, J. (2015). *"Pink tax" encarece produtos voltados para mulheres*. Folha de Sao Paulo. https://www1.folha.uol.com.br/mercado/2015/07/1651761-pink-tax-encarece-produto-para-mulheres.shtml.

D'Alessandro, M. (2016). *Economía feminista: Cómo construir una sociedad igualitaria (sin perder el glamour)*. Sudamericana.

De Barbieri, T. (2004). "Más de tres décadas de los estudios de género en América Latina." *Revista Mexicana de Sociología* 66: 197–214. https://doi.org/10.2307/3541450.

Department of Consumer Affairs. (2015). *From Cradle to Cane: The Cost of Being a Female Consumer: A Study of Gender Pricing in New York City*. New York City Department of Consumer Affairs.

Evia, M.J. (2015). *Impuesto rosa: definición y ejemplos*. Expok Comunicación de Sustentabilidad y RSE. https://www.expoknews.com/impuesto-rosa-definicion-y-ejemplos/.

Federici, S. (2010). *Calibán y la bruja: Mujeres, cuerpo y acumulación originaria*. Traficantes de Sueños.

Gallego, J. (2009). "La construcción del género a través de la publicidad." *Actas Del Congreso La Construcción Del Género En La Publicidad En El Siglo XXI*.

Idealo Magazín. (2016). "Tasa Rosa: Productos de mujer hasta un 24% más caros." *Idealo*. https://www.idealo.es/magazin/tasa-rosa-pink-tax-en-espana/.

Lagarde, M. (2005). *Los cautiverios de las mujeres: madresposas, monjas, putas, presas y locas*. Universidad Nacional Autónoma de México.

Lamas, M. (2015). "Usos, dificultades y posibilidades de la categoría género." *Revista de Estudios de Género La Ventana*: 10–61.

Martínez Navarro, G., Manzano Antón, R., and Bouza, G. (2018). "Identidad de género, consumo y discriminación a través del precio." *Revista Latina de Comunicación Social* 73: 385–400. http://www.revistalatinacs.org/073paper/1261/20es.html.

Medina, M.A. (2016). *¿Existe en Colombia el "impuesto rosa"?* El Espectador. https://www.elespectador.com/noticias/economia/existe-colombia-el-impuesto-rosa-articulo-617821.

Observatorio de Coyuntura Económica y Políticas Públicas. (2017). *PINK TAX: "El impuesto que las mujeres pagan solo por ser mujeres."* Observatorio de Coyuntura

Económica y Políticas Públicas. https://docs.wixstatic.com/ugd/4d12aa_98b50aab3
cd64179955afob139d18c93.pdf.

Organic Law for the Defense of Consumers, (2015).

Parkin, M., and Loría, E. (2010). *Microeconomía: versión para latinoamérica* (9na ed.).
Pearson educación.

Pérez, I. (2017). "Consumo y género: una revisión de la producción historiográfica re-
ciente sobre América Latina en el siglo XX." *Historia Crítica* 65: 29–48.

Rodriguez Enriquez, C. (2015). "Economía feminista y economía del cuidado: Aportes
conceptuales para el estudio de la desigualdad." *Nueva Sociedad* 256(3): 1–15.

Scott, J., and Lamas, M. (1992). "Igualdad versus diferencia: los usos de la teoría post-
estructuralista." *Debate Feminista* 5: 85–104.

Soley-Beltran, P. (2012). "Muñecas que hablan. Ética y estética de los modelos de belle-
za en publicidad y moda." *Revista de Dialectología y Tradiciones Populares* 68(1):
115–146.

United Nations. (1948). *Declaración Universal de Derechos Humanos.* ONU.

United Nations. (1981). *Convention on the Elimination of All Forms of Discrimination
against Women.* UN. https://www.un.org/womenwatch/daw/cedaw/text/econven-
tion.htm

Varian, H.R. (1989). "Price discrimination." *Handbook of Industrial Organization* 1:
597–654.

World Bank. (2018). *Atlas de los Objetivos de Desarrollo Sostenible 2018: Basado en los
Indicadores del Desarrollo Mundial.* World Bank. https://doi.org/10.1596/978-1-4648-
1250-7.

CHAPTER 8

Political Representation of Women in the Ecuadorian Legislature

Gabriela Gallardo

> Political leaders take our money, lead us to wars, and write the laws that govern our lives. Should they include in their ranks men and women, rich and poor, teachers and slaves? For most of world history, the answer is no. Men ruled; women worked in the home. Women's interests were represented by their husbands and fathers. The same was true for members of ethnically subordinate groups: the conquerors would take care of the colonized, the rich of the poor, the whites of the blacks, and so on and so forth.
>
> HTUN 2004: 439

1 Introduction

Historically, democracy was a function of patriarchal institutions where there was no room for women to participate in politics, as only men made decisions. It was a political society exclusively for men. It was impossible to believe that women could one day rule. In 1861, John Stuart Mill penned a seminal work in political science, 'Considerations on Representative Government,' noting that women were excluded from political rights such as suffrage just because they were women (Mill 2004).

It was not until 1893 that women were first allowed to vote, that was in New Zealand. In 1929, Ecuador became the first Latin American country to put women's suffrage into practice (National Geographic 2019). Matilde Hidalgo de Procel, an Ecuadorian doctor, was the first woman to vote in Latin America in 1924 (Adams 2014).

In other words, it was only less than a century ago that women began to participate in elections in Ecuador and in terms of occupying positions of political representation, just like men, that occurred much later and the extent to which it has occurred is still in dispute. Today only one country, Bolivia, has reached the milestone of having 50% women in parliament. On average, across Latin America, 28.8% of elected parliamentarians are women. Whilst this is far short of an equitable situation, it is better than what currently prevails elsewhere around the world. It is important to reflect that this demonstrates that political institutions continue to be dominated by men. In other words men represent the political elite (Hughes 2013).

Due to this unequal situation, in recent years the political representation of women has received particular attention among different governments and institutions around the world. For example, the empowerment of women and specifically the number of women in parliaments is a metric used by the United Nations in the construction of its Gender Inequality Index (GII) (UNDP 2019). In addition, several governments have introduced quota policies to promote the participation of women in their legislatures. Women's quotas represent a formal mechanism that regulates the inclusion of women in parliaments (Krook 2008) and, as a legal instrument, they have served to generate positive changes in the participation of women in Latin America (Schwindt-Bayer 2010).

For example, following the introduction of a quota system on this basis, in 2013, 38% of Ecuadorian parliamentarians were women, one of the highest proportions in the region. In addition, on May 24, 2013, for the first time in history, three women positioned themselves as the highest authorities of the National Assembly. While representation has not yet reached 50 per cent in the Ecuadorian parliament, the period 2013–2017 showed unprecedented results for improvements in women's political representation.

However, it is important to question whether the increase in women in parliament may only be a victory in terms of numbers, and not necessarily reflective of a pro-women agenda. Indeed, Felipe Burbano de Lara (2004) suggests that female politicians in Ecuador do not translate gender disputes into their agendas. To explore this, it is important to understand that women are not a homogeneous group (Celis et al. 2008) and that representation must be understood through their diversity.

Thus, there are debates in the literature concerning whether or not there is a causal relationship between who the representatives are (descriptive representation) and what they do as representatives (substantive representation) (Celis et al. 2008; Childs 2008; Dolan and Ford 1995; Dovi 2002; Mackay 2008; Mansbridge 2005; Tremblay and Pelletier 2001).

Schwindt-Bayer (2010) notes that women's representation may vary according to legislative environments. Therefore, the purpose of this study is to explore how female legislators represented the National Assembly of Ecuador 2013–2017, which will lead us to delve deeper into the political representation of women.

2   Theoretical Framework

The main objective of this section is to open the door to the theoretical debate on women's political representation. For that, the theory on Hanna Pitkin (1967) and the framework of Schwindt-Bayer (2010) will be discussed on the basis of three dimensions that allow appreciation of the panorama of political representation. This is then augmented by taking an intersectional approach pursuant of a holistic understanding of women's realities.

2.1   *Political Representation*
The etymological origins of the word 'representation' refer to re-presentation, making the present again (Pitkin 1967). But what is the political representation of women? Almost all contemporary studies (Celis et al. 2008; Childs 2008; Kurebwa 2015; Schwindt-Bayer 2010) on the representation of women are based on the concept put forward by Hanna Pitkin (1967) in her book 'The Concept of Representation.'

For Pitkin (1967), the word representation is linked to the idea of democracy, describing a diversity of definitions based on particular political theories; from which, she concludes that on the basis of there being no single definition, the most vital element necessary to understand what the word means is to know in what and how it is used. For that, she proposes that representation should be imagined as a photograph taken from different angles. These angles are seen as four dimensions, namely formalist, descriptive, symbolic, and substantive representation.

Pitkin, along with other political scientists, based much of her debate on the statements that Thomas Hobbes (1909) presented in his seminal book 'The Leviathan.' This book, originally published in 1651, is based on the theory of the social contract which is identified as a modern political idea rooted in the principles of popular sovereignty and government accountability to the people. However, women were excluded from this social contract, so his book refers exclusively to the representation of men. For Hobbes, the only people who could reach the position of being government representatives were men. The word 'women' was totally absent and at that time it was unthinkable that a woman could govern a nation. This famous book is a clear example of the exclusion of women in political science.

Similarly but surprisingly, Pitkin (1967) does not incorporate the representation of women into her concept. Her book ignores women in political representation. By contrast, nowadays, several investigations concerning women in political representations, such as those mentioned above, are based on Pitkin's concept. However, most of this research on women's representation has focused exclusively on Western democracies (Celis and Childs 2012; Childs 2008; Dolan and Ford 1995; Krook 2008; Tremblay and Pelletier 2001).

Bucking this trend, Leslie Schwindt-Bayer (2010), professor of political science at Rice University, presents research on women's political representation in Latin America using Pitkin's concept of political representation. Thus, for the present research which seeks to explore the political representation of women in Ecuador, the book 'Political power and women's representation in Latin America' by Leslie Schwindt-Bayer (2010) will be the guide. Her book provides a framework for what are formal, substantive, descriptive, and symbolic dimensions of representation and how to examine them. It compares the political representation of women in some Latin American parliaments, but not in the Ecuadorian context.

2.2   Women's Political Representation by Leslie Schwindt-Bayer

Leslie Schwindt-Bayer (2010) introduces a specific concept on the political representation of women:

> Women's representation is not just about explaining how women get elected or what kinds of policies they produce once there. Instead, it is a multifaceted and integrated concept comprised of the gendered nature of electoral institutions (formal representation), the presence of women in legislatures (descriptive representation), the way in which women represent (substantive representation), and citizen perceptions of that representation (symbolic representation). To fully understand women's representation, it is necessary to examine all of these dimensions of representation and the ways in which they influence one another.
>
>   p. 32

That is, the following aspects of political representation must be observed, including how they relate to each other.

2.2.1   Formal Representation

Leslie Schwindt-Bayer (2010) argues that electoral rules affecting descriptive representation are formal representation par excellence. That is, rules that have an effect on those who can be chosen as representatives. Specifically, Schwindt-Bayer mentions the case of how formal rules affect women in legislatures through two types of electoral institutions: proportional electoral rules and women-specific electoral institutions. The latter refers to quotas for women.

Women's quotas are a formal rule that some countries maintain in their national laws to regulate the inclusion of women in politics. They are required to be implemented by political parties, the government, or political institutions pursuant of meeting the obligation to have a certain percentage of women on their lists. The ultimate goal here is to increase the presence of women in politics (Schwindt-Bayer 2010).

On this, it is worth emphasizing that most scholars such as Mona Lee Krook (2008), Schwindt-Bayer (2010), and Miki Kaul Kittilson (2005) who study women's quota policies refer to 'gender quotas,' but focus only on the presence of women rather than the different genders that this 'gender' social construction includes. Being a woman refers to being a particular gender but there are a diversity of genders.

Leslie Schwindt-Bayer (2010) argues that the inclusion of women's quotas has led to the election of more women in Latin American legislatures. Similarly, Kittilson (2005) states that in most cases the implementation of quotas is "followed by a dramatic increase in women's parliamentary participation" (p. 638).

Jane Mansbridge (2005) emphasizes that quotas are necessary to promote women's participation in politics. However, the women's quota promotes the inclusion of women in politics, but not of all women. As summarized by Celis et al. (2008), many feminists explicitly recognize the heterogeneity of women as a group, observing that there is no empirical or theoretical plausibility to the idea that women share the same personal experiences. Therefore, for inclusion it is vital to bear in mind that women are not a homogeneous group.

However, this does not happen in practice. Mala Htun (2012) states that women's quotas are not intended to represent all women. For example, women of African descent are less represented in Latin American politics. In Brazil, in 2012, only 1% of parliamentary seats were held by women of African descent, despite constituting 25% of the total Brazilian population. In Colombia, in the same year, women of African descent did not get any seats in the Colombian House of Representatives, although they represented 6% of the population.

2.2.2   Descriptive Representation

What does a representative legislature look like? It should resemble those represented, reflecting them without distortion. The legislature could be selected so that its composition corresponds exactly to that of the entire nation and Pitkin (1967) mentions that, according to some proportionalists, the assembly must maintain the most accurate image of the country possible.

"*Descriptive* representation focuses on the composition of the legislature and the extent to which its diversity mirrors diversity in society" (Schwindt-Bayer 2010: 6). In other words, it refers to the representativeness of the system. Legislatures may be descriptively representative based on territorial correspondence (Marsh and Wessels 1997) but they may also be representative in terms of social characteristics such as race, ethnicity, class, and gender (Norris and Franklin 1997).

Leslie Schwindt-Bayer (2010) mentions that descriptive representation is the determining factor as legislatures reflect diversity in the electorate. She suggests that formal institutions that emphasize proportionality and representativeness produce legislatures that are representative of the diversity of society (Schwindt-Bayer 2010).

But does identity matter in the acts of the representatives? Jane Mansbridge (2005) argues that descriptive representation by women improves substantive outcomes for women in all policy areas.

Two questions then arise. Does the Ecuadorian legislature reflect the diversity of women? Who are the women who govern Ecuador?

2.2.3   Substantive Representation

Substantive representation is the activity of representing with respect to "what the representative does and how he does it, or in some combination of these two considerations" (Pitkin 1967: 143). For Leslie Schwindt-Bayer (2010) substantive representation relates to the way elected officials act for their constituents through "the activities of representing and their responsiveness to the political concerns of their constituents" (p. 6).

In this dimension, a debate is opened as to whether or not women represent the women of the country in their actions. Some scholars argue that electing women to legislative offices is different to electing male legislators, as women will raise concerns about gender equality, sponsor equality bills, sit on women's affairs committees, and bring women's perspectives into legislative debates (Schwindt-Bayer 2010). However, other scholars doubt that the presence of women translates into actions in favor of the "unstable category 'women' and their contestable 'interests'" (Mackay 2008: 125).

However, women may be more interested in representing women as they have faced the same historical discrimination (Mansbridge 2005). Along these lines, some academics point out that it is only women who assume a feminist identity, those who care about women; feminist identity being something transcendental in the representation of women. Studies by Dolan and Ford (1995) and Tremblay and Pelletier (2001) argue that feminist women promote a pro-women agenda. Dolan and Ford (1995) conclude that most women who maintain a feminist identity tend to prioritize legislative issues in favor of women. It should be noted that this identity is recognized and defined through the self. For example, in Ecuador not all female representatives identify themselves as feminists but it is they who assume this position or not, which would have consequences for their legislative actions.

In conclusion, the current theoretical framework of representation explains representation from different dimensions and as such contrasts with alternative theoretical approaches which cast representation from a single point of view. Schwindt-Bayer (2010) mentions that this representation framework generates more precise conclusions vis-à-vis the representation of women. For example, by concentrating only on the descriptive dimension, the result in some countries might be that women's representation is improving only because of the increase in the number of women in parliament. However, when examining these same countries through a substantive representation lens, the result could be different, as women legislators do not necessarily respond to a pro-women agenda.

Importantly, this theory allows the connection between different aspects of representation. For example, formal representation has implications for descriptive representation and descriptive representation for substantive representation. In Ecuador, formal representation influences who sits in the National Assembly and in turn who (the identity of the representatives) influences the actions of representation. The model would be as presented in Figure 8.1, excluding the symbolic dimension:[1]

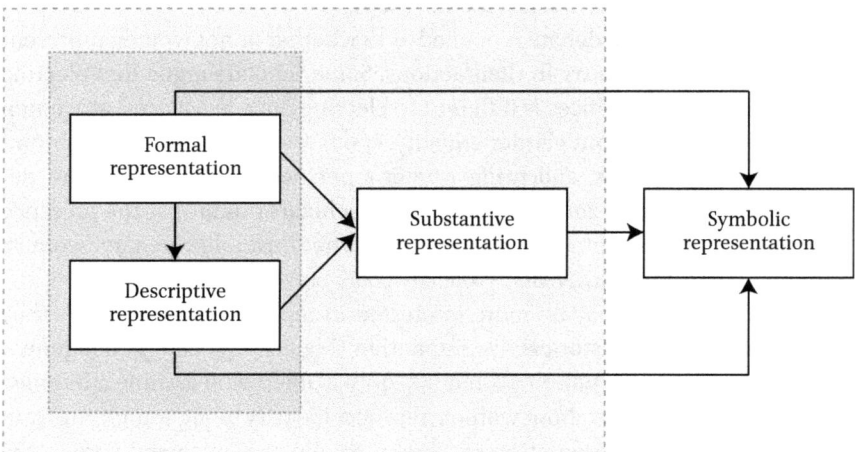

FIGURE 8.1   Integrated Model of Representation
             SOURCE: SCHWINDT-BAYER (2010)

---

1   The symbolic dimension is excluded despite being part of the model proposed by Pitkin and Schwindt-Bayer given that the present research focuses on the perspective of women legislators, and not of citizens.

It is important to note the limitations of Leslie Schwindt-Bayer's framework (2010). One of them concerns the common mistake of limiting gender with women. Second, analysis of descriptive representation in that framework refers to women in general, assuming that women are a homogenous category, without diversity. For that reason, this investigation seeks to augment this framework through due consideration and incorporation of 'intersectionality.'

2.3   Intersectionality

The representation of women must be seen from its level of plurality. The first feminist to introduce the term 'intersectionality' was Kimberlé Crenshaw in 'Mapping the Margins: Intersectionality, Identity Politics, and Violence Against Women of Color,' where she highlights how society has hidden the vulnerability of women, especially black women. Crenshaw establishes links between individual identity and collective identity (Crenshaw 1990).

However, intersectionality may be defined in different, even contradictory, terms. Patricia Hill Collins and Sirma Bilge (2016) propose the following definition of intersectionality, which appears to be accepted by the majority of scholars working in this domain.

> Intersectionality is a way of understanding and analyzing the complexity in the world, in people, and in human experiences. The events and conditions of social and political life and the self can seldom be understood as shaped by one factor. They are generally shaped by many factors in diverse and mutually influencing ways. When it comes to social inequality, people's lives and the organization of power in a given society are better understood as being shaped not by a single axis of social division, be it race or gender or class, but by many axes that work together and influence each other.
>
> p. 2

The importance of using intersectionality as a framework for analysis is based on the most important aspects of contemporary feminist thinking that has been concerned with the issue of differences through understanding the effects of race, class, and gender on women's identities, experiences, and struggles.

Intersectionality can take many forms, one of which is as an analytical tool which facilitates exploring how a case can be understood by many factors that operate together in diverse and mutually influencing ways (Collins and Bilge 2016). For example, how women represent in politics depends on different factors. The use of intersectionality as an analytical tool highlights how gender, race, class, sexuality, and citizenship influence outcomes.

Collins and Bilge (2016) present contemporary debates on the connection between identity and intersectionality. For example, in contemporary society, race and gender can operate as visible identities (Alcoff 2005). However, identity in broad terms is not something that is observed, instead, it is intra-subjective because it refers to how each individual recognizes him or herself. For example, the concept of 'women' can be recognized through different versions (Alcoff 2005). Intersectionality proposes a combinatorial approach to recognize the diversity of identities (Collins and Bilge 2016).

Identity can also influence politics in a form of resistance. The politics of identity can be conceived as an essential tool for resisting historical oppression, identity as a political place but not as an essence. It should be noted, however, that identity politics has been criticized for being associated with radical separatists and that this can affect democracy. For classical liberal political theory, the initial ego state is conceptualized as an abstract individual without a group (Alcoff 2005), as if women were radicalized and represented only women who forget the common good among citizens. This theory supports not separating citizens into groups, but do women representatives seek exclusively to separate and legislate for and by women? Conversely, identities in intersectionality may not separate people, but connect them. Intersectionality as an analytical tool creates a broader understanding of individual and collective identities; identities that can build a collective 'we' (Collins and Bilge 2016).

By understanding the limitations of Leslie Schwindt-Bayer's Women's Representation framework, this research seeks to acknowledge and incorporate the diversity of women, from different identities and personal experiences, using identity as a basis. This research presents intersectionality as a way of framing the diverse interactions of identities and personal experiences in the context of the representation of women, especially of five different women in Ecuadorian politics.

3   Methodology

3.1   *Questions*

The overall question to be resolved is how did the five female legislators, which form the sample of this study's respondents, represent in the National Assembly of Ecuador between 2013 and 2017? To explore and answer this question, the political representation of women is observed and questioned from three perspectives, answering the following sub-questions:

1. What were the electoral standards for women's representation in the 2013–2017 National Assembly? Are quotas important?
2. How was the National Assembly constituted in terms of the presence of women?
3. What is the identity of the representatives?
4. How did women act as legislators?
5. What was the relationship between the descriptive representation of the five female legislators and their substantive representation?

3.2   Data Selection

The case study is framed in terms of the National Assembly of Ecuador in the 2013–2017 legislative period. This period is chosen because it had the largest presence of female representatives compared to any other time in Ecuadorian history. Qualitative data derived from interviews and secondary data were used to analyze political representation. The qualitative information obtained made it possible to capture the feelings, values, and perceptions that influenced the behaviors of the five female legislators.

The overarching criterion for selecting the five female legislators concerned a diversity objective. Thus, each of them was selected for being from a different political party, different ideology (from left to right), different ethnicity, and different province (covering almost all geographical regions of Ecuador). Added to this, the aim was to select the most recognized individuals at the national level subject to meeting this overall diversity objective. For example, Lourdes Tibán is recognized worldwide as an indigenous legislator; Gabriela Rivadeneira as the most voted legislator of the Alianza País movement and President of the 2013–2017 Assembly; Cristina Reyes as a recognized assemblywoman of the traditional right-wing party of Guayas province; Mae Montaño as an outstanding right-wing Afro-descendant assemblywoman who has been in the country's political life for several years; and Gabriela Díaz as the country's youngest assemblywoman in an Ecuadorian Amazon province.[2]

The secondary data utilized herein include the electoral laws within which the representatives were elected and the proposed laws presented by each of the five selected assembly members during the period 2013–2017.

---

2   A limitation in this selection is the lack of any women explicitly representing a non-heterosexual orientation, since no legislator presented herself in such terms. Likewise, the social class of interviewees could not be identified.

TABLE 8.1   Overview of interviewees

Name	Political Party	Ideology	Region	Province	Race
Gabriela Rivadeneira	Alianza País	Left	Sierra (highland region)	Imbabura	Mestizo
Mae Montaño	CREO	Right	Coast	Esmeraldas	Afro-Ecuadorian
Lourdes Tibán	Pachakutik	Left	Sierra	Cotopaxi	Indigenous
Cristina Reyes	Partido Social Cristiano	Right	Coast	Guayas	Not specified
Gabriela Diaz	Avanza	Center	Amazon	Pastaza	Not specified

The interviews conducted were designed using an intersectional methodology. This type of interview made it easier to identify how gender, race, class, personal experiences, self-identification, geographic origin, and other elements influence responses. All questions were open-ended so as not to constrain responses.

3.3   Data Analysis

The interview data were analyzed using thematic analysis and discourse analysis. Thematic analysis is a method used to observe, find, explore, and report issues within the data. In this type of analysis, the meaning of a topic can be divided into a set of subtopics. This method helps to classify the data obtained through a consistent coding strategy and to produce a thematic network that synthesizes and interprets information. For example, issues such as 'women's quota,' 'Feminism,' and 'identity' emerged from the data.

The second part of the analysis examines the legislative initiatives presented by the five Assembly members between 2013–2017. Specifically, the motives behind these legislative initiatives are analyzed using discourse analysis to understand their political intent. This discourse analysis was carried out based on the 'What is the Problem?' approach put forward by Carol Bacchi (1999). She considers that policy-making is "a struggle over meaning and significance" (Bacchi 1999: 19). In addition, she establishes that a public policy seeks to illustrate a certain range of problems, types of ideas, and even silences. Through the following questions, Bacchi (1999) proposes to investigate the background of a certain policy: What is the problem? What are the assumptions underlying this representation? What are the effects produced? Who is likely to benefit from this representation? What is left without problems in this representation? How would the answers differ if the problem were represented differently?

Thus, the laws presented by the assembly members were analyzed through these questions, which helped to understand their reasons for introducing and supporting these policy initiatives and therefore their position on certain problems.

4   Results

4.1   *Formal Dimension*
4.1.1   Electoral Rules
Electoral institutions are the rules that define how the electoral process works, and these rules can help or hinder women's participation (Schwindt-Bayer 2010). So how do these rules work in Ecuador? Ecuadorian law establishes that citizens vote for the president and legislators. For the latter, the electoral system is configured so that individuals are elected to represent different regions (provinces), on a first-past-the-post or majority basis. The regional system means that candidates must be selected by the different regions in the country rather than being imposed top-down.

The system also stipulates that 50% of the candidates on the electoral lists must be women,[3] promoting equal representation of women and men in terms of nominations and appointments to the public service, to management and decision-making bodies, and in political parties and movements (article 3). The first paragraph of article 99 establishes that parity is obligatory (Código de la Democracia 2009).

The greatest advance observed by virtue of the extant Code of Democracy, introduced in 2009, is the increase in female participation. The fact that the lists establish a percentage of 50% women and 50% men, is unprecedented in the history of Ecuadorian and Latin American legislation.

Another substantial improvement is to expressly provide for alternation. These regulations stipulate that representatives of the National Assembly must maintain a strict format of equity, parity, alternation, and sequencing between women and men. In contrast to other electoral laws, this rule clearly expresses the sequence of woman-man-woman.[4]

---

3   The Democracy Code is the prevailing law that has regulated elections since April 27, 2009.
4   In the past, alternation was not clearly specified, so the system lent itself to maneuvers so that, in the lists, a man was often specified first, followed by a woman (Vega 2005).

However, it is also important to mention that Ecuadorian legislation concerning quotas does not specify anything in favor of minorities. No quotas are established for Afro-descendants or indigenous people. By contrast, unlike Ecuador, in the legislation of Colombia, Venezuela, and Bolivia seats are reserved for indigenous or Afro-descendant people (Htun 2012).

4.1.2   Legislators' Opinions on the Quota
The five interviewees agreed that the women's quota has been fundamental in increasing the participation of women in the Ecuadorian parliament. For example, Mae Montaño pointed out that quotas help to include people who have suffered historical discrimination: "groups that have suffered historical discrimination and inequalities need affirmative action to help redress that process."

However, everyone also agreed that the use of quotas or how they are designed can be improved. Three of the women emphasized the importance of accompanying the quota policy with gender-sensitive training. The indigenous assembly member, Lourdes Tibán, presents three plausible proposals for reforms to improve the electoral system in relation to women's participation. The first proposal is to link women with collectives through a collective quota, that is to say, the collective of women becomes the objective to be met, not the person. The second proposal is to have affirmative actions in favor of indigenous people pursuant of increasing their representation in the Assembly. Finally, she mentioned the possibility of changing from mandating parity (or 50% women's quota) in election results rather than just lists. For her part, Gabriela Díaz proposes to include quotas for young people, since in her opinion too few young women participate in politics.

4.2   *Descriptive Dimension*
4.2.1   Overview of the Composition of the National Assembly 2013–2017
A parliament involves incorporating all citizens and reflecting their diversity. It can be descriptively representative in terms of geographical correspondence and can also be representative in relation to characteristics such as race, ethnicity, class, or gender (Schwindt-Bayer 2010). Taking these parameters into account, how has the Ecuadorian parliament been shaped with respect to women? In what follows, the composition of the National Assembly in 2013 is described.

In the 2013 elections, 1,434 citizens participated as candidates. Of this number, 665 were women, 46.4% of the total. Of the 143 candidates elected as legislators for the period 2013–2017, only 55 were women, or 38.5 per cent. However, this still represented the highest proportion of women ever elected to

TABLE 8.2   Number of women in the Ecuadorian parliament (1996–2013)

Standard	Year	Number of women
Before women's quota	1996	5
After women's quota	1997	7
After 20% quota	1998	16
Parity between men and women	2013	55

parliament in Ecuador (CNE 2015). Table 8.2 below represents the number of women over the years in relation to the standards in force.

It can be concluded that the implementation of the quota heralded substantial change. From 5 women in parliament in 1996 to 16 in 1998 (immediately after implementation of the 20% women's quota) (Vega 2005), and then a jump to 55 women elected in 2013 (CNE 2015) with parity. Although not the only factor, it is certain that the quota policy contributed to the increase in the number of women in the Ecuadorian parliament. This finding supports Kittilson's (2005) thesis that quotas are a good mechanism for improving women's numerical representation. Likewise, it can be verified that there is a relationship between formal representation and descriptive representation, we could denote it as a causal relationship.

On the composition of the National Assembly it is important to note that, first, women did not occupy 50% of the candidacies in the electoral lists despite being mandatory. Second, the women who participated the most and obtained legislative seats were adults between the ages of 30 and 65 (CNE 2015). Third, whether and the extent to which there are diverse sexual preferences among women in the legislature is unknown. Fourth, the majority of women legislators came from the country's main provinces. Fifth, Alianza País was the political party that presented the most female candidates culminating in the most women elected to the Assembly (CNE 2015). Sixth and finally, the indigenous and Afro-Ecuadorian population was not adequately reflected in the number of legislators for 2013–2017 and there is little information on women in terms of their ethnicity or nationality. As Mala Htun (2012) mentions, women's quotas may not represent all women such as, for example, Afro-descendants who are underrepresented in Latin America in general, and as can be observed herein, this applies to Ecuador.

4.2.2   Identities of Five Female Legislators

Given that women are not a homogeneous group, there is no empirical or theoretical evidence that supports commonalities between women's personal

TABLE 8.3   Identities of five female legislators

Name	Race	Gender	Personal Characteristics	Origin	Age	Other
Gabriela Rivadeneira	Mestizo	Woman	Convinced Passionate	Otavalo	Young	Feminist Socialist
Lourdes Tibán	Indigenous	Woman	Multifaceted	N/A	N/A	Mother Public Official
Cristina Reyes	N/A	Woman	Strong	Guayaquil	Young	
Mae Montaño	Black	Woman	Simple	N/A	N/A	Social activist
Gabriela Diaz	N/A	Woman	N/A	Amazon	Young	Against Rafael Correa

Note: N/A = Not available

experiences (Celis et al. 2008) so it is pertinent to explore who the women who governed during 2013–2017 are from their own histories.

Table 8.3 delineates the characteristics of the five assembly members based on what was discerned from the interview data.

All interviewees replied that they consider themselves to be women, none mentioned any other gender. The indigenous and black respondents mentioned their ethnicity as essential characteristics, unlike the others. The three youngest assembly members mentioned the characteristic of being young. One of them noted being a mother as an important characteristic. The silences are also significant. To elaborate, none of them referred to their social class, nor did they mention their sexual orientation, and very little importance was given to their political party or ideology. It can be concluded that all the assembly members self-identified with different characteristics. None of them identified only with being a woman, but also as black, indigenous, mestizo, adult, young, *otavaleña* (from Otavalo), *guayaquileña* (from Guayaquil), *amazónica* (from the Amazon region), mother, etc.

Regarding their feminist identity, four of the interviewees identified themselves as feminists, while one of them did not. Not all women are feminists but the chances of women legislators considering themselves feminists as mentioned by Dolan and Ford (1995) are greater. Gabriela Díaz, who does not consider herself a feminist, and Cristina Reyes, who said she is a feminist strictly in defense of women's rights, mentioned the word 'radicalism,' pointing to a cultural discourse of how Feminism is interpreted in Ecuador.

As another important point to note, women have different conceptions and motivations to consider themselves feminists. Mae Montaño, for example, considers herself a "feminist at heart" since she had not been "academically instructed" to become a feminist. The legislator told how her personal story of being the daughter of a single mother who suffered psychological and physical abuse by her partner, motivated her feminist identity. On the other hand, Lourdes Tibán replied that she considers herself a feminist but "in her way" based "on the complementarity between women and men."

Dovi (2002) mentions that to have a relationship with constituents (i.e., the group they claim to represent and were elected to represent), women must recognize each other as belonging to a historically disadvantaged group. Indeed, the four women who identified themselves as feminists recognized that they came from a disadvantaged group because they were women. Each of them narrated different situations where they were discriminated against because they were women.

At the same time, they noted that from their position of representation they tried to represent all Ecuadorians and not only women. None responded that they exclusively represented women. It is not surprising that politicians mention that they represent all citizens. Schwindt-Bayer (2010) points out that female representatives recognize the need to represent all constituents, not just women. But do their identities influence their activities as legislators? The following section will describe their work in this respect and analyze the relationship between the descriptive and substantive representations of the 2013–2017 assembly members.

4.3   *Substantive Representation*

Substantive representation, as mentioned above, is 'action for' Schwindt-Bayer (2010); these are actions that are performed in the name of representation. Two elements were used as the basis to analyze this dimension, which Schwindt-Bayer (2010) provides in her framework: "An Integrated Model of Women's Representation" (p. 6–32).

4.3.1   Creating Policy: initiatives of Law

In the period 2013–2017, the five assembly members presented several bills. It is important to inquire what intentions or motivations the legislators had to present these bills so as to know how they represented Ecuadorians politically. In the following matrix, a summary of their reasons or intentions is presented based on what was discerned from the interview data in conjunction with Bacchi's (1999) discourse analysis model.

TABLE 8.4   Motivations of law initiatives

Name	Laws Presented	Main motivation
Lourdes Tibán	Reform of the Organic Code of Territorial Organization, Autonomy and Decentralization (*Código Orgánico de Organización Territorial, Autonomía y Descentralización, COOTAD*).	To protect small landowners by distinguishing them from large landowners. It mentions the traditional practice of rural people inheriting small pieces of land to build small houses.
	Reform of the Organic Law on Land Transport, Traffic, and Road Safety (*Ley Orgánica de Transporte Terrestre, Tráfico y Seguridad Vial*).	Provide a transportation solution to indigenous communities.
	Law on Intercultural Practice for Humanized Childbirth in the National Health System (*Ley de Práctica Intercultural para el Parto Humanizado en el Sistema Nacional de Salud*).	Promote ancestral knowledge including the indigenous worldview of complementarity between men and women and the community. It is based on her personal experiences vis-à-vis giving birth to her three children.
	Reform to the Organic Law of the Legislative Function (*Ley Orgánica de la Función Legislativa*).	Improve the legislative debate.
	Labor Code Reform (*Código del Trabajo*).	Promote a special retirement outcome for women. Change self-employment to a special regime.
Gabriela Rivadeneira	Organic Law for the Use of Cannabis for Medical and Therapeutic Purposes (*Ley Orgánica para el Uso del Cannabis con Fines Médicos y Terapéuticos*).	Attend the request of a group of young people. Attend to a health problem.
	Reform to the Organic Law of the Legislative Function (*Ley Orgánica de la Función Legislativa*).	Resolve legislative procedures as President of the Assembly.
	Organic Law of Humanized Childbirth (*Ley Orgánica de Parto Humanizado*).	Promote women's reproductive rights and promote childbirth practices that she observed in Otavalo.
	Organic Law for the Strengthening of Popular Consultation and Political Participation (*Ley Orgánica para el Fortalecimiento de la Consulta Popular y la Participación Política*).	Harmonize laws as President of the National Assembly.

TABLE 8.4   Motivations of law initiatives (*cont.*)

Name	Laws Presented	Main motivation
	Organic Law on the Protection of Property Rights and Privacy of Personal Data (*Ley Orgánica sobre la Protección de los Derechos de Propiedad y Privacidad de Datos Personales*).	Protect citizens' information.
Mae Montaño	Organic Law for the Defense of Urban Entrepreneurs (*Ley Orgánica para la Defensa de los Emprendedores Urbanos*).	Protect workers in the informal sector who are vulnerable to harassment by the police. She mentions her personal experience whereby her mother as a single parent used to sell food on the streets informally.
	Reform to the Organic Law of the Legislative Function (*Ley Orgánica de la Función Legislativa*).	Improve the legislative debate.
	Organic Law for the Promotion of Entrepreneurship (*Ley Orgánica para la Promoción del Emprendimiento*).	Addressing the social problem of unemployment, especially regarding women. In her interview she said, "I believe that we are obligated from the Assembly to generate rights that are useful for the people and the law tries to give facilities to the entrepreneur. We cannot have a society where the young population is unemployed, where women heads of household have to become informal, where unemployed men become informal, where the Afro-Ecuadorian population is among the poorest in the indigenous country, etc. So, what we want with this is to push entrepreneurship and make life easier for the Ecuadorian, the Ecuadorian entrepreneur to generate their own resources, so that they does not depend on the state, on subsidies." She mentions women and the Afro-Ecuadorian population.
	Reform to the Communication Law (*Ley de Comunicación*).	Control the 2013–2017 government for abuses of freedom of expression.

TABLE 8.4   Motivations of law initiatives (*cont.*)

Name	Laws Presented	Main motivation
Cristina Reyes	Reform to the Organic Law of the Legislative Function (*Ley Orgánica de la Función Legislativa*).	Improve certain legislative procedures.
	Law for the Promotion of Juvenile Entrepreneurship (*Ley para la Promoción de Emprendimiento Juvenil*).	Encourage young people as productive engines. She mentions that her intention with this law was "to benefit the young people."
	Reform of the Seventh Transitional Provision of the Organic Law of Public Electricity Service (*Ley Orgánica del Servicio Público de Energía Eléctrica*).	Based on a meeting with firefighters in Guayaquil.
	Law on the reform of the Labor Code (*Código del Trabajo*).	Take care of retired people's requests.
	Reform of the Organic Law on Citizen Participation and Social Control (*Ley Orgánica de Participación Ciudadana y Control Social*).	Encourage volunteering, especially among young people.
	Reform of the Social Security Law (*Ley de Seguridad Social*).	Control the 2013–2017 government so that it does not unduly use Social Security funds.
Gabriela Diaz	Reform to the Organic Law of the Legislative Function (*Ley Orgánica de la Función Legislativa*).	Improve the legislative debate.
	Reform of the Higher Education Organic Law (*Ley Orgánica de Educación Superior*).	Solve problems concerning the post-compulsory education of young people. She mentions as an example that the young people of Pastaza must migrate to other provinces to study at university.
	Student Technological Law (*Ley Tecnológica Estudiantil*).	Supporting young people to access technology and thus promote better education.
	Reform to the Tourism Law and the Civil Aviation Law (*Ley de Turismo* and *Ley de Aviación Civil*).	Controlling airfare prices. She mentions the Amazon and Galapagos.

As can be observed in Table 8.4, three assembly members (Rivadeneira, Tibán, and Montaño) mentioned women as a beneficiary group in their bills. For example, the Law of Humanized Childbirth focused on women. Likewise, the youth were a group noted in the motivations of three assembly members: Cristina Reyes, Gabriela Rivadeneira, and Gabriela Díaz. The latter focused two of their three laws on young people. For her part, Tibán presented laws to address problems of indigenous populations. In the same way, Mae Montaño mentions the Afro-Ecuadorian population. Within the motivations for introducing policy initiatives, one can also find personal experiences such as childbirth mentioned by Lourdes Tibán or being the daughter of a single mother by Mae Montaño. Ideology also plays an important role, especially for women from right-wing parties such as Montaño and Reyes.

4.3.2   Work in the Territory

Although policy-making is considered "the most important part of a legislator's job, representatives also build relationships with constituents in their electoral districts. It is through their interaction with constituents that they learn what issues and problems are most important to citizens" (Schwindt-Bayer 2010: 153). As a result, questions related to work outside the office (such as their meetings and local visits) were asked to the five selected female assembly members.

The five legislators responded that the meetings they held were with all kinds of citizens. Expressly, Mae Montaño and Lourdes Tibán indicated that the doors of their offices were open to all kinds of citizens not specifically to women. In the interview, Tibán noted that Parliament should represent all Ecuadorians, not just indigenous people or just women.

In the same way, all the assembly members responded that they endeavored to travel all over Ecuador, but there were places to which they gave particular importance. For example, Cristina Reyes emphasized Guayaquil. In the same way, Gabriela Diaz showed her preference for the Pastaza work district. Montaño also mentioned the province of Esmeraldas. In other words, the provinces from which they hail receive particular attention.

4.4   *Descriptive-Substantive Representation Relationship*

What is the relationship between the descriptive and substantive representations of the five women? The present case shows that there is a strong relationship in this respect for the five female Assembly members in the Parliament of Ecuador 2013–2017. Figure 8.2 below shows the relationship between women's identities and their actions in the legislature.

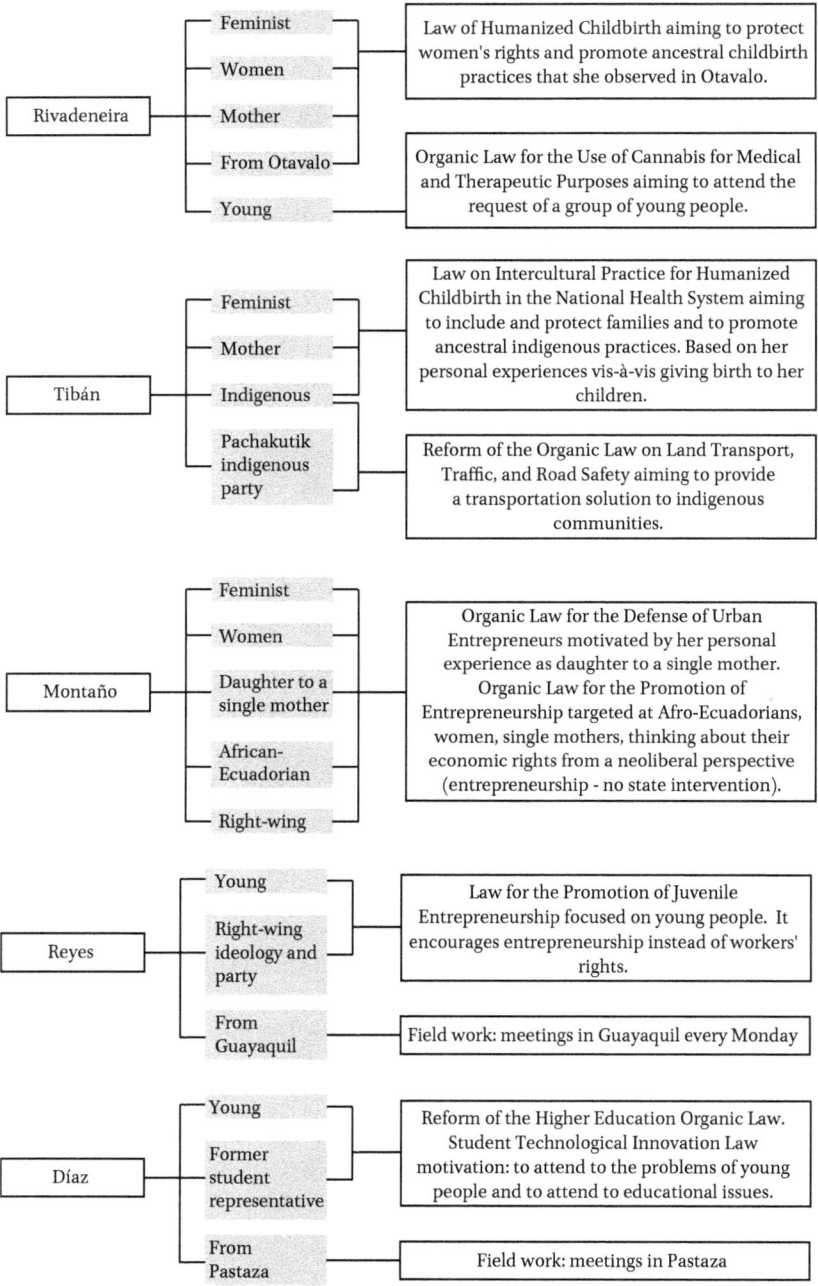

FIGURE 8.2 Identities-laws

As can be seen in Figure 8.2, the five women acted in accordance with their identities. Thus, the present case supports the assertion of Dolan and Ford (1995) and Tremblay and Pelletier (2001) that women with feminist identities promote a pro-women agenda. This case shows that the assembly members who responded with a feminist identity in the interviews presented women in their motivations of laws and, by contrast, the legislator who did not self-identify as feminist instead emphasized other motivations. For example, Gabriela Rivadeneira, who emphasized her strong feminist identity, introduced a particular law to address women's rights.

However, sharing a feminist identity does not mean sharing the same vision when legislating; there are other elements that can co-determine this vision. For example, Lourdes Tibán and Gabriela Rivadeneira (both with a feminist identity) presented the same issue of law on 'humanized childbirth,' but there were evident differences in their motivations. Rivadeneira saw women as the main beneficiaries of the law, while Tibán considered women but also family and community as beneficiaries. The latter mentions that childbirth should be seen as a community act in the complementarity between men and women, from an indigenous worldview. On the other hand, Rivadeneira defined childbirth as a decision solely for women. In addition, Tibán referred to indigenous practices and the birth of her three children while Rivadeneira referred to practices she learned about in Otavalo.

In addition, members of marginalized groups such as Afro-descendants and indigenous women make their difference in the legislature by serving minorities. Melanie M. Hughes (2013) argues that "members of marginalized groups in visible positions of power may have broad societal effects" (p. 23). Mae Montaño, who considers herself a feminist at heart and was motivated to be a feminist by her mother's experiences, also presented motivations for policy initiatives based on her life history. The reason she wanted to protect urban and informal entrepreneurs was based on the fact that her mother, as a single parent, used to sell products on the streets, and she mentioned the Afro-Ecuadorian people several times. In the same way, Lourdes Tibán made her work visible to indigenous struggles, but not exclusively.

Age is also relevant: the three youngest female legislators presented laws to address actions in favor of 'young people' such as the law for young entrepreneurs, laws related to education, and laws related to the legalization of Cannabis. Gabriela Diaz emphasizes several times that the youth were the main group she tried to attend to; she was the youngest woman in the National Assembly.

Also, the place where they come from was taken into account. In terms of her motivations as well as the focus of her out-of-office work, Cristina Reyes

mentioned Guayaquil, where she was born. The clearest example in this respect is attributable to Gabriela Díaz. In terms of her work and motivation for
tabling policy interventions, she mentioned the Amazon several times, particularly the province of Pastaza where she comes from.

Not all interviewees stressed their ideological position or political party, but
almost all act according to their political perspective. Mae Montaño, for example, in presenting the Organic Law in Defense of Entrepreneurship expresses her right-wing position: "of no State intervention in the economy even in
unemployment." At the same time, Cristina Reyes, of a right-wing party and
ideology, presents the Law of Entrepreneurship and Reform to the Law of
Communication, the latter in favor of press freedom.

Leslie Schwind-Bayer raised the question of whether female legislators
represent women and, if not, who they represent (Schwindt-Bayer 2010).
Through the present case it can be observed that none of the women affirmed or acted exclusively to represent women or to do so in a special way,
but rather to represent different citizens. Their actions were based on the intersectionality of identity: being a woman, belonging to a certain ethnicity,
being a certain age, having a particular ideology, personal experiences, and
coming from a particular geographical area, whether or not she has a feminist
identity.

5   Conclusions

In response to the question as to whether the women legislators of the National Assembly 2013–2017 represented politically according to their gender or
not, the answer is yes and no. Several factors influenced their representation, including the political context, the country's rules/institutions and their
identity.

With respect to electoral norms, the present case study corroborates that
women's quotas in Ecuador are an essential tool for the inclusion of women in
the legislature, being a non-unique but principal factor explaining the increased number of women in the National Assembly. Assembly members interviewed assert that women's quotas are still necessary in women's political
representation. However, their efficacy remains to be reviewed in the political
arena, as despite their intention to achieve parity, less than 50 per cent of
the seats in the Ecuadorian legislature are occupied by women. Nevertheless, although parity remains to be achieved, due notice should be made of the
fact that the current electoral rules have promoted the inclusion of women
from different provinces of the country. Having yet to discuss new inclusion

mechanisms, the legislators interviewed propose to include quotas in the results, including youth quotas, as well as initiatives to promote political training
for women.

In terms of the descriptive dimension, the five assembly members interviewed identified themselves as women, however, it was not the only personal
characteristic they mentioned. The identities of the interviewees can be conceived as a complex skeleton between their feminist identity, gender, race, age,
geographical origin, ideology, and personal experiences. You cannot separate
being a woman from being indigenous or young. There is no hierarchy between
personal characteristics; these different identities operate together and are different in each person. Four of the five female legislators considered themselves
feminists, agreeing that women are more likely to consider themselves feminists, although they do not conceive Feminism in the same way. This research
shows how conceptions and reasons for being feminists are understood in different ways. Women are a heterogeneous category and should be addressed in
political representation from that perspective.

Moving on to the relationship between descriptive and substantive representations, the empirical data garnered from the interviews reveal that the
identities and personal experiences of representatives are important in the
way they legislate. Their motivations for introducing particular policy initiatives were largely based on their personal identities, their personal experiences, as well as their work in their constituencies. Considering that their identities are complex, multifaceted, diverse, and interconnected, their legislative
work was varied. An excellent example of this is how Lourdes Tibán, who
claims to represent all Ecuadorians, presented her personal experiences of being a mother as one of her policy motivations, but also being a woman, and
being indigenous, were motivators for her in this respect. Their identities cannot be separated and defined exclusively in terms of being women and, therefore, their work in the National Assembly cannot respond to a single face of
their identity either.

With regard to the framework for women's political representation proposed by Schwindt-Bayer (2010), two important elements can be highlighted.
First, Schwindt-Bayer focuses her analysis on the differences between women
and men in legislatures, but neglects to present the differences between wom-
en legislators themselves. As this research shows, women are not a homogeneous category. Gender identity may not be the only reason for representing in
a particular way; it may be related to other factors such as race, age, personal
experiences, and feminist identity. In the future, political scientists studying the representation of women should consider merging the Schwindt-
Bayer framework with an intersectional perspective, which will render it

possible to observe all women in a way which is more reflective of their empirical realities.

Second, it is important to emphasize that political representation cannot be appreciated from a single perspective. The different dimensions proposed by Hanna Pitkin and used by Leslie Schwindt-Bayer are recommendable since political representation is interconnected between formal, descriptive, and substantive considerations. For example, the case of women's political representation in Ecuador's Parliament 2013–2017 shows how formal representation through electoral rules had positive effects on women's participation in Ecuador. Similarly, who these legislators are (descriptive representation) affects their actions (of substantive representation). Therefore, for completeness, formal, substantive, and descriptive dimensions need to be acknowledged and incorporated pursuant of a meaningful model of representation.

The intersectional analysis helped to understand and examine the complexity of the five female legislators, understanding that several elements come together in their representation. The intersection has the necessary ingredients for a robust feminist theory, since it fosters complexity. Further research is needed to explore how the Ecuadorian parliament is composed, preferably through intersectoral lenses, to observe which groups in Ecuadorian society are being ignored or excluded. The number of women in the National Assembly is not sufficient to analyze women's political participation. Similarly, quotas that have been widely discussed should go beyond the number of women in office; could the solution be to include an intersectoral debate on them in parliament?

References

Adams, J. (2014). *Women and the Vote. A world history.* Oxford University Press.

Alcoff, L.M. (2005). *Visible identities: Race, gender, and the self.* Oxford University Press.

Código de la Democracia. (2009). http://www.lexis.com.ec/wp-content/uploads/2018/07/LI-LEY-ORGANICA-ELECTORAL-CODIGO-DE-LA-DEMOCRACIA.pdf.

Bacchi, C.L. (1999). *Women, policy and politics: The construction of policy problems.* Sage.

Burbano de Lara, F. (2004). "El impacto de la cuota en los imaginarios masculinos de la política." *Reflexiones Sobre Mujer y Política: Memoria Del Seminario Nacional "Los Cambios Políticos En El Ecuador: Perspectivas y Retos Para Las Mujeres,"* p. 89.

Celis, K., and Childs, S. (2012). "The substantive representation of women: What to do with conservative claims?" *Political Studies* 60(1): 213–225. https://doi.org/10.1111/j.1467-9248.2011.00904.x.

Celis, K., Childs, S., Kantola, J., and Krook, M.L. (2008). "Rethinking women's substantive representation." *Representation* 44(2): 99–110. https://doi.org/10.1080/0034489 0802079573.

Childs, S. (2008). *Women and British party politics: Descriptive, substantive and symbolic representation.* Routledge.

CNE. (2015). *Indicadores de Participación Política de la Mujer Ecuatoriana. En las elecciones 2002–2014.* Dirección Nacional de Estadística Institucional y Electoral. http://cne.gob.ec/documents/Estadisticas/Investigaciones/participacinmujer2002–2014 feb-2015.pdf.

Collins, P.H., and Bilge, S. (2016). *Intersectionality.* John Wiley & Sons.

Crenshaw, K. (1990). "Mapping the margins: Intersectionality, identity politics, and violence against women of color." *Stanford Law Review* 43: 1241–1299. https://doi .org/10.2307/1229039.

Dolan, K., and Ford, L.E. (1995). "Women in the state legislatures: Feminist identity and legislative behaviors." *American Politics Quarterly* 23(1): 96–108. https://doi.org/10.11 77/1532673X9502300105.

Dovi, S. (2002). "Preferable descriptive representatives: Will just any woman, black, or Latino do?" *American Political Science Review* 96(4): 729–743. https://www.jstor.org/ stable/3117507?seq=1.

Hobbes, T. (1909). *Hobbes's Leviathan. Ed. WG Posgon Smith.* London: Oxford University Press.

Htun, M. (2004). "Is gender like ethnicity? The political representation of identity groups." *Perspectives on Politics* 3: 439–458. https://www.jstor.org/stable/3688807.

Htun, M. (2012). *Desventaja interseccional e inclusión política: cómo lograr que un mayor número de mujeres afrodescencientes ocupe cargos de elección popular en América Latina.* BID.

Hughes, M.M. (2013). "Diversity in national legislatures around the world." *Sociology Compass* 7(1): 23–33. https://doi.org/10.1111/soc4.12010.

Kittilson, M.C. (2005). "In support of gender quotas: Setting new standards, bringing visible gains." *Politics & Gender* 1(4): 638–645. https://doi.org/10.1017/S1743923X0523 0192.

Krook, M.L. (2008). "Quota laws for women in politics: Implications for feminist practice." *Social Politics* 15(3): 345–368. https://doi.org/10.1093/sp/jxn014.

Kurebwa, J. (2015). "A review of Hanna Pitkin's (1967) conception of women's political representation." *International Journal of Scientific and Research Publications* 5(11): 50–60. http://www.ijsrp.org/research-paper-1115/ijsrp-p4710.pdf.

Mackay, F. (2008). " 'Thick' conceptions of substantive representation: Women, gender and political institutions." *Representation* 44(2): 125–139. https://doi.org/10.1080/ 0034489080207960.

Mansbridge, J. (2005). "Quota problems: Combating the dangers of essentialism." *Politics & Gender* 1(4): 622–638. https://doi.org/10.1017/S1743923X05220196.

Marsh, M., and Wessels, B. (1997). "Territorial representation." *European Journal of Political Research* 32(2): 227–241. https://doi.org/10.1111/ajps.12403.

Mill, J.S. (2004). *Considerations of Representative Government 1861*. http://www.guten berg.org.

National Geographic. (2019). *Fechas clave en la historia para conseguir el voto femenino* (Issue January 20th, 2019). National Geographic España. https://www.national geographic.com.es/historia/grandes-reportajes/fechas-clave-historia-para -conseguir-voto-femenino_12300/1.

Norris, P., and Franklin, M. (1997). "Social representation." *European Journal of Political Research* 32(2): 185–210. https://dosi.org/10.1111/1475-6765.00338.

Pitkin, H.F. (1967). *The concept of representation* (Vol. 75). Univ of California Press.

Schwindt-Bayer, L.A. (2010). *Political power and women's representation in Latin America*. Oxford University Press.

Tremblay, M., and Pelletier, R. (2001). "More women constituency party presidents: A strategy for increasing the number of women candidates in Canada?" *Party Politics* 7(2): 157–190. https://doi.org/10.1177/1354068801007002002.

UNDP. (2019). *Gender Inequality Index* (2018th ed.). http://hdr.undp.org/en/content/ gender-inequality-index-gii.

Vega, S. (2005). "La cuota electoral en Ecuador; nadando contracorriente en un horizonte esperanzador." In M. León (Ed.), *Nadando contra la corriente. Mujeres y cuotas políticas en los países andinos* (pp. 169–206). UNIFEM; UNFPA; UNIVERSIDAD NACIONAL; IEP; CIDEM; FLACSO ECUADOR.

PART 3

Rural and Indigenous Women in Ecuador

∴

CHAPTER 9

The Invisible Economy of Ecuadorian Peasant Women

Ana Valeria Recalde-Vela and Daniel Zea

1 Introduction

In various cultures throughout the history of humanity, women have held the social function of family caretaker, particularly caretaker of children. Women have also held an important role in the historical development of food (León 2007). But whenever we think 'who is the peasant woman?' two aspects stand-out: gender and socio-spatial location. However, this identity is also charged with various contemporary connotations associated with poverty, discrimination and other marginalized identities like indigenous identity, especially in regions of the world like Latin America. This chapter interprets the peasant woman as a socially constructed category throughout history which personifies an extremely important actor, whose crucial contributions are often forgotten within agriculture, food and agrobiodiversity, in Ecuador and throughout the world.

Peasant women are actors who, throughout history, have contributed to ecological sustainability by fostering agrobiodiversity and food cultures, therefore contributing to cultural, economic, social and biological reproduction of humanity. But peasant women have been marginalized and besieged, as their economy has always existed at the margin of capitalism. The central role of women in bringing about 'discoveries and research' linked to food is a contemporary vindication from global peasant movements during the Nyéléni Forum in 2007 (León 2007). Peasant women have served this fundamental role to humanity, together with peasant men, who are of course equally important and play a complementary role. However, this chapter considers peasant women's economy as the starting point for analyzing profound agrarian, environmental and social crises, and consequently for analyzing the multiple responses from social movements, such as the struggle to achieve food sovereignty. Mainly because traditionally peasant women's economies enter into direct and more profound conflict with capitalism than men's economies, as this chapter will explain.

Within all societies, gender categories have a purpose oriented towards achieving a division of knowledge and labor that may facilitate biological and social reproduction[1] of the family, community, etc. In fact, within all societies and cultures, women possess particular knowledge about certain aspects of agriculture, biodiversity and food. Even so, they are usually also discriminated when it comes to learning and regarding the social value of the knowledge they may possess (Agrawal 1995).

FAO (1997) defines gender as follows:

> GENDER refers not to women or men per se, but to the relations between them, both perceptual and material. Gender is not determined biologically, as a result of sexual characteristics of either women or men, but is constructed socially. It is a central organizing principle of societies and often governs the processes of production and reproduction, consumption and distribution.
>
> p. 2

Whereas gender roles are defined by FAO (1997) as follows:

> GENDER ROLES are the socially ascribed roles of women and men, which vary among different societies and cultures, classes and ages, and during different periods in history. Gender-specific roles and responsibilities are often conditioned by household structure, access to resources, specific impacts of the global economy, and other locally relevant factors such as ecological conditions.
>
> p. 2

According to FAO there is a need to differentiate labor according to gender, knowledge, contributions and necessities of women and men within State policy and programs, given that both are important actors in the global production of food and in conservation and management of biodiversity (FAO 2004). Differentiation of knowledge and labor through gender in agrarian economies began to be noticed in the topic of environment and development since the 1992 Rio Earth Summit which gradually turned into a discourse about "the role of gender social relations in shaping resource use and management

---

1 Biological reproduction refers also to demographic reproduction of a population, whereas social reproduction is wider in the sense that it considers the reproduction of a society within tis cultural, economic and social aspects too.

and possibilities of sustainable development" expressed in the 2002 World Summit (Elías 2016: 2). Elías (2016) confers a different definition of gender as:

> The culturally and socially constructed differences found within the meanings, beliefs, practices associated with 'femininity' and 'masculinity' which may vary from a social context to another, but that also embodies a relationship between men and women 'created and negotiated dynamically.'
>
> p. 2

The use of the term 'sexual division of labor' has become popular throughout the years. However, if we understand the definitions of 'men' and 'women' from the perspective of 'gender' and not biological aspects, 'sexual division of labor' is flawed. Therefore, we use 'gender division of labor.' Within agrarian studies, gender is analyzed by framing the 'Agrarian Question of Gender,' one of the many contemporary agrarian questions which considers how social gender relations are shaped through accumulation, production and rural politics, but also vice versa; how rural accumulation, production and politics are configured through social relations of gender (Akram-Lodhi and Kay 2010). The Agrarian Question of Gender contests how gender dynamics are negotiated within certain rural settings, that either allow or hinder the continuity of peasant economies.

Generally, and in various societies, gender division of labor consists in the productive work (meaning paid labor) and reproductive work (unpaid labor) which are usually carried out by men and women respectively. Friedrich Engels (1972) understood social reproduction of labor[2] as the production of human beings, 'propagation of the species,' or labor which allows households and communities to 'send productive members into the world' (Collins 2014) also called 'care economy' by feminist economists. This shows that a significant chunk of household labor is not calculated as it consists of unpaid work, but if it were included in economic measures, the GDP would increase significantly. In the case of peasant women, as important as their role is in the production of food, in adding value to food, and as a whole to rural economies, it is often invisible (FAO 2009). The dichotomy between productive and reproductive economies, key to the capitalist paradigm, is in fact artificial because both types of

---

2   We must distinguish between social reproduction used in a broader manner which includes reproduction of social relationships, culture, class, economy, technology, etc. Whereas social reproduction of labor refers to the 'care economy' within the domestic world geared towards the reproduction of labor in the service of capitalism.

labor require work, effort and time. The difference is that productive work holds an elevated social value as it is waged and results in purchasing power, whereas reproductive work does not. For instance, Ecuador's GDP does not take into account labor fulfilled by women in family gardens,[3] and while the agricultural sector represented 13.2 per cent of the GDP in 2010 (Carrión and Herrera 2012), it could have been higher due to this shortcoming in the construction of indicators.

To make sense of gender division of labor, the Agrarian Question of Gender must be approached from the complexity of rural social relations, which tend to be even more conservative than in urban settings. This heightened conservativism often results in the generalized over exploitation of women in rural production and accumulation processes. In Ecuador, rural women constitute almost 50% of the total rural population, however, in 2006 they received only 21.33% of the total rural income (León 2007). Furthermore, they work more hours on average than men, but suffer a higher rate of underemployment and have less access to resources such as land, as they are owners of only 12.71% of all agricultural land in Ecuador (FIAN Ecuador 2018). Finally, peasant women have less access to resources such as credit, water and seeds (Leon 2017).

This chapter explores how modes of rural production and accumulation change, from the perspective of gender dynamics, as the capitalist frontier expands in the countryside. Despite the social and economic value that women deliver in terms of nutrition, conservation of biodiversity, food security and food sovereignty, the Ecuadorian State embarked on an exclusionary project of agrarian capitalist expansion by applying certain changes in the production matrix that pushes peasant women's economies back. State policies that accompanied this change have eroded peasant women's economies because they incentivize the productivist model which is centered exclusively on producing commodities. Simultaneously, the State has left unprotected an important sector by not providing differentiated incentives geared towards food sovereignty, where peasant women's economies could have more opportunities of survival together with family agriculture.

2   Theoretical Framework

This research uses the theoretical framework proposed by Collins (2014) who offers a feminist perspective 'to open up the black box of the commodity.'

---

3   Family gardens are equivalents to a family orchard or diversified plots.

Collins questions the fact that almost all research regarding commodity chains is dominated by neoclassical economic theory from a positivist perspective and therefore she suggests a critical approach to analyzing commodity chains (Collins 2014). She bases her analysis on Marx's definition of commodities as 'containers of hidden relationships' that are less apparent when production is moved to the Third World, and notes that "examining the materiality of their production and circulation [...] allows us to recover some of what neoclassical economics makes us forget: living, breathing, gendered, and raced bodies working under social relations that exploit them" (Collins 2014: 27).

One of the black boxes that Collins (2014) opens is the subsidy of reproductive labor traditionally carried out by women, which not only includes the care economy but also the daily work of consumption, cooking, cleaning, paying bills, talking to teachers and doctors, among other necessary social transactions for household function, beyond other activities to supplement household income or reduce costs during hard times. Moreover, this invisible and undervalued economy serves for the "reproduction of capitalist workers, allowing employers to lower wage costs by indirectly exploiting the labor of women in the home." Therefore, household production becomes a type of "capitalist 'reproduction' " in the service of capital (Collins 2014: 34).

On the one hand, some argue that reproductive work "operates outside the discipline of capitalist institutions and implements its own definitions of quality and value" (Collins 2014: 34) while others suggest that it is not only foreign but also "immune to the direct domination of capital" or that it conserves a degree of autonomy (p. 35). However, we argue that in the case of peasant women's economies, the subsidy that they provide with their reproductive work is not all that flexible or immune to capitalism. An immediate argument that supports this is that an important element within reproductive work of peasant women is traditionally embodied in a physical space (resource and territory), the family gardens, where she produces a significant portion of household food and agrobiodiversity. Peasant women's work is valuable not only for the household or immediate community, but also for the environment, agrobiodiversity, food sovereignty and therefore for the world.

In regions as South Asia and sub-Saharan Africa women play a key role in the traditional seed systems for growing their crops. In these cases, up to 90% of the planting material used in smallholder agriculture is "seed and germ plasm produced, selected and saved by women, and it is predominantly women who grow and preserve underutilized species which local communities use to supplement their diets" (De Schutter 2009: 15–16). There are intellectual and activist currents like essentialist ecofeminists (Shiva 1988) who argue that women are closer to nature because they are mothers and caretakers. However, other ecological feminist schools of thought (Agarwal 1998; Warren 1966) and constructivist Ecofeminism (Puleo 2015; Warren 1966), criticizes this stance and argues that this is also a historical social construction that equates to a gender division of labor. Furthermore, it is important to recognize that peasant men have had an important role too in the conservation and reproduction of agrobiodiversity and world food sovereignty.

Notwithstanding, women supply between 60 and 80% of food production in the poorest countries and around 50% on a world scale (FAO 2018; León 2007). They also provide 43% of total agricultural labor (FAO 2018). During the Women's Forum, summoned by the World March of Women, which took place on the eve of Nyéleni World Forum, rural and peasant women's organizations from all over the world reclaimed the importance of their economy. Since the invention of agriculture they have experimented, hybridized seeds, selected edible and non-edible food. They have also preserved foods and invented and refined diets, cuisine (León 2007). In Latin America, women work effectively within the set of activities of family agriculture: preparing the soil, cultivating, harvesting, raising animals, among others (including the transformation of products and handcrafting). However, given their reduced social status, all other activities are considered an extension of their role as wife and mother (Siliprandi 2015).

During an interview with Stalin Herrera, an expert in agrarian studies from the Institute of Ecuadorian Studies (IEE) he revealed that, in general, peasant women's economies in Ecuador are linked to the 'sphere of diversity' in their practices and knowledge. Herrera (December 14, 2018) argues that:

> Women's economies are linked to the economy of care and to productive diversity (because they take care of family gardens). Their practices and roles within family agriculture are linked to certain elements that a family farm depends on for agrobiodiversity. For instance, who select seeds, thresh them, etc., are regularly women. The family garden where the productive diversity for consumption exists, and the diversity of medicinal, ornamental plants, or plants that help care for the farm, are all in the hands of women, in addition to the care of animals.

Indeed, women manage plots that are on average between a third and 50% smaller than the regular ones (FAO 2011a). However, in general they manage more diversity within their economies than their male counterparts who usually focus their labor towards productive, remunerated and formal labor contracts under vertical integration schemes. Nevertheless, there is a lot of variation regarding the different types of peasant family economies or family farmer economies, and therefore also regarding the different possible combinations in terms of gender division of labor. Gender division of labor can vary among regions and peoples in Ecuador. Here, each family composes their household economic strategy in a manner that is complementary, coordinated with men's individual strategies (S. Herrera, personal communication, December 14, 2018).

This chapter does not seek to describe some or all forms of local level peasant household organization. Instead, it attempts to depict a national level image by providing general strokes regarding peasant women's economies with respect to the conflict generated by State agrarian policy which puts them in severe disadvantage.

3   Methodology

The methodology used here consists of the theoretical framework proposed by Collins (2014), combined with the use of relevant literature and data extracted through personal interviews. The purpose of using this methodology is to open up commodities' 'black box' which is constructed through the process of vertical integration of peasant family farmer economies, and to reveal the effects of State agrarian policy (which is exclusively directed towards productivist commodity export economy) on peasant women's economies.

4   Results and Analysis

4.1   *Peasant Family Economy and Its Social Reproduction*
Vertical integration (or variations such as contract farming) became widespread in Ecuador since the nineties, as a mechanism used by agrarian capitalism to further the productivist model promoted since the seventies which sought to break pre-capitalist relations of production (Herrera 2009). Vertical integration is and has been a mechanism through which agrarian capitalism is able to control resources such as land, water and soil fertility fostered by peasants through generations. Instead of buying lands and hiring laborers, companies hire peasant families who own the land and resources themselves, who then produce industrial foods that companies can buy, therefore shifting externalities inherent to the agro-industrial model to the peasantry. Vertical integration, in many cases occurs through contracts where the industry or company stipulates which products, their quality, quantity, when and even how they must be produced using certain technologies (FAO 2013a). Usually, the adoption

of technologies is required within the contract, which companies themselves sell like kits that include seeds and pesticides. In turn, this creates dependency on these technologies for peasant farmers once they have been adopted. Peasants thus become integrated into a global chain of commodity production, but usually at the expense of the diversity of family farms or plots/gardens, given that the magnitude of the investment and dependency that this change in production model catalyzes, leaves no alternative but to continue down the path of monoculture production.

The relationship between the expansion of the capitalist frontier vis-à-vis non-capitalist forms of production like the peasant economy, has been studied since the beginning of the XX century in Russia. Lenin (1982) argued that because peasants are subjugated to commodity markets, they tend to lose their lands with the expansion of capitalism in the countryside. Lands then become concentrated in the hands of a few capitalist farmers and part of the peasantry is forced to join the proletariat. The surviving peasantry must shift towards new configurations of rural inhabitants in differentiated social classes as a result of the inevitable process of depeasantization (Lenin 1982). Now, there is another thesis carried forward during the same time in Russia belonging to Chayanov and other rural social theorists who criticized Lenin's posture regarding polarizing social differentiation or his so-called classical dualism thesis (Van Der Ploeg 2007). Chayanov, the father of family farming, argued that the differentiation of the peasantry is rather demographic and cyclical, and it is able to persist under conditions where a capitalist farmer would not survive because peasant households are based on subsistence and self-exploitation during difficult times (less food and more work hours) (Thorner 1988). Lastly, the survival of peasant household depends on family labor, therefore on the consumer-laborer and consumer-non laborer ratios (cyclical and demographic) within the home (Thorner 1988).

For the International Year of Family Farming 2014, the FAO (2013) defined it as:

> [A] means of organizing agricultural, forestry, fisheries, pastoral and aquaculture production which is managed and operated by a family and predominantly reliant on family labor, including both women's and men's. The family and the farm are linked, co-evolve and combine economic, environmental, reproductive, social and cultural functions.
>
> p. 2

In Latin America, the discussion around family farming and peasant economies is several decades old and is adopting operative dimensions with the formulation of public policy in several countries, directed towards family farming in 'symbiosis' with academic debates (Martínez 2013). These debates are centered in the survival of peasant economies but also around possible ways to insert them into markets without necessarily de-structuring them (Martínez 2013). In Ecuador, agriculture is one of the main sources of employment and income for rural populations—which represents 30% of the country's population. However, this segment of the population has experienced noticeable sociodemographic changes which depict the progressive loss of agriculture's importance and, for the same reason, of traditional peasant employment (Martínez 2013).

Revising this debate through the Agrarian Question of Gender helps us understand with further detail the profound value that the invisible economy of peasant women has within family farming and what threatens it. The expansion of agrarian capitalism in its more contemporary forms, such as contract farming, results in that the State may not acknowledge families who are vertically integrated as family farmers. In this process the State does not have to acknowledge the importance of women in agriculture and can then classify these family production nuclei as small-scale agro-industrial producers. This renders women's economy even more invaluable and invisible, because by making sense of small-scale industrial production, the State considers the productivist aspect exclusively. Thus, danger of displacing women here is even greater as data shows that peasant family farming has a higher percentage of women's participation at 25%, while medium-scale agriculture admits 23% and commercial agriculture includes only 14% women (FIAN Ecuador 2018).

Generally, there may be various typologies of family farming where peasant-family economic units make use of various strategies and combinations of 'pre-capitalist' (subsistence) economies and 'capitalist' (productivist) economies. Meillassoux (1975) argued that the 'domestic community,' as is the peasant woman's economy, is preserved, exploited and is used by capital. Meaning that it represents a 'subsidy' (Collins 2014) that is not endogenous to capitalism (belongs to a pre-capitalist mode of production) and helps producing a surplus that can be appropriated allowing capital to expand. In Ecuador, this subsidy is observed through data from a national survey on the use of time 'Encuesta Específica del Uso del Tiempo' (EUT 2012) which shows that women on average allocate "four times more time in non-paid labor than men" and in rural areas they work on average 25:33 hours per week more than men (FIAN Ecuador 2018). However, they suffer more underemployment in rural areas (84%) compared to men (69%) and own only 12.71% of land on average (FIAN Ecuador 2018).

Meillassoux also argued that, in some capitalist countries, this care-economy subsidy is secured by the State through social welfare services, but in developing countries families depend on pre-capitalist economies for the reproduction of labor—meaning in the traditionally non-productivist economy of women (O'Laughlin 1977). When we think of Ecuador's agro-export economy geared towards supplying countries in the Global North with products like cocoa, banana, oil palm, etc., what happens is that capital extracts value enriching markets in the Global North by appropriating the subsidy provided by peasant women in the Global South. However, it is necessary to clarify that peasant women's labor is not infinitely illimited and elastic (Pacheco 2010) and that a large part of women's economies have spatial limitations (the garden or plot). And as long as the agro-export industrial model that uses monocultures expands, there is less space in peasant territories for peasant women's economies. As Herrera (December 14, 2018) explained in the above-mentioned interview:

> Peasant women are the ones who are constantly negotiating with the agro-industrial model of production. So, as long as vertical integration value chains advance and subordinate small producers to commodity chains like maize, cocoa, palm, sugar cane, or whatever, the farm tends to reduce the space for production and reproduction of women's economies.

The spheres of production of biodiversity and food sovereignty therefore have been reduced in a process incentivized by the State for over a decade now. Thus, in terms of development and Good Living, it is clear that agrarian policies which are non-differentiated and do not take into account gender dynamics deepen unequal relations of power between men and women in the countryside as peasant women lose their economies, their source of production.

4.2 The Economy of the Peasant Woman and the Ecuadorian State

Historically, Ecuador has been a producer of commodities. According to the Observatory of Economic Complexity (OEC 2018), in 2017 the most exported five non-petroleum products were banana, flowers, crustaceans, cocoa and tuna. Out of these products the first four are commodities while tuna is semi-processed. Like the majority of countries in the region, Ecuador fits in the periphery of the world economic order which supplies the global north with raw materials. Acosta (2016) explains that Ecuador's mode of production is a 'primary export capitalism' up to this day, given that an extractivist mode of accumulation was imposed since colonial times in function of the demand from emerging capitalist centers in the West.

> Some regions were specialized in the extraction and production of commodities, while others assumed the role of manufacturers, often using

the natural resources from impoverished countries. The result of this process is the immovable effectiveness of the primary accumulation exporters where extractivism is one of its manifestations.
    ACOSTA 2016: 3 (translated by the authors)

This mode of extraction and production of resources, imposed since the colonial times, is still present in Ecuador and it is reflected in the country's industrial and economic development programs. The majority of these programs lack a social perspective in that they poorly respond to local socio-economic needs and are mainly directed to maximizing productivity. The agricultural sector is not an exception.

For a decade, Rafael Correa's government (2007–2017), embarked on a 'change in the productive matrix' directed towards improved efficiency and quality (Bravo 2016). Some of its main objectives were to move beyond the commodity export model and broaden the scope of processed and semi-processed products for export in international markets. Nevertheless, Bravo (2016) argues that the new productive matrix consisted on several strategies for homogenizing the country's production, citing the case of livestock production. According to the same author, that meant a 'death sentence' for peasant production. In this context, next section will analyze how the change in the productive matrix, together with legislation and policies in place have impacted peasant women's economies.

4.3   Policies and Laws Directed Towards the Agricultural Sector

Government planning geared towards inducing a change in the productive matrix nevertheless respond to current demands from the international markets which position Ecuador as a periphery, thus demanding still mostly commodities. Herrera (December 14, 2018) explains that the National Planification and Development Secretariat (SENPLADES) imposed specific Territorial Development Plans which established strategic zones within the National Development Plans for 2009–2013 and 2014–2017. Here, they defined five areas for productive development in agriculture and allocated the mass production of commodities (monocultures) in certain provinces. This resulted in a material reduction in the diversity of production which is directly linked to women's economies. The main commodities destined for monoculture expansion include bananas, maize, cocoa, sugar cane and oil palm.

Furthermore, there are currently no programs directed specifically towards the development of peasant women's economies and funding for projects related to food sovereignty barely exists. This section analyses the project 'Ecuadorian Agricultural Policy—Towards a Sustainable Rural Territorial

Development 2015–2025' which was elaborated by the Ministry of Agriculture and Livestock (MAG). This program evaluated the state of agriculture presenting solutions to increase agroindustrial productivity. It also analyzes, from a social perspective, that most peasant farmers, including women, suffer from low levels of education and lack access to finance services, while recognizing their importance in economic, social and territorial development of the agricultural sector.

Agricultural policies between 2015–2025 (MAG 2014) are based on four strategic objectives:

1.   To contribute to reducing poverty and socio-economic inequality of rural inhabitants, particularly improving the social inclusion of those small and medium-scale farmers residing in the countryside.

2.   To improve the contribution of agriculture in order to guarantee the food security and food sovereignty of the Ecuadorian population (in the present and future).

3.   To enhance the contribution of agriculture in territorial development, and national economic growth with social inclusion.

4.   To support the change in the productive matrix, in terms of substituting primary and agricultural imports, diversifying export supply, and generating a primary base for agroindustrial development.

As a first observation we find that none of the objectives specifically address gender issues nor include gender as a key aspect. Regarding the first objective, its field of action only refers to how conditions should be generated for generational relief, promotion of productive chains, access to rural support services (infrastructure and roads) and improvements in the living conditions of peasant farmers (health, nutrition, education, housing, water for human consumption, basic sanitation, etc.) (MAG 2014).

The second objective, which refers to food sovereignty, does not make specific reference to incentivizing peasant women's economies, although it is usually women who guarantee a level of sovereignty in family farming. In fact, none of the objectives recognize peasant women's economies, given that no field of action which may encourage the development of family gardens is established. Nor do the objectives recognize women's central role in fostering agrobiodiversity, food security and food sovereignty. The fourth objective confirms the Ecuadorian government's tendency towards productivism, given that it reinforces the pursual to increase productivity and agroindustrial development from its primary base. This translates into the exclusive promotion of monocultures, the standardization of plantations (production models) and international conditions for trading these agrodinsutrial products. But in an attempt to change the country's productive matrix, these agricultural policies only reinforce Ecuador's position as a producer of raw materials or commodities.

One of the main criticisms to the Agricultural Policies 2015–2025 is that, although they identify and acknowledge various socio-economic deficiencies of women in agriculture, they still focus primarily on improving factors of productivity. The Inter-American Institute for Cooperation on Agriculture (IICA 2014: 11) explains that rural women constitute one of the driving forces in maintaining the economy of their territories and share responsibility in the development, stability and survival of their families. This is because they are food producers associated with family farming, and due to the role they play in the decision-making regarding the use and distribution of household income. The role of peasant women described by IICA can be found in the document 'Agricultural Policies 2015–2025.'

For the design of agrarian policies between 2015–2025, the MAG (2014) identified 16 problems within the agricultural sector. Among them are low productivity within the various forms of productive organization, a high dependence on imported capital goods, the lack of capacity to promote conditions to achieve productive diversification and creation of added value, and human talent that lacks skills and training.

The issues pointed out here are solely concentrated on increasing productivity of plantations at a national scale. Perhaps the only aspect that considers a social aspect is the recognition that the Ecuadorian peasantry has "talent that lacks skills and training." However, this denies that there is valuable ancestral knowledge that the Ecuadorian peasantry may possess as this knowledge does not align with the productivist agenda that has followed the Green Revolution. But, even more prominent is that gender inequality is explicitly excluded from these key areas of improvement, and therefore so is peasant women's struggle to maintain their economy. Thus, by marginalizing peasant women's economies from public policies, the Ministry of Agriculture ignores yet another form of increasing production at national level. FAO (2011b) explains that:

> Reducing the "gender gap" in agriculture can lead to a significant increase in production: FAO's report on 'The state of agriculture and food 2010–2011' determined that women could increase their crop yields between 20 and 30 percent if the gender gap in order to access agricultural inputs were to close. This increase could raise agricultural production in developing countries by 2.5–4 percent, which at the same time could reduce the number of people suffering from food insecurity around the world by 12–17 percent.
>
> p. 102 (translated by the authors)

The Ecuadorian government thus lacks clear guidelines to attempt to break the aforementioned dichotomy, that men are the main producers and women have reproductive and caretaker functions. These dynamics will continue to accentuate within the agricultural sector, deepening the deficiencies between genders. Therefore, this will continue to directly affect the well-being of the rural population by limiting the capacity of peasant women to improve their economy—an economy which deeply contributes to agroecological sustainability, agrobiodiversity, food security and nutrition and food sovereignty in the country.

The 2015–2025 policy project presents proposals for zoning the production of commodities that require a conventional agriculture monoculture model. This project divides Ecuador's 24 provinces into seven zones. The purpose of zoning is to exploit the resources according to the conditions offered by each area, to promote the cultivation of commodities that are already dominant in the sector, as well as the most 'adequate' (taking into account soil conditions), with the purpose of increasing the productivity of each zone (MAG 2014). At the same time, it imposes the standardization of production methods and the use of agricultural inputs for the production of these commodities responding to the demands of the Global North instead of generating a policy that is suitable with the needs and reality of cultural diversity from the country itself.

In addition, two relatively new laws—the 'Organic Law on Agrobiodiversity, Seeds and Promotion of Agriculture (LOASFAS) and the 'Animal and Agriculture Health Law'—respond to the needs of countries that import the majority of Ecuadorian products. These laws tend to harmonize all norms regarding Ecuadorian sanitary and phytosanitary guidelines aligned with the conditions established by World Trade Organization (WTO) for the trade of commodities. Responding once again to conditions demanded by the Global North, Principle A of the Animal and Agriculture Health Law specifies the following:

> Harmonization: To establish phytosanitary and animal health guidelines based on common national and international standards from several countries, with the purpose of protecting people's health and life, guaranteeing food sovereignty, animal welfare or preserving plant safety and facilitating international trade.
>
> LOASFAS 2017: 2 (translated by the authors)

'Harmonizing' crop and seed production processes constitutes a direct attack against the biodiversity of peasant family gardens. Since it is women who generally run family gardens, these new regulations represent gender barriers for product access in local markets. In this way, the State indirectly discourages diversified production and promotes monocultures, directly damaging the capacity to generate resources from peasant women's economy. This capitalist onslaught (global and national) over women's economies causes physical changes to their territory and their mode of production, forcing them to shift towards being cheap labor force as a way of adapting to the same production model, the monoculture.

State policies for the agricultural sector promote a model of vertical integration of small producers into agroindustrial schemes as a way of responding to the needs of the macro plan of 'changing the productive matrix.' Consequently, these conditions force small farmers to exchange the heterogeneity and biodiversity of their territories with monocultures, forcing them to transform or reduce the space destined for gardens, which are used for the production of food consumed by the peasant family, and are usually managed by women. These events negatively affect the decision-making power of women within the peasant family economy given that their productive and reproductive role becomes even more limited. There are other consequences, such as a decline in the quality of food and nutrition of the family, given that the peasant family cannot be fed through monoculture production.

In 2009, the National Assembly of Ecuador passed a law called 'Organic Law of the Food Sovereignty Regime' (LORSA), which explains the following in Article 1:

> The objective of this law is to establish the mechanisms through which the State may fulfill its obligation and strategic objective of guaranteeing individuals, communities and peoples the self-sufficiency for healthy, nutritious and culturally appropriate foods on a permanent basis.
>
> LORSA 2009: 1 (translated by the authors)

The creation of a law such as LORSA during the time, showed that the Ecuadorian State held priorities framed under the principle of food sovereignty to establish a regime for social development of the agricultural sector. This law promotes the conservation of biodiversity, the environment, nutrition and food. It also stipulates that, in terms of food, 'quality' is more important than quantity. However, there is no clear alignment between 'agricultural policies 2015–2025,' the national development plans for the agricultural sector and LORSA. The change in the productive matrix, together with national development plans, the Agrobiodiversity and Seeds Law and the agricultural policies designed by the Ministry of Agriculture, promote monoculture expansion and the standardization of plantations nationwide, which contradicts the regime established within LORSA.

In order to construct agrarian policies that are truly based on the needs of Ecuadorian people in terms of social, economic and nutritional wellbeing that are expressed in the LORSA, a differentiated approach should exist. Policies which differentiate between the peasant families' economies that supply the necessary food and nutrition for the Ecuadorian citizen on the one hand, and the agro-export economy on the other. At this point, food sovereignty is built by the State exclusively as a discourse, given that the productivist focus of agricultural policies is increasingly limiting the centers of production of a true food sovereignty. Furthermore, another way in which food sovereignty becomes discouraged is when the State considers peasant women exclusively objects of social welfare through subsidies to the care economy (e.g. education and health) instead of considering them empowered subjects of autonomous and diverse food production (S. Herrera, personal communication, December 14, 2018). Although it is a positive thing that the State invests in social welfare, it is also a mechanism that demobilizes social organization and articulation around food sovereignty. Finally, it causes a significant level of fragility in these care economies, given that during times of economic crisis or government deficit, these subsidies are withdrawn, leaving peasant women more unprotected.

5   Conclusion

Food sovereignty, as a concept, has more affinity with peasant women's economies because it prioritizes local commercialization, promotes freedom from the dependence on green revolution technologies, proposing instead agroecology. Therefore, it advances agrobiodiversity and prioritizes healthy food and nutrition for local producers and consumers, setting the rights of peoples before the rights of companies.[4] This chapter was set out to elucidate that, although food sovereignty appears in the Constitution of Ecuador and is backed by national organic legislation such as LORSA, when it comes to policy implementation, there is almost no effort to fulfill the food sovereignty regime. There are in fact no clear policies directed towards food sovereignty or peasant women. The productivism approach captures almost the full budget of the Ministry of Agriculture, so we question: how much of this budget in fact directed toward peasant and indigenous family agriculture, or actions to guarantee food sovereignty? Scholars around the globe have studied the implementation of food sovereignty in Ecuador. Edelman (2017) for instance questions 'how much

---

4   For more information, search for 'The Six Pillars of Food Sovereignty.' 1. It focuses on food for people. 2. It values food producers. 3. It localizes food systems. 4. It puts control locally. 5. It builds local knowledge and skills. 6. It works with nature (Vía Campesina, 2007).

food sovereignty can you get for one million dollars?' referring to the insignificant budget of COPISA[5] in 2016 which has since then declined greatly.

Moreover, various laws related to food sovereignty which were created with COPISA through a method of rural citizens' participation (including the Water Law, Land Law, Communes' Law and the Agrobiodiversity and Seeds Law) were totally modified by the National Assembly before their approval. These laws then shifted their focus in support of agro-extractivist interests, and all have serious gaps in terms of gender[6] perspective. Particularly, the Agrobiodiversity and Seeds Law provoked public outrage from rural and urban social movements and it was women leaders from indigenous movements such as ECUARUNARI[7] who led processes of organization and mobilization to pressure the government to negotiate certain points of this law—especially regarding Article 57, which allowed genetically modified organisms to enter the country (A. Naranjo, personal communication, November 30, 2018). For this and many other reasons, it is contentious to assume that peasant women have been passive actors when facing the processes that de-structure family farming through vertical integration into global commodity markets. This is an assumption that has often been reproduced in academia, for which many have been criticized, such as Meillassoux (1975).

As a matter of fact, peasant women not only worldwide, but also in Ecuador, have been protagonists in proposing many alternatives to the hegemony of productivist rural economies. A notable example are the proposals that emerged at the IV National Meeting of Rural Women organized by several peasant and indigenous organizations in Ecuador. The proposals that emerged here are linked to a construction of food sovereignty that is parallel to that of the State, led through the empowerment of women and focused on local needs. Firstly, during the meeting women expressed the need for local community-care systems to assist women when they must leave their communities—as an alternative system of childcare support. Second, they established the urgent need to respond to the State regarding certification and phytosanitary conditions that limit the commercialization of a greater diversity of healthy produce with nutritional and cultural value. In addition, they established the need for reclaiming spaces in local markets for peasant production. Therefore, they proposed the creation of a National Peasant Fair accompanied by the

---

5 'Conferencia Plurinacional e Intercultural de Soberanía Alimentaria' translates to Plurinational and Intercultural Conference on Food Sovereignty.

6 With the exception of the Land Law which has not achieved its desired distribution effect (Herrera 2018).

7 In particular, the current vice-president of ECUARUNARI Blanca Chancoso and others like Carmita Losano.

creation of an agroecological certification established by peasant organizations themselves; parallel and alternative to State certification schemes that only favor agro-industrial products. Finally, they decided reclaiming the garden as a territory and recovering native seeds through seed exchanges.

It is important to recognize that the productivist orientation of the Ecuadorian State is a difficult paradigm to fracture without profound questioning of the primary-export production modality. Nowadays, Ecuador is still operating as part of a periphery that responds to the demands of the Global North. This reality has been materialized in the policies and laws directed towards the agricultural sector, and in many ways exacerbated through actions such as the signing of the Free Trade Agreement (FTA) with the European Union.

The main critique of this chapter is that the current model for development and regulation of the agricultural sector excludes peasant women's economies, which is a really important economic sector of the country—even if it is apparently invisible, its contribution is immense. The development of peasant women's economies not only empower rural women by turning them into subjects of (diverse) production, it also guarantees income for an important part of the rural population and it ensures that rural households are able to send productive members to the world. Even though the Ecuadorian State does recognize structural social problems in relation to gender within agriculture, its orientation towards extractivism deepens the marginalization of women. Future agricultural regulations should construct differentiated policy from a gender perspective, in order to support and respect agrobiodiversity within peasant territories. Failing to create differentiated policy through the exclusive promotion of monoculture and standardized production as the only method to improve the levels of productivity violates and impoverishes peasant territories and households. Likewise, future policy should promote peasant women's economies and food sovereignty by centering development around people rather than commodity markets. A final criticism is that there is a significant limitation in terms of the availability of data regarding the wellbeing of rural women. A comprehensive agrarian census has not been carried out since 2000 in Ecuador. The information available comes from a few surveys such as the Survey of Surface and Continuous Agricultural Production (ESPAC) (2002–present) and others.

References

Acosta, A. (2016). "Las dependencias del extractivismo: Aporte para un debate incompleto." *Aktuel Marx* 20: 1–22. http://www.biodiversidadla.org/Documentos/Las_dependencias_del_extractivismo._Aporte_para_un_debate_incompleto.

Agarwal, B. (1998). "Environmental management, equity and ecofeminism: Debating India's experience." *The Journal of Peasant Studies*: 55–95. https://doi.org/10.1080/03066159808438684.

Agrawal, A. (1995). "Dismantling the divide between indigenous and western knowledge." In *Development and Change* (pp. 413–439). https://doi.org/10.1111/j.1467-7660.1995.tb00560.x.

Akram-Lodhi, A.H., and Kay, C. (2010). "Surveying the agrarian question (Part 2): current debates and beyond." *The Journal of Peasant Studies* 32(7): 255–284. https://doi.org/10.1080/03066151003594906.

Ley Orgánica del Régimen de la Soberanía Alimentaria (LORSA). (2009). https://www.soberaniaalimentaria.gob.ec/pacha/wp-content/uploads/2011/04/LORSA.pdf.

Ley Orgánica de Agrobiodiversidad, Semillas y Fomento de Agricultura (LOASFAS). (2017). http://www.fao.org/faolex/results/details/es/c/LEX-FAOC168628/.

Bravo, E. (2016). *La regulación empresarial de la producción campesina.* Editorial Universitaria Abya-Yala. http://www.digitaliapublishing.com/a/58984/la-regulacion-empresarial-en-la-produccion-de-alimentos--impactos-en-la-vida-campesina.

Carrión, D., and Herrera, S. (2012). *Ecuador Rural del Siglo XXI: soberanía alimentaria, inversión pública y política agraria.* Instituto de Estudios Ecuatorianos. https://biblio.flacsoandes.edu.ec/shared/biblio_view.php?bibid=129843&tab=opac.

Collins, J. (2014). "A Feminist Approach to Overcoming the Closed Boxes of the Commodity Chain." In W. Dunaway (Ed.), *Gendered Commodity Chains* (pp. 27–37). Stanford University Press. https://doi.org/10.1515/9780804788960-007.

De Schutter, O. (2009). *The right to food: seed policies and the right to food: enhancing agrobiodiversity and encouraging innovation.* UN Digital library.

Edelman, M. (2017). "The Future of Food and Challenges for Agriculture in the 21st Century: debates about who, and with what social, economic and ecological implications we will feed the world." *Elikadura* 90: 1–20.

Elías, M. (2016). "Distinct, shared and complementary: gendered agroecological knowledge in review." *CAB Reviews* 11(40): 1–16. https://doi.org/10.1079/PAVSNNR201611040.

Engels, F. (1972). *Origin of the Family, Private Property and the State.* London, Pathfinder Press.

FAO. (1997). *Gender: key to sustainability and food security.* Food and Agriculture Organization. http://www.fao.org/News/1997/introG-e.htm.

FAO. (2004). *Building on Gender, Agrobiodiversity and Local Knowledge.* http://www.fao.org/docrep/007/y5608e/y5608e00.htm#Contents.

FAO. (2009). "Cerrar la Brecha: El Programa del FAO para la igualdad de género en la agricultura y el desarrollo rural." In *Food and Agriculture Organization.* FAO.

FAO. (2011a). *Desarrollo de cadenas de valor sensibles al género.* A. Pedro, H. David, E. Krivonos, and J. Morrison (Eds.). Food and Agricultura Organization.

FAO. (2011b). *El Estado Mundial de la Agricultura y la Alimentación: Las Mujeres en la Agricultura Cerrar la brecha de género en las áreas del desarrollo.* http://www.fao.org/docrep/013/i2050s/i2082s00.pdf.

FAO. (2013a). *Smallholder integration in changing food markets.* http://www.fao.org/docrep/018/i3292e/i3292e.pdf.

FAO. (2013b). *International Year of Family Farming 2014. Master Plan* (final version). http://www.fao.org/fileadmin/user_upload/iyff/docs/Final_Master_Plan_IYFF_2014_30-05.pdf.

FAO. (2018). *Las mujeres alimentan al mundo.* Food and Agriculture Organization. http://www.fao.org/argentina/noticias/detail-events/es/c/1146615/.

FIAN Ecuador. (2018). *Mujeres Rurales y Tierra en Ecuador: Es Hora de Cerrar Las Brechas de Género en el Campo.*

Herrera, S. (2009). *Nabón: Entre las Mujeres y el Gobierno Local.* IEE—IRDC—PRIGE-PP—Municipio de Nabón.

IICA. (2014). *Agricultura, oportunidad de desarrollo en las Américas plan de mediano plazo 2014–2018.* M.G. Víctor Villalobos Héctor Iturbe, Yanko Goic and M.Á.A. y F. Sancho (eds.). http://repiica.iica.int/docs/b3333e/b3333e.pdf.

Lenin, V.I. (1982). "The Class Differentiation of the peasantry." In Harriss, John (Ed.), *Rural Development: theories of peasant economy and agrarian change* (pp. 130–139). London: Routledge.

León, I. (2007). *Mujeres agricultoras: Gestoras de soberanía alimentaria.* https://nyeleni.org/spip.php?article335.

Leon, X. (2017). *Feminismo y Buen Vivir: Utopías Decoloniales.* (PYDLOS). http://dspace.ucuenca.edu.ec/bitstream/123456789/27831/1/feminismo%20y%20buen%20vivir%20pdf%20PARA%20IMPRESION%20(1).pdf.

Martínez, L. (2013). "Agricultura Familiar en el Ecuador informe del Proyecto Análisis de la Pobreza y de la Desigualdad en América Latina Rural." *Centro Latinoamericano Para El Desarrollo Rural RIMISP*: 147.

Meillassoux, C. (1975). *Femmes, Greniers et Capitaux.* Maspero.

Ministerio de Agricultura y Ganadería. (2014). *La Política Agropecuaria Ecuatoriana: Hacia el desarrollo territorial rural sostenible 2015–2025.* http://servicios.agricultura.gob.ec/politicas/La PolíticasAgropecuariasal2025Iparte.pdf.

O'Laughlin, B. (1977). "Production and Reproduction: Meillassoux's Femmes, Greniers et Capitaux." *Critique of Anthropology* 2(3): 3–32. https://doi.org/10.1177/0308275X7700200802.

OEC. (2018). *Country profile: Ecuador—Trade Balance.* https://oec.world/en/profile/country/ecu/.

Pacheco, M. (2010). "Agroecología y Feminismo." *Diálogos Instituto Para El Desarrollo Rural de Sudamérica (IPDRS)*: 44.

Puleo, A. (2015). *Ecología y género en diálogo interdisciplinar.* Madrid: Plaza y Valdés.

Shiva, V. (1988). *Staying Alive Women, Ecology and Survival in India*. Indraprastha Press.

Siliprandi, E. (2015). "Una Mirada ecofeminista sobre las luchas por la sostenibilidad en el mundo rural." In Puleo, Alicia, *Ecología y Género En Diálogo Interdisciplinar* (pp. 279–290). Madrid: Plaza y Valdés.

Thorner, D. (1988). "Chayanov's Concept of the Peasant Economy." In A.V. Chayanov, *The Theory of Peasant Economy*. The University of Wisconsin Press.

Van Der Ploeg, J. (2007). *The peasant mode of Production Revisited*. Rural Development. http://www.jandouwevanderploeg.com/NL/publicaties/artikelen/the-peasant -mode-of-production-revisited/.

Vía Campesina. (2007). Nyéléni Declaration Sélingué, Mali: Forum for Food Sovereignty. https://nyeleni.org/DOWNLOADS/Nyelni_EN.pdf.

Warren, K. (1966). "Ecological Feminist Philosophies." *University of Virginia: Indiana University Press*.

Inequality of Income and Job Satisfaction in Ecuador between Genders and Ethnic Groups

Diana Cabrera, Edwin Espinoza and Ana Oña

1 Introduction

This chapter provides a theoretical and empirical analysis of income inequality, working conditions, and satisfaction between genders and ethnic groups in Ecuador. The importance of studying these differences lies in the fact that they generate and entrench salient problems of inequity, inequality, and lack of inclusion that Ecuador has experienced and endured since the colonial period. This study contributes to analyses of well-being and development in Latin America, which have been pursued for many years because of the persistence of problematic and inequitable economic realities.

For decades, Latin American economies have sought to address internal problems of inequality and low incomes through different economic interventions in their public policies. Thus, starting at the beginning of the 20th century, countries applied policies targeted at industrialization by import substitution, state interventionism, and even the nationalization of the means of production in countries such as Cuba. However, even though some improvements were duly noted, structural inequities persisted. Then, starting in the 1980s, development paradigms shifted to those that advocated the lowering of tariff barriers and the free functioning of market forces. This was a period associated with the exacerbation of inequities.

More recently, alternative postulates have been put forward, some of which are autochthonous like the *Sumak Kawsay* or *Buen Vivir* (Good Living) in Ecuador. This new vision of goals and objectives for the economy was embodied in the Constitution of Ecuador (2008) and in the National Development Plans for 2009–2013 and 2017–2021, the former being the National Plan for Good Living (SENPLADES 2009) and the latter being the All Life Plan (SENPLADES 2017), which the State constructed as an action guide for the implementation of public policies.

Buen Vivir, according to the Ecuadorian Constitution, refers to the search for a harmonious relationship between State, society, market, and nature; where the idea of development leaves aside the emphasis on the mercantile to focus on human beings. Thus, an economic system oriented toward solidarity and inclusivity that fosters decent employment and uproots the economy to service society, and not capital (SENPLADES 2009, 2017).

The goals of these plans also included achieving gender and ethnic equity, defending the generation of decent employment, productivity, and competitiveness as well as the consolidation of a social and solidarity-based economic system (SENPLADES 2009, 2017).

Studies on wage discrimination by gender in Ecuador have shown that such discrimination exists in almost all branches of activity although to different extents (Benítez and Espinoza, 2018). In 2018, the average wage of men was 20% higher than that of women, according to the Technical Secretary of the National Council for Gender Equality in Ecuador (Consejo Nacional para la Igualdad de Género), as reported in two of the most popular newspapers in the country (El Comercio 2019; El Telégrafo 2018). In the same way, for the period between 2007–2015, it was revealed that labor satisfaction in Ecuador was related to well-being and productivity. Thus income, structural labor market changes, social security, formalization, and work conditions turn out to be relevant around this category (Grijalva et al. 2017).

Hence, in what follows, we seek to analyze the fulfillment of these goals (gender and ethnic equity) by exploring the most relevant statistics on the subject. In this connection, sections 2–4 of this chapter analyze the categories of gender and ethnicity from a theoretical perspective, which allows us to understand their political scope within Ecuador. The fifth section presents the methodology. The sixth section focuses on an empirical exploration of the employment situation of the aforementioned categories in terms of occupation, wage inequality, conditions, and satisfaction with working life in Ecuador in 2018. For this purpose, data from the National Survey of Employment, Unemployment and Underemployment (ENEMDU) are used (available from the National Institute for Statistics and Censuses, INEC). Finally, the seventh section presents a synthesis of the most important findings, reflections, and recommendations on this interesting and relevant subject in Ecuador—a megadiverse, multicultural, and unequal country at the same time.

2   Labor Differences between Genders and Ethnicities: the Capitalist Accumulation Process

The capitalist system operates with intrinsic and structural differences between social classes. These differences are manifested in the type of activities, the harshness of these, hours of work, but above all in the income received.

However, labor differences are not found only between social classes. Members of the same social class, socioeconomic sector, income quintile, or other ways of differentiating them, exhibit gender differences. Thus, men tend to have higher positions of power and higher salaries than women. Added to this is the fact that women's tasks include domestic work that adds to their efforts in the productive system, but without receiving compensatory remuneration. This housework, generally assigned to women, generates values that are neither accounted for nor paid for within the prevailing capitalist system, which nevertheless appropriates them.

Karl Marx (1977) argued that the capitalists may safely leave the burden of reproduction of the working class to the laborers themselves. Furthermore, Marxist feminists have long argued that values generated in domestic work are transferred to the capitalist, since the woman carries out work in the home (food, clothing repair, and cleaning) that replenishes workers, prepares them for the day in the factory, and that the capitalist does not cover with the salary that the worker receives.

Federici (2010), for instance, advances (but also sometimes criticizes) Marx's ideas and argues that domestic work is appropriated by the capitalist system and is a fundamental part of the accumulation process. In other words, the value generated by women's work is dispossessed by the system of capitalist accumulation. As argued by her:

> (...) the power difference between women and men and the concealment of women's unpaid work behind the screen of natural inferiority, has allowed capitalism to vastly expand "the unpaid part of the working day," and to use (male) wages to accumulate female work. In many cases, they have also served to divert class antagonism to an antagonism between men and women. Thus, primitive accumulation has been above all an accumulation of differences, inequalities, hierarchies and divisions that has separated workers from each other and even from themselves.
>
> pp. 76–77[1]

Furthermore, this is linked to the idea that labor is not simply a commodity or a factor of production but encompasses complexities greater than those assigned by conventional economics. As Polanyi (1947) argued, labor is artificially converted into a fictitious commodity; a resource not created in the

---

1   Translated from the original Spanish text.

production process, but codified as the labor force or factor of production, and is exploited in the process of capital accumulation.

Therefore, if labor differences between genders are referred to, it is women who have the greatest burden of time (Carrasco 2006; Consejo Nacional para la Igualdad de Género 2015; León 2003; Picchio 1992; Rodríguez Chaurnet 1996) by taking—in many cases—not only material sustenance to the home, but also for their additional and permanent work in matters of care and nutrition; problems to which are added the salary inequalities that persist (their salary is usually lower than that of men) and the type of work they can access, which is generally routine and precarious.

In addition, it can be observed that, even in the upper economic strata, women are frequently removed from positions of leadership and direction. This warns that, although more fortunate than their gender partners from lower socioeconomic strata, women from higher such strata also suffer some degree of discrimination in their work roles.

3   Labor Differences between Genders, But Also between Ethnicities

The working conditions of women are structurally plagued with disadvantages. But if the category 'ethnicity' is added to this inter-gender analysis, the results are even more concerning.

Thus, the Latin American capitalist system has, in addition to the assignment of roles by gender, a structural assignment of labor roles by ethnicity in which some are more favored than others. Native, autochthonous, or 'indigenous' ethnicities are among the least favored by Ecuador's labor structure; while people of European descent tend to have higher incomes than others. Thus, it would be observed that gender differences have very different effects on the quality of life of people from different ethnic groups.

This problem has been taken into account by the Ecuadorian authorities and attempts have been made to remedy it, but so far no substantive results have been achieved. It is possible that these failures are due to the fact that the approach used to propose solutions is contaminated by western ethnocentrism, or that simply the structure of the system is not compatible with the solutions; and that the capitalist system is, inevitably, a machine for assigning social roles.

The Ecuadorian State, for its part, in the new Constitution of 2008, took up proposals from the indigenous worldview such as the *Sumak Kawsay* or *Buen Vivir*. However, in practice, public policies seem to aim to integrate indigenous people into the westernized working life of cities, into the established productive system in which their ethnic status is almost always a disadvantage.

For this reason, 'indigenist' state policy has received strong criticism accusing it of being an attempt to homogenize and even subordinately integrate the indigenous into the capitalist system prevailing in modern cities. Bretón Solo de Zaldívar (2013) is of the opinion that state *indigenism* is:

> a set of initiatives promoted by the public powers to stimulate the "modernization" of the "backward" or "traditional" collectives and their integration into the "national society," [...] the indigenist policies intended to desindianize the indigenous people, to deny at the end of the process the cultural alterity for the sake of the construction of an imagined (and imaginary) national community.
>
> p. 74[2]

By integrating themselves into salaried working life, indigenous people are thwarted by the disadvantages derived from the social prejudices that assign them roles at the low levels of the salary scale and power. The same happens with black people, mulattoes, *cholos, montubios,* and other non-white ethnic groups in Ecuador, and even with many whites of low socioeconomic status.

Hence, it is evident that the capitalist system has now overlapped the lags of racial discrimination of pre-capitalist colonial times, in which ethnicity or race determined social position and tasks. Throughout this chapter it will be shown that there is still a predetermined assignment in the Ecuadorian labor world, where ethnicity and gender are significant determinants of income, status, and conditions.

Thus, the labor market not only excludes women from jobs traditionally performed by men, it also prioritizes the participation of whites, or as many whites as possible, in jobs with better incomes and little risk of physical harm. Meanwhile, those who are of African descent (blacks, mulattoes, and afro-Ecuadorians), *montubios,* and indigenous people,[3] are almost condemned to

---

2 Translated from the original Spanish text.

3 It should be clarified that the way in which ENEMDU classifies the ethnic groups to which respondents belong does not necessarily refer to physical racial characteristics. The information is obtained from the question "How do you consider yourself?"; and this refers to how the respondent identifies according to their customs and culture. For this reason, there is a division between afro-Ecuadorians, blacks and mulattoes; it is also observed that the *montubios* are not an ethnic or racial group, but a very heterogeneous group of peasants of the Ecuadorian coast, who in general are mestizos, and in some provinces have Caucasian

exhausting, dangerous, and poorly paid tasks. Therefore, as long as these role assignments remain in force, the *Sumak Kawsay* will not go beyond mere discourse or 'embellishment' in the Constitution.

4   The Assignment of Labor Roles in the Capitalist Accumulation
          Process: Ethnicity and Gender as Determinants of Labor Status

Orthodox economic theory commonly views human labor as a factor of production that is combined with other factors (land and capital) to produce the commodities that give life to the process of accumulation. Workers have different abilities according to their physical constitution. Thus, the combinations that can be made of the work factor, end in the specialization of the human being in various tasks according to sex, height, physical strength, and so on.

Thus, when human skills are selected according to gender to optimize them in the productive process, it results in a certain degree of labor determinism by sex. The man, the male human being, is often seen to endure work that requires high physical effort and risk, and exhausting hours of night work. Therefore, the tasks of force and risk are assigned to men. Women, on the other hand, have been relegated to purely domestic and caring roles, to repetitive and tedious tasks of little physical effort in factory production, food preparation, cleaning, and so on. However, both types of tasks, assigned to men and women, are also reserved for people of low socioeconomic status who, in general, in the case of Latin America, belong to non-white ethnic groups.

White men from socioeconomic sectors with high incomes have reserved for themselves the positions of direction, leadership, decision making, and better incomes in the productive process. This also applies to white women, although to a lesser extent than men. This results in certain spaces in the productive system already having in advance a list of gender and even racial characteristics, informally assigned, for who is going to occupy them.

Therefore, the capitalist system follows a logic of (theoretical) work factor optimization that has resulted in a division or assignment of roles by gender, in

physiognomic characteristics. Also, other inhabitants of the Ecuadorian coast identify themselves as afro-Ecuadorians, as a form of political vindication of their roots; however, physiognomically they are mulatto and even have indigenous ancestry. Likewise, some mestizos identify themselves as indigenous and some whites even define themselves as mestizos. In short, this is not a specifically racial-phenotypical categorization, but rather a cultural one, which, although related to the former, is not necessarily the same in Ecuador.

which men have certain advantages over women. Further, evolution of the system has generated an ethnic segregation that, perhaps without any logic of optimization, relegates non-white people to subordinate roles and to less pleasant and poorly paid tasks.

The attempt to explain these work assignments by ethnicity can lead to intense controversy. Thus, authors such as Rushton (1996) and Herrnstein and Murray (2010), when they studied inequalities in income levels between ethnic groups in developed countries, ended up attributing them to differences between intellectual capacities that they assumed to be of biological origin. This generated a strong debate and even rejection on the part of the academic community.

Other authors such as Gunnar Myrdal (1962; 1979) have studied differences in opportunity and income among ethnic groups in the United States, and attributed them to vicious cycles in which the lack of opportunities for blacks led to low incomes and precarious jobs and these, in turn, led to few opportunities for advancement, again.

In the case of Latin America, there are multiple studies on the subject of social differentiation by ethnic groups. Bello and Rangel (2000), Valenzuela and Rangel (2004), Flórez et al. (2003), and De Ferranti et al. (2003), have analyzed the inequities, exclusion, inter-ethnic inequalities, and social costs generated by such differentiation. There are also authors who have researched this topic by combining gender and ethnicity differences, such as Valenzuela (2003). All of these various outputs serve as a reference for the present study.

Nearly all extant research on the subject conducted in Latin America, points to persistent lags in the racial caste division of the European colonial period as the cause of socio-economic inequalities between ethnicities or races.

It would be complex and laborious to explain the roots of this phenomenon and especially its continuity over time. Perhaps, in the case of Ecuador and Latin America, the reasons for these vicious circles are to be found in inherited customs and beliefs; that is, in informal institutions that were derived from the formal institutions of the colonial past.

There seems to be a general conviction that white people are more intellectually cultivated, more trustworthy, more respectable, and more responsible than members of other ethnic groups. Therefore, as a corollary to this belief, non-white people are perceived as less worthy of roles that need those qualities. This forms a vicious circle of poverty, marginalization, violence, and so on.

Using Myrdal's thesis (Myrdal 1959; 1979), one could say that in Ecuador there is a cumulative circular causation that perpetuates and deepens the problem of ethnic discrimination. Thus, the opportunities that non-white people have to achieve better qualities and qualifications are reduced and the circle is fed back to supposedly confirm prejudices.[4]

However, this chapter does not attempt to delve into the causes of these social differences between ethnicities and genders, but rather to show that they also exist in Ecuador, through descriptive and inferential (econometric) analyses.

5 Methodology

The data used in this chapter emanate from the ENEMDU (National Survey of Employment, Unemployment and Underemployment) as of June 2018, which can be found on the website of the National Institute of Statistics and Censuses of Ecuador (INEC). Missing data and data from respondents with incomes greater than $999,999 were eliminated.

After processing, data are available for 23,734 respondents; 61.65% are men and 38.35% are women. The ethnic distribution of the respondents is described as follows: 6.41 per cent of the respondents are indigenous, 1.08 per cent are afro-Ecuadorian, 0.99 per cent are black, 0.83 per cent are mulattoes, 4.92 per cent are *montubios*, 84.59 per cent are mestizo (mixed-heritage), 1.13 per cent are white and there is a small percentage (0.04 per cent) in the 'other' category.

Job satisfaction is a qualitative variable which is important because it can determine emotional state (Locke 1976) and affective response (Muchinsky 1993). The survey used in this case took into consideration ENEMDU's question on '*how he/she feels at work*' which is answerable using '*Happy*' or '*Not happy*,' with the latter being demarcated as either '*Not very happy*,' '*Unhappy*' or '*Totally unhappy*.'

Processed statistical data showing inequality in income from labor, working conditions, and job satisfaction between genders and ethnicities in Ecuador will be presented in the form of tables, accompanied by descriptive analyses.

Then, econometric estimates will be described and discussed to delve deeper into the causes of labor differences between genders and ethnicities.

---

4 *Economic Theory and Underdeveloped Regions* is a work in which Myrdal (1959) seeks to explain the differences between developed and underdeveloped regions. In this text he sets out the idea of the principle of circular causation and social change. Although it is not the main topic, in this same work the situation of blacks in North America is analyzed pursuant of identifying the reasons for the vicious circle in which one was poor because one was black and because one was black one was poor. Thus, this resonates with the circular causation principle for analyzing socioeconomic differences between ethnicities.

To foreground that analysis, the following considerations warrant noting related to database handling:

- The construction of the employment indicators was based on syntax provided by the official entity (INEC).
- The variable 'real labor income' was considered, which is constructed by INEC. The natural logarithm of this variable was used to stabilize the variance.
- The education variable was constructed as a function of level of instruction and years.
- Outliers were eliminated from the age and income variables.
- The model was adjusted considering the hourly income variable given the inequalities in hours worked between men and women.

Usual tests were performed and, consequently, White standard errors were used to account for heteroscedasticity.

6   Results

This section will be divided into four subsections. The first subsection presents the occupations to which each ethnic group and gender are dedicated. The second subsection presents data on the employment situation of respondents as to whether they work informally, are underemployed, or are in suitable jobs. The third subsection presents inequalities in labor income between genders and ethnicities, and the average income of women as a percentage of that of men. The fourth subsection provides a statistical description of the causes of satisfaction/satisfaction in the working life of those surveyed, by gender and ethnicity. The fifth subsection presents econometric estimates of how gender and ethnicity affect the income of respondents.

6.1   *Occupational Categories*

Table 10.1 shows the percentage of respondents who are laborers, employers, self-employed, or domestic employees. These activities were chosen among others presented by the ENEMDU survey for expository purposes, i.e., because they are representative of the socioeconomic conditions of the individuals engaged in these activities. Other categories are not shown.

Laborer—Men tend to these tasks more than women. However, *montubio*[5] men are the most involved in this type of work (respective to their same ethnic self-portrayal) with 49.19% of male *montubio* respondents classed as laborers.

---

5   Singular (masculine) for 'montubios.'

TABLE 10.1 Occupations by ethnicity and gender

Ethnic self-identification	Occupation categories by sex (%)							
	Laborer		Employer		Self-employed		Domestic employee	
	Men	Women	Men	Women	Men	Women	Men	Women
Indigenous	16.96	6.03	1.49	0.97	56.85	62.06	0.40	3.70
Afro-Ecuadorian	20.71	3.42	0.71	5.13	31.43	35.90	0.00	12.82
Black	26.81	4.12	2.90	2.06	28.26	46.39	0.00	9.28
Mulatto	23.02	2.78	1.59	6.94	27.78	47.22	0.00	6.94
Montubio	49.19	4.92	3.14	1.23	29.14	63.11	0.22	12.70
Mixed Heritage	17.52	2.94	4.60	2.60	33.62	43.34	0.35	6.66
White	14.12	3.03	8.24	6.06	40.59	40.40	0.00	4.04
Total	19.60	3.19	4.26	2.58	34.90	44.85	0.33	6.73

SOURCE: INEC (2018)

White men are the least likely to participate in this category (only 14.12% of white male respondents work as laborers.)

Employer—Overall, 4.26% of men are employers which, although a small percentage, is greater than that of women, 2.58%. In relative terms, it is observed that white men dedicate the most to these activities, with 8.24%.

Self-employed—This is the category with the highest participation of both men and women in the aggregate; in this case women have higher participation (44.85%) than men (34.90%). In relative terms, indigenous men are the ones who participate the most in this category, with 56.85 per cent. The women who participate most in this category are the *montubias*[6] at 63.11%.

Domestic employee—This category is the one that most reflects differences in the allocation of tasks by gender, although participation in it is small. Male participation is very low, at 0.33%, with the figure for women registering at 6.73%. In other words, women participate 20 times more than men. It is also important to note that 12.82% of afro-Ecuadorian women are domestic

---

6 Feminine (plural) for 'montubio.'

workers, 12.70% of the *montubias*, 9.28% of black females, and 6.94% of the *mulattas*[7] also dedicate to those activities.

6.2   Underemployment, Informality, Adequate Employment, Domestic Employment

Indigenous people are the group with the highest incidence of informal employment, in relative terms, with 65.90% of those surveyed working in the informal sector. The second largest ethnic group in this respect is the *montubios* with 64.18% The group with the lowest incidence of informal employment relative to their ethnic self-identification was the *mestizos* with 37.31% (Table 10.2).

The *montubios* were the group who were least likely to be in adequate employment, only 25.71% of those surveyed defined their employment situation as adequate; they are followed by indigenous people with 31.60%. Whites had the highest proportion of people in suitable employment, at 55.02%.

TABLE 10.2   Employment situation by ethnicity and gender

| Ethnic self-identification | Employment situation (%) | | | | | | | | |
| | Informal | | | Underemployment | | | Adequate employment | | |
	Men	Women	Total	Men	Women	Total	Men	Women	Total
Indigenous	65.67	66.34	65.90	20.04	14.40	18.13	36.11	22.76	31.60
Afro-Ecuadorian	43.57	29.91	37.35	28.57	25.64	27.24	48.57	47.01	47.86
Black	44.20	43.30	43.83	28.26	26.80	27.66	46.38	30.93	40.00
Mulatto	37.30	47.22	40.91	23.81	33.33	27.27	46.03	36.11	42.42
Montubio	64.0v3	64.75	64.18	42.15	20.49	37.62	27.84	17.62	25.71
Mixed Heritage	37.72	36.68	37.31	18.51	17.78	18.22	57.36	45.66	52.73
White	39.41	34.34	37.55	19.41	21.21	20.07	56.47	52.53	55.02
Total	41.43	39.14	40.55	20.34	18.02	19.45	53.76	43.49	49.82

SOURCE: INEC (2018)

a   In Ecuador, employment is sub-divided into 5 categories by the INEC: adequate employment, underem
    ployment, non-remunerated employment, other non-adequate employment, and unclassified. In addi
    tion, from a different perspective, employment could be sub-divided into employment in the formal and
    in the informal sectors.

---

7   Feminine (plural) for 'mulatto.'

The *montubios* are also the ethnic group with the highest percentage of underemployment, at 37.62%. The second largest group in this respect is afro-Ecuadorians with 27.66%, followed by mulattoes and afro-Ecuadorians.

In terms of gender, men tend more towards informality, with 41.43% working in the informal sector compared to 39.14% of women. Men are also more likely to be underemployed at 20.34%, with 18.02% of women in this category. However, men are more likely to be in adequate employment, with 53.76% compared to 43.49% for women.

6.3 Inequality in Income and Working Conditions between Genders and Ethnic Groups

The first observation is that the *montubios* are the group with the lowest income, receiving $330.27 per month. The group with the second lowest average income is indigenous people, with $335.14. The highest wage group is occupied by whites with a monthly average of $616.99 (Table 10.3).

The last time this analysis was carried out, in 2014 (Cabrera et al. 2016), indigenous people were the lowest salary group, followed by the *montubios*; this time, these positions are switched.

In terms of gender income inequalities, the biggest gap between male and female income from labor is observed with respect to the *montubios*; the women in this group earn 73.16 per cent of what men of the same ethnicity earn. They are followed by indigenous women with 76.87% of the income compared to men of their ethnicity (Table 10.3).

TABLE 10.3   Average monthly income by ethnicity and gender

Ethnic self-identification	Average Income (US $ per month)			Average income of women as a percentage of the average income of men of the same ethnic group
	Men	Women	Total	
Indigenous	363.54	279.44	335.14	76.87%
Afro-Ecuadorian	484.77	473.68	479.72	97.71%
Black	439.18	341.71	398.95	77.81%
Mulatto	434.90	369.85	411.25	85.04%
Montubio	349.91	255.99	330.27	73.16%
Mixed Heritage	580.72	461.24	533.36	79.43%
White	652.91	555.31	616.99	85.05%
Total	548.84	444.90	508.97	81.06%

SOURCE: INEC (2018)

Women overall earn 81.06% of what men earn (Table 10.3). Although this is problematic it is nevertheless an improvement compared to the findings of the earlier study in 2014, where the figure was 79.70%. However, it must be taken into account that men work, on average more hours than women per week (INEC 2018). Thus, hourly income is preferred as indicator and used in section 6.6.

6.4   Differences in Satisfaction with Working Life

Mestizos are the ethnic group happiest with their work, with 75.19% of those interviewed expressing satisfaction, followed by whites with 74.72%. The group with the lowest percentage of people happy with their work is the *montubios* at 65.35%, followed by indigenous people at 65.55% (Table 10.4).

The ethnic group with the most respondents who reported being totally dissatisfied with their work was the mulattoes with 4.04%, followed by whites with 3.35% (INEC 2018).

If all forms of dissatisfaction are aggregated, it can be observed that the group with the greatest dissatisfaction is the *montubios* with 34.65%, followed by indigenous people with 34.39% (Table 10.4).

If this analysis is divided by gender, it is observed that women are the happiest gender with their work, with 77.01%. However, if differences by gender and ethnicity are observed, it is noted that women self-identified as mulatto

TABLE 10.4   Job satisfaction by ethnicity and gender

Ethnic self-identification	How does people feel about their job (%)					
	Happy			Unhappy		
	Men	Women	Total	Men	Women	Total
Indigenous	64.24	68.09	65.55	35.66	31.91	34.39
Afro-Ecuadorian	69.29	81.20	74.71	30.71	18.80	25.29
Black	73.91	67.01	71.06	26.09	32.99	28.94
Mulatto	73.02	61.11	68.69	26.98	38.89	31.31
Montubio	62.79	75.00	65.35	37.21	25.00	34.65
Mixed Heritage	73.41	77.90	75.19	26.58	22.07	24.79
White	75.29	73.74	74.72	24.12	26.26	24.91
Total	72.10	77.01	73.98	27.87	22.97	25.99

SOURCE: INEC (2018)

are the ones that reported being unhappy with their work the most, with 38.89% of those surveyed; followed by black women with 32.99%, and indigenous women with 31.91%. The men who are *happiest* with their work are the whites with 75.29%. The ethnic group of men most *unhappy* with their work is the *montubios* with 37.21%, followed by indigenous with 35.66% (Table 10.4).

6.5   Causes of Labor Unease and Categories of Occupation

Table 10.5 shows that men are, on average, more *dissatisfied* with their work than women. The biggest reason for discontent for both sexes is low income, and the second biggest reason is poor prospects for progress. Here, men outnumber women in all categories, except in discontent over poor labor relations, where women have a higher percentage.

This highlights that two issues are of particular concern to men over women: the harmful environment and possible accidents. Here, the percentage of dissatisfied men is, respectively, 3 to 1 and 5 to 1 higher than that of women. However, it should be noted that in both cases, these concerns are not prominent among white men whilst being more accentuated among mulattoes and *montubios*.

6.6   Inferential Analysis

To corroborate the descriptive findings, both by gender and ethnicity, an inferential (econometric) model is used in which the natural logarithm of hourly

TABLE 10.5   Reasons for labor dissatisfaction by gender

Reasons for dissatisfaction	Men (%)	Women (%)
Low income	26.39	21.85
Many hours of work	4.74	3.14
Inconvenient schedules	1.72	1.23
Work overload	2.34	1.87
Not having stability	11.05	7.59
Harmful environment	2.30	0.76
Working on the street	1.24	0.79
Possible accidents	1.65	0.31
Daily activities	3.21	3.06
Low possibilities of progress	16.89	13.57
Poor working relationships	0.60	0.69
Total unhappy	**27.87**	**22.97**

SOURCE: INEC (2018)

income is the dependent variable with age, age squared, sex, ethnicity, marital status and education as independent variables. An intercept and idiosyncratic error term are included as standard.

Four iterations are shown in Table 10.6: the first up to the 20th percentile of income, the second up to the 40th percentile, the third up to the 60th percentile, and the last up to the 80th percentile. That is to say, in the first group we find the people with the lowest incomes and we ascend as the percentiles advance. The upper quartile was not included due to the low reliability of data at this end of the distribution. Being a woman is associated with having a significantly lower income than man, until the 60th percentile. It is also evident that being married is associated with a higher income compared to all other relationship categories, controlling for other relevant factors. In terms of ethnicity, all have higher incomes than indigenous people. In other ethnic groups such as black, mulatto, *montubio*, and mestizo, as income increases this gap decreases.

TABLE 10.6 Percentile regressions

Variables	Q1	Q2	Q3	Q4
Gender: Women	-0.126***	-0.089***	-0.071***	-0.070***
Age	0.021***	0.022***	0.026***	0.027***
Age squared	-0.000***	-0.000***	-0.000***	-0.000***
Years of education	0.037***	0.041***	0.045***	0.053***
Civil status (Ref. cat.: married)				
Separated	-0.044***	-0.073***	-0.101***	-0.126***
Divorced	-0.051*	-0.063**	-0.035	-0.018
Widow(er)	0.038**	-0.037	-0.056***	-0.058
Civil union	-0.025*	-0.049***	-0.072***	-0.095***
Single	-0.099***	-0.113***	-0.125***	-0.135***
Ethnicity (Ref. cat.: indigenous)				
Afro-Ecuadorian	0.091*	0.138**	0.158***	0.125***
Black	0.230***	0.157***	0.107***	0.038
Mulatto	0.116***	0.115***	0.138*	0.078**
Montubio	0.215***	0.164***	0.117***	0.111***
Mixed Heritage	0.207***	0.189***	0.141***	0.091***
White	0.216***	0.233***	0.195***	0.250***
Another ethnicity	0.531***	0.450***	0.559***	0.888
Constant	-0.178***	-0.062*	0.022	0.156***
Number of observations	24,158	24,158	24,158	24,158

TABLE 10.6 Percentile regressions (*cont.*)

Variables	Q1	Q2	Q3	Q4
Pseudo-R-squared	0.1148	0.1254	0.1401	0.1822
Prob > F	0.0000	0.0000	0.0000	0.0000

Note: *** $p < 0.01$, ** $p < 0.05$, * $p < 0.1$

Table 10.7 presents results from three regressions. The first with the total number of respondents, the second with employed individuals, and the third only with those considered to be in adequate (full) employment. In all three regressions, being a woman is associated with having less income than being a man,

TABLE 10.7 Regressions by type of employment

Variables	All	Employed	Full Employment
Gender: Women	−0.096***	−0.096***	−0.015
Age	0.024***	0.024***	0.010***
Age squared	−0.000***	−0.000***	−0.000*
Years of education	0.047***	0.047***	0.044***
Civil status (Ref. cat.: married)			
Separated	−0.099***	−0.099***	−0.125***
Divorced	−0.045**	−0.044**	−0.049*
Widow(er)	−0.025	−0.025	−0.095***
Civil union	−0.072***	−0.073***	−0.093***
Single	−0.133***	−0.133***	−0.102***
Ethnicity (Ref. cat.: indigenous)			
Afro-Ecuadorian	0.142***	0.141***	0.058
Black	0.140***	0.139***	−0.020
Mulatto	0.103***	0.102***	−0.029
Montubio	0.153***	0.152***	0.005
Mixed Heritage	0.152***	0.151***	0.001
White	0.240***	0.239***	0.042
Other ethnicity	0.609***	0.608***	0.283
Constant	−0.041	−0.037	0.516***
Number of observations	24,158	24,126	11,820
Pseudo-R-squared	0.242	0.241	0.261
Prob > F	**0.000**	**0.000**	**0.000**

Note: *** $p < 0.01$, ** $p < 0.05$, * $p < 0.1$

but this difference is smaller for those respondents in full employment. In terms of ethnicity, being black, mulatto, *montubio*, white, and other ethnicity is associated with having a significantly higher income than being indigenous, controlling for other factors in the equation. However, this situation is not significant in full employment. In all three regressions, there is a positive relationship between education and income.

7   Discussion and Concluding Remarks

Focusing on the descriptive statistics, in terms of ethnic groups, the *montubios* have the lowest incomes, the highest wage inequalities by gender in income, the lowest adequate employment, and the highest underemployment. Further, the *montubios* participate the most as laborers; almost half of the *montubio* men exercise this labor role. The *montubios* are also the group most dissatisfied with their work.

Indigenous people are the group that tends more towards informal work, they have the second lowest incomes and the second highest wage inequality by gender. Indigenous people are also the second most dissatisfied with their work.

The men who are happiest with their work are the whites, and the least happy are the *montubios*. Women tend to be happier with their work than men, yet mulatto women are the least happy.

Overall, a higher proportion of men have feelings of dissatisfaction with their work compared to women. The biggest reason for discontent, in both genders, is low income.

There are some noteworthy observations regarding gender differences and labor discontent. A higher proportion of men than women report being discontent across all of the reasons for labor discontent analyzed, except in the issue of labor relations, which is the only one in which women are more discontent than men.

The greatest differences are found with respect to issues of harmful environments and occupational accidents, which are much broader concerns among men than among women. Further, these concerns are more ingrained among male *montubios* and mulattoes, and of little incidence among white men. That is to say, although men are more likely than women to hold risky jobs in harmful environment, men of certain ethnicities tend so even more.

Men participate more as employers than women. Among men, it is the whites who are the most likely to be employers. Further, a higher proportion of white women are employers than non-white men. This reveals that, here, ethnicity is more important than gender.

The data reveal that women tend to work in domestic service at a much higher rate than men; women's participation in this category is 20 times higher than that of men. This is the employment category with the highest percentage differences in participation by gender. But, just as was the case above, the role of domestic employees is also more nuanced if ethnicity is considered because it is the women *montubias* and those of African descent (afro-Ecuadorian, black, and mulatto), who participate most in this category.

Let us now focus on the determinants of the hourly income considered in this study. When other relevant factors such as age, marital status and years of education are considered, as in Tables 10.6 and 10.7, being a woman is still associated with having lower incomes, whether or not one has adequate employment. Furthermore, ethnicity was proven to matter. Being indigenous is associated with lower levels of income compared to the other categories considered. In contrast, being white and from a different ethnicity than the listed in this study is associated with the highest levels of income.

Based on the foregoing, some central conclusions can be drawn. The *montubios* and indigenous peoples are the most disadvantaged ethnic groups in Ecuador. To understand the significance of this, it must be borne in mind that the *montubios* are generally descendants of the aborigines, mestizos, and poor whites of the Ecuadorian coast, whose ancestors have historically been alienated from the ownership of land and means of production. Likewise, the indigenous people are descendants of the poor indigenous peasants of the Ecuadorian Sierra (Andean region), who, like the *montubios*, suffered a long process of several centuries of alienation of their lands and properties. The ancestors of the current members of these groups constituted the mass of cheap labor of the mostly agricultural economy of the Ecuadorian Coast and Sierra from the colonial period well into the republican period. In both cases, both the *montubio* and the indigenous peoples have an automatic identification with poverty, as well as with marginality, within the social prejudices in Ecuador.

Therefore, the historical continuity of these ethnic groups at the bottom of the income distribution, in the most precarious and least satisfactory tasks, reveals how little the distribution of wealth and social roles among ethnic groups in Ecuador have changed two centuries after the end of the colonial period.

In addition, women continue to be paid less than men, and this gap worsens in the case of non-white women. It is also observed that non-white men are more disadvantaged than white women. Therefore, while gender inequalities are important within the labor market, so are ethnic differences. This forms a picture of inequalities that reveals continuities that originated in the colonial period and have not yet been overcome.

Therefore, to understand Ecuadorian labor differences, the postulates presented in the theoretical framework of this article, relating to labor differences between men and women, need to include differentiations by ethnicity, as well as a historical analysis of their causes. As proposed by authors such as Federici (2010), there is a concealment of the appropriation of the values created through women's unpaid work, as well as an asymmetry of power unfavorable towards them. However, when analyzing the case of Ecuador, both men and women of non-white ethnicities have greater difficulties than white men and white women in gaining access to positions of power. This does not deny the validity of Federici's assertions, but it is an example of how the study of Ecuador and Latin America needs its own theoretical constructions that particularize in their characteristics and unfailingly consider the ethnic differences between the studies of gender differences.

It is also noted that Myrdal's theses (1959, 1979) are still valid and applicable to the study of the socio-economic reality of Ecuador. There is a vicious circle, a cumulative circular causation, which has not been broken despite the very long period of time that has elapsed between the colonial period and the present. Indigenous people, Afro-descendants, and other previously disadvantaged ethnic groups continue to be disadvantaged nowadays; and their low incomes will likely be a key difficulty for their descendants to emerge from these unfavorable positions. Ruminating further on this is beyond the scope of this chapter, but this certainly represents fruitful terrain for future research.

Thus, it is observed that the differences in income and positions in the division of labor among social classes, which theorists such as Marx pointed out, and which his followers studied, need to be augmented by considerations of ethnic differences, at least in the case of Ecuador. This is so, because in Ecuador the labor roles and therefore positionings in social strata are determined by the ethnic category to which an individual belongs.

As a final conclusion, it can be said that being a woman continues to be a disadvantage in the workplace in Ecuador and this condition worsens if one is also indigenous, *montubia*,[8] or of African descent. Being a man of those ethnic groups is also a disadvantage and almost a determinism in the lowest positions of the labor scale.

This study is understandably limited to analysis of data provided by the survey to which reference is made. Therefore, the conclusions and questions that arise from this work need to be corroborated and answered, respectively, by

---

8   Feminine (singular) for 'montubio.'

those surveyed, to whom there is no access. Key questions in this respect are as follows. What are the difficulties that an afro-Ecuadorian, black, or mulatto woman encounters in accessing a well-paid job? As a woman, do you consider that the color of your skin has been a factor against you when it comes to obtaining a better job? Are interpersonal relationships with those who can help you improve your social position more difficult for you because of your culture or ethnicity? Have you experienced situations where your status as an indigenous or black man locks you into certain types of low-paid and low-skilled jobs? As stated, these are questions that can only be answered by those who have experienced the problem; therefore, they require fieldwork that goes beyond the boundaries of this study.

Nevertheless, this work has important practical and policy implications. This is so, because, in Ecuador, studies on racial socioeconomic differences are resisted and, indeed, are considered a kind of taboo of which one avoids speaking, in a society that is supposed to be egalitarian, democratic, and liberated from colonialism. Therefore, the greatest contribution of this study lies in what it can do toward breaking down these barriers pursuant of reasoned debate and understanding.

References

Constitution of Ecuador. (2008). https://www.asambleanacional.gob.ec/sites/default/files/documents/old/constitucion_de_bolsillo.pdf.

Bello, M., and Rangel, M. (2000). *Etnicidad, "raza" y equidad en América Latina y el Caribe.*

Benítez, D., and Espinoza, B. (2018). *Discriminación salarial por género en el sector formal en Ecuador usando registros administrativos.* (No. 6; Cuaderno de Trabajo). https://www.ecuadorencifras.gob.ec/documentos/web-inec/Bibliotecas/Libros/Discriminacion_salar_por_genero_sec_for_Ecu.pdf.

Bretón Solo de Zaldívar, V. (2013). "Etnicidad, desarrollo y 'Buen Vivir': Reflexiones críticas en perspectiva histórica." *European Review of Latin American and Caribbean Studies*, 95, 71–95. http://doi.org/10.18352/erlacs.9231.

Cabrera, D., Espinoza, E., and Rodríguez, Z. (2016). "Diferencias salariales y satisfacción laboral entre géneros y etnias en el Ecuador." *Revista Científica ECOCIENCIA* 3(4): 1–26.

Carrasco, C. (2006). *Estadístiques sota sospita: proposta de nous indicadors de l'experiència femenina.* Generalitat de Catalunya: Institut Català de les Dones.

Consejo Nacional para la Igualdad de Género. (2015). *Logros de la Revolución Ciudadana en Clave de Género.*

De Ferranti, D., Perry, G., Ferreira, F., Walton, M., and Coday, D. (2003). *Desigualdad en América Latina y el Caribe: ¿ruptura con la historia?*

El Comercio. (2019). *La brecha salarial de género en Ecuador se encuentra en un 20%.* https://www.elcomercio.com/actualidad/brecha-salarial-mujer-ecuador-igualdad.html.

El Telégrafo. (2018). *Las mujeres gana 20% menos de salario que los hombres.* https://www.eltelegrafo.com.ec/noticias/economia/4/mujeres-desigualdad-salarial.

Federici, S. (2010). *Calibán y la bruja: Mujeres, cuerpo y acumulación originaria.* Traficantes de Sueños.

Flórez, C.E., Medina, C., and Urrea, F. (2003). "Los costos de la exclusión social por raza o etnia en América Latina y el Caribe." *Coyuntura Social* 29. https://www.repository.fedesarrollo.org.co/handle/11445/1061?show=full.

Grijalva, A.M., Palacios, J.C., Patiño, C.E., and Tamayo, D.A. (2017). "Los factores asociados a la satisfacción laboral en Ecuador en 2007 y 2015 utilizando la Encuesta Nacional de Empleo, Desempleo y Subempleo." *Analítika* 13(1): 7–45. https://www.ecuadorencifras.gob.ec/documentos/web-inec/Revistas/Analitika/Anexos_pdf/Analit_13/1.pdf.

Herrnstein, R.J., and Murray, C. (2010). *The bell curve: Intelligence and class structure in American life.* Simon and Schuster.

INEC. (2018). *National Survey of Employment, Unemployment and Underemployment.* INEC. https://www.ecuadorencifras.gob.ec/enemdu-2018/.

León, M. (2003). *Mujeres y Trabajo: cambios impostergables.* REMTE.

Locke, E.A. (1976). *The nature and causes of job satisfaction, in Dunnette. Handbook of industrial and organizational psicology.* Rand McNally College Ed.

Marx, K. (1977). *El capital. Crítica de la economía política.* Ediciones AKAL.

Muchinsky, P.M. (1993). *Psychology applied to work* (4a. ed.). Pacific Grove Publishing Company.

Myrdal, G. (1959). *Teoría económica y regiones subdesarrolladas.* Fondo de Cultura Económica.

Myrdal, G. (1962). "An American Dilemma." In M.W. Hughey (Ed.), *New Tribalisms: The Resurgence of Race and Ethnicity* (pp. 61–72). Palgrave Macmillan UK. https://doi.org/10.1007/978-1-349-26403-2_5.

Myrdal, G. (1979). *Teoría Económica y Regiones Subdesarrolladas* (1a edición). Fondo de Cultura Económica.

Picchio, A. (1992). *Social reproduction: the political economy of the labour market.* Cambridge University Press.

Polanyi, K. (1947). *La Gran Transformación. Crítica del liberalismo económico* (2007 Quipu). Quipu.

Rodríguez Chaurnet, D. (1996). "La valoración del trabajo doméstico: algunas reflexiones." *Problemas Del Desarrollo* 2(109): 101–113.

Rushton, J.P. (1996). *Race, evolution, and behavior: A life history perspective.* Transaction Publ.

SENPLADES. (2009). *Plan Nacional del Buen Vivir (PNBV) 2009–2013.* https://www .planificacion.gob.ec/plan-nacional-para-el-buen-vivir-2009-2013/.

SENPLADES. (2017). *Plan Nacional del Buen Vivir (PNBV) 2017–2021.* https://www.plani ficacion.gob.ec/wp-content/uploads/downloads/2017/10/PNBV-26-OCT-FINAL_6K .compressed1.pdf.

Valenzuela, M.E. (2003). "Desigualdad de género y pobreza en América Latina." In M.E. Valenzuela (Ed.), *Mujeres, Pobreza y Mercado de Trabajo: Argentina y Paraguay (Proyecto: Género, Pobreza y Empleo en América Latina)* (pp. 15–66). Organización Internacional del Trabajo.

Valenzuela, M.E., and Rangel, M. (Eds). (2004). *Desigualdades entrecruzadas: pobreza, género, etnia y raza en América Latina.* Oficina Regional de la OIT para América Latina y el Caribe.

CHAPTER 11

Southern Craftswomen: Weaving Networks in the Solidarity Economy

María Anchundia, Wendy Mora and Sayonara Morejón

Whether in the countryside or the cities, rivers or forests,
women's daily practices are at the same time
of resistance to the attacks of the patriarchal capitalism on life,
and of the construction of the world we want to live in.

NOBRE (2015)

∴

1   Introduction

Ecuador in 2008 was the scene of two events that marked ruptures and advances at the national and local levels, in which women's participation was a determining factor. In a referendum, the people approved a Constitution that, for the first time, included the popular and solidarity economy (article 283),[1] as part of the economic system. In a small rural town in the south, called *El Retiro*, located in Machala canton, El Oro province, a group of women with ancestral knowledge about the use of the banana stem in handicrafts, decided to form the Association of Agro-artisanal Women (AMA), assuming the principles of solidarity and reciprocity.

At the national level, the constitutional changes were no coincidence, but the product of intense days of debate and the mobilization of social organizations and women's movements, especially in the south of Ecuador. On the other hand, the emergence of the Association of Agro-artisanal Women was, among other reasons, the result of a decade-long organizational process involving the women of El Oro, who had influenced the design of public policies to strengthen their economic autonomy.

---

1 See Constitution of the Republic of Ecuador. Chapter 4, Section 1, Article 283, second paragraph.

The women of the south are diverse, consisting of *montubias*, indigenous peoples, afro-descendants, mestizas, farmers, fisherwomen, shrimp gatherers, banana and cocoa workers, guardians of the mangrove swamps and ecosystems, teachers, merchants, artisans, and community fund managers. Drawing on this diversity they initiated organizational processes to defend and exercise their rights, which then became important in influencing the emergence of solidarity economy initiatives.

The crafts produced by the members of the Association, taking advantage of a natural resource that is abundant in that territory, not only placed them as producers of cultural goods, but also as generators and carriers of knowledge, particularly ancestral knowledge, of their peoples (Instituto de Patrimonio Natural y Cultural & Ministerio de Industrias y Productividad 2010). Concomitantly, principles of solidarity were incorporated in production and marketing processes, thus contributing to the construction of another world, where the priority is not profit, but cultural recovery and wellbeing.

This experience, which is a reflection of the significant participation of women in the solidarity economy, does not focus exclusively on economic remuneration, but values learning, coexistence, and the possibility of dealing collaboratively on issues such as violence against women, reproductive health, and fundamental rights. The solidarity economy in dialogue with the feminist economy creates a possibility to overcome the fragmentations between economics and politics and its practices constitute a political economy of resistance (Nobre 2015).

For the present study we started from the perspective of feminist economics, because it allows us to identify the inequalities that exist in a capitalist and patriarchal model, for example, the disparities arising from the sexual division of labor, which constitutes the material basis of women's oppression, assigning them unpaid reproductive work but which, being naturalized as a feminine activity, is not recognized either fairly or symbolically, and much less are policies implemented to render it sustainable. Feminist economics makes this work, and the relationships between this work and paid work, visible. At the same time, it shows how women reconcile these two types of work in a context of tensions, whilst proposing to overcome this conflict by re-defining work from the perspective of the sustainability of life and not profit (Nobre 2015).

Another contribution of feminist economics to this study is that it allows us to identify how economic policies have differentiated impacts between men and women. For example, the implementation of credit policies without considering that women do not have access to ownership of certain resources, will contribute to the exclusion of this resource to women, if applied indiscriminately.

In addition, we take a solidarity economy approach. Several studies have been carried out in this respect. Singer (2000) explains that this is a mode of production and distribution created and recreated periodically by those who are marginalized by the labor market. The solidarity economy, he adds, is a continuous creation of workers in struggle against capitalism, with the possibility to surpass capitalism because of the inherent virtues and advantages of a solidarity approach. For Gaiger (2007) it is a new logic of development, building another economy and focusing on values of solidarity and reproduction of life.

The concepts of feminist economics and the solidarity economy, therefore, allow us to make women visible as economic actors, developing alternative economic practices whose pillars are based on solidarity and collective decision-making.

Against this background, the objective of this chapter is to identify the factors that influenced the emergence of the AMA, the strategies developed to sustain it for a decade, and its contributions to the solidarity economy and the initiation and maintenance of feminist leadership.

The methodology used in this chapter seeks to make women's jobs visible, assuming that both paid and unpaid jobs are part of the economy, thus departing from the concept of employment that only incorporates paid jobs. To make visible the work carried out by women at the provincial level, time-use data are utilized to quantify and understand the differential composition of the working days of men and women, with the aim of highlighting inequalities.

Also, to study the contributions of AMA craftswomen to the solidarity economy, field work has been carried out over a number of years involving interviews, focus groups, and meetings with the craftswomen.

In the next section we begin by explaining the context in which this solidarity economy initiative arises in what is called the 'banana capital of Ecuador,' the province of El Oro. Then we explain the road travelled in the establishment and evolution of the Association of Agro-artisanal Women and finally the impacts that this productive and solidarity initiative generates at the local and regional levels in terms of female leadership.

2   Bananas, Handicrafts, and Women Movements in the Province of El Oro

The coastal province of El Oro, located on the southern border of Ecuador and endowed with fertile lands, has been the scene of various export booms that have contributed to the economic growth of the country. These events, which generated substantial profits, especially for large exporters, excluded producers from the benefits of the surplus. Faced with this situation, in recent decades, Orense workers have developed other types of economies that do not aim to make a profit, but instead seek to improve their living conditions, and especially because of women, initiatives based on the principles of solidarity have been strengthened.

The process by which this province became incorporated into the world market began in the middle of the twentieth century because of reduced banana production in Central America. This posed an opportunity because of the fertility of Orense lands. Following the crisis of the 1920s, these lands, which were formerly cocoa plantations, were converted in the 1940s and dedicated to the new export product: bananas.

Before the Second World War, this market was largely supplied by the United Fruit Company and Standard Fruit Company with production located in Costa Rica, Guatemala, Honduras, and Panama. Moreover, around a third of total production occurred in other countries such as Mexico, Nicaragua, Cuba, Dominican Republic, Haiti, and Belize. From 1948 onwards, Ecuadorian exports replaced those of the latter group, while those of the former were maintained until 1964. Countries displaced from the world market, especially by the fungal pathogen known as Panama disease, as well as by cyclones, never recovered the important position they had in the pre-war period. Until 1964, Ecuador continued to supply 25% of the international demand, slightly surpassing the four Central American exporters combined (Larrea 1987).

Thus, the confluence of ecological, socio-economic, and political factors determined that the comparative costs of the country and the province remained favorable in relation to traditional suppliers worldwide.

This boom, which lasted between 1948 and 1965, generated several impacts at the national level, among them, the Ecuadorian economy entered a long process of sustained growth: GDP evaluated at constant prices showed an annual cumulative growth rate of 5.6% between 1948 and 1954 and 4.8% between 1954 and 1965 (Larrea 1987). Banana exports represented between 30% and 40% of total exports (Figure 11.1).

Figure 11.1 shows how banana exports during the boom period rose from $2,761,000 in 1948 to $68,951,000 in 1964. Concomitant with this growth, income disparities grew, and although banana workers contributed to the wealth, their living conditions deteriorated (Larrea 1987).

Other impacts of the boom in the period included migration from the Sierra (Andean region) to the Coast, accelerated urbanization in Machala (the provincial capital), the strengthening of local governments, and in the early 1960s, the dissolution of pre-capitalist relations in agriculture and the strengthening of the import substitution process, which was evidenced by the emergence of particular banana agro-industries.

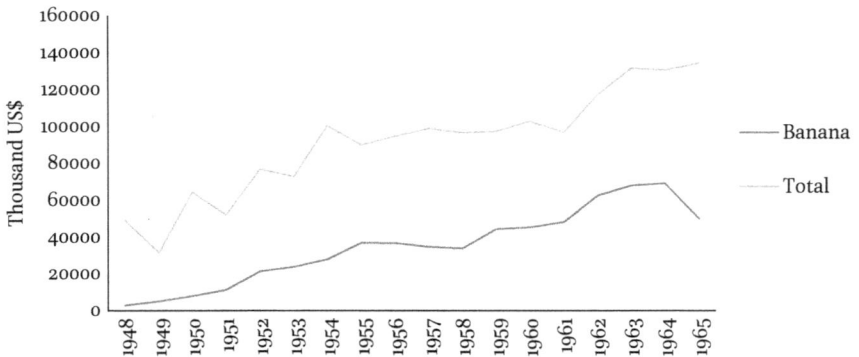

FIGURE 11.1 Total exports and banana exports from Ecuador, 1948–1965
SOURCE: CENTRAL BANK OF ECUADOR (BCE, 2002)

In the following years, although banana exports continued to be significant in the traditional sector, oil companies began to predominate, starting in 1972. From the mid-1980s, when the neoliberal model was adopted, the concentration of wealth in the hands of exporters became reinforced, while at the same time society and rural economies were restructured.

During this period, non-agricultural rural activities in Latin America grew significantly in terms of employment and income. While, in the early 1980s, less than a quarter of the rural population was engaged in off-farm activities, by the end of the 1990s this had increased to two-fifths, devoted mainly to the service sector (Kay 2009), with rural women participating substantially, through their incorporation into commerce, handicrafts, and as personal service workers.

In the province of El Oro as well as in Latin American rural areas more generally, the growth of non-agricultural employment is apparent, as evidenced by national census figures referring to the occupations of the economically active population (Figure 11.2).

Figure 11.2 shows that over a thirty-six-year period there were changes in the structure of the economically active population. In 1974 farmers and skilled workers pre-dominated (51%), followed by officers and artisans (9%). However, by the year 2010, first place was held by traders and service workers (18%), followed by officers and artisans (12%), with farmers in third place (8%). The agricultural sector declined not only in percentage terms, but in absolute terms as well, moving from 40,149 to 21,710 workers. It should be emphasized that people employed in so-called elementary occupations appear to pre-dominate in 2010. However, this is likely erroneous in the sense that the National Institute

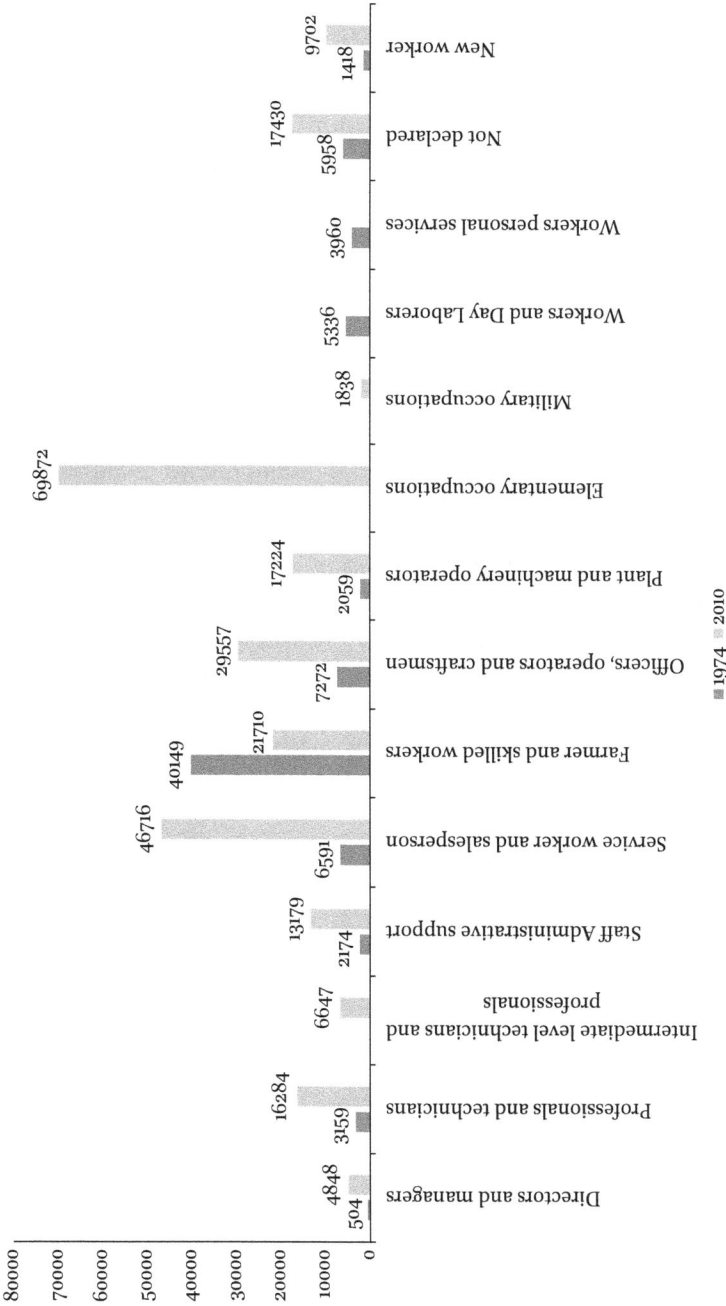

FIGURE 11.2: Economically active population in El Oro Province, 1974 and 2010

SOURCE: NATIONAL INSTITUTE OF STATISTICS AND CENSUSES (INEC 1974, 2010)

of Statistics and Censuses (INEC) includes people engaged in agriculture, as well as artisans who do not use machinery in this category.

Another change observed is the growing number of women joining the economically active population in recent decades, as can be seen in Figure 11.3.

As a result of neoliberalism, labor flexibilization modified the participation of men and women (Kay 2009). A first consequence of the new model and the crisis experienced by Ecuador at the end of the last century was the rural-urban migration of men, which led to an increase in female heads of households and a growing incorporation of women into paid work, especially in banana and shrimp companies, respectively carrying out activities in processing and peeling. In most cases these were low wage jobs without social benefits, that is, access to employment occurred in precarious conditions. Other sources of income were found by developing ventures in non-agricultural industries, including commerce and handicrafts, as shown by the 2010 Census data.

This growing participation of women in the labor market made visible the tensions between the time demanded by paid work and that devoted to care work (Carrasco 2003), both for children and the elderly. This is important because historically such care work has been invisible and attributable to patriarchal patterns and the sexual division of labor.

In recent years, feminist organizations have succeeded in better highlighting the conflicts in their working days. The State's response has been the application of time use surveys, which have shown that women are overloaded in terms of work. If we look at the results of the survey conducted by the National

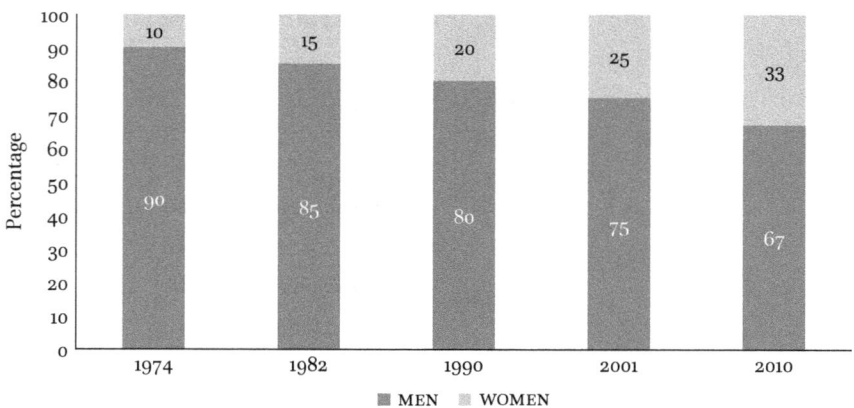

FIGURE 11.3 Economically active population by gender in El Oro Province, 1974–2010
SOURCE: INEC (2010)

Institute of Statistics and Censuses and the National Council of Women (CONAMU) in 2007 in the province of El Oro, we see that the overall weekly workload is 60 hours for men, while that of women is 73 hours, reflecting the time devoted to care activities which are assumed by women to a greater extent than men (Pérez et al. 2008).

Feminist economics provides us with a lens to identify and explore, through the study of time-use, asymmetries in the distribution and valuation of each type of work, which have adverse effects on gender equality and women's autonomy (Jain 2013). Against this background, the right to equality and the State's obligation to apply affirmative action measures, established in article 11, paragraph 2, of the Constitution, should be expressed in State plans and budgets for the financing of care centers, in terms of infrastructure and operations, to reduce this overload of work. On the one hand this would create better conditions for women to pursue other activities, as is the case with artisans, and, on the other, it would rightly acknowledge that it is incumbent on the State to assume co-responsibility in terms of care.

The absence of such policies, both from central and local governments, has contributed to a worsening of inequality in the province, despite contributions and initiatives from the working population. Land ownership and export earnings have become even more concentrated in the elite, and large income inequalities and social divisions remain as a result. These inequalities have motivated the formation of a strong social movement both at the level of banana workers and other branches of production in the province, which have been organized on the basis of principles that privilege solidarity over profit.

Another fact that affects the emergence of new productive organizations is that, since the province of El Oro is located in a border area, the population that lives there has faced the deleterious impacts of armed conflicts with the neighboring country, Peru, and has also been part of the peace proposals.

In 1999, after the peace agreements between Ecuador and Peru, the women's organizations of El Oro joined those of the other border provinces and formed the Committee for the Development of Border Women (*Comité de Desarrollo de Mujeres de Frontera*, in Spanish), CODEMUF, which brought together more than 100 women's organizations from the provinces of El Oro, Loja, Morona Santiago, Pastaza, and Zamora Chinchipe. Collectively, various ethnic and social sectors were represented. CODEMUF was established in Vilcabamba, Loja province, on April 25, 1999, within the framework of the Meeting of Women's Organizations of the Southern-Eastern border of Ecuador. It contributed to the strengthening of women's organizations that demanded economic, social, and cultural rights (CODEMUF 2001), at the same time pressing for public funding to bolster the productive initiatives of the women's organizations of the border, among them those of the artisans.

This process led to the strengthening of women's organizations in cantonal capitals and in urban and rural parishes in the south, with the aim of proposing public policies and projects centered on the participation of women's organizations for the improvement of living and working conditions in border areas.

In addition, the southern provinces, including El Oro, have a tradition of associativity, of the formation of cooperatives that will have an impact on the constitution of associations of women producers. This is evidenced through the formation of women's organizations fighting for economic, social, and cultural rights in the 1990s. The Movement of Women of El Oro (MMO) is particularly noteworthy in this respect. Since 1997, initiatives developed by the MMO have focused on the defense and enforceability of women's economic, social, and cultural rights, as well as on the creation of solidarity credit organizations and food supply and sovereignty organizations such as *Taleguita Solidaria*. These are organizations in which the artisans of El Retiro parish and other cantons in the province that make up the AMA have been integrated. This process contributes to the strengthening of other women's organizations and coincides with the approval of a Constitution that incorporates the solidarity economy as part of the economic system.

3   The AMA: Ancestral Knowledge, Solidarity, Care, and
        Feminist Leadership

The context described and discussed above shows us the external factors that converged to provide the space and motivation for the emergence of the Association of Agro-artisanal Women: the proximity to raw material, the banana crisis, the neoliberal policies that expelled large numbers of farmers from their main occupation, the need for a Constitution such as that of 2008 that recognizes the solidarity economy, and finally the strengthening of women's organizations that question the neoliberal and patriarchal model and demand economic rights for equal access to productive resources with policies that strengthen their productive initiatives.

To these factors others are added. In the province of El Oro, at the beginning of the 21st century, various craft associations emerged in which women are linked. According to the 2010 Census, out of an economically active population of 255,007 people, 83,175 are women and of these 3,593 are artisans (INEC 2010). Using products derived from the environment, and that were not used

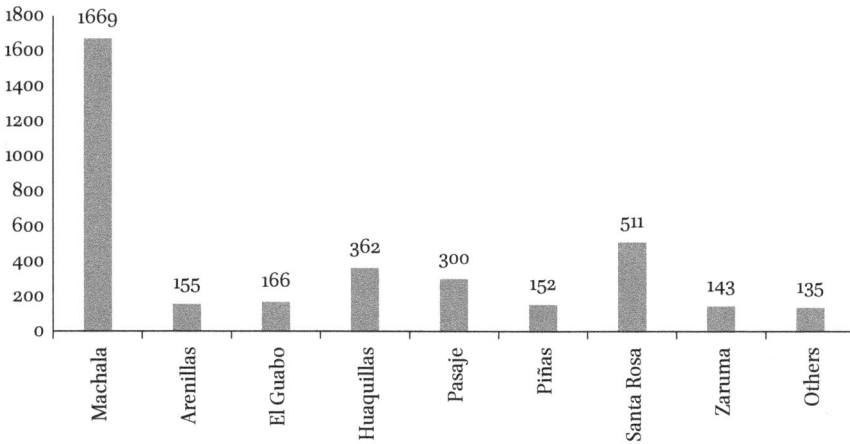

FIGURE 11.4 Female artisans in El Oro province by cantons, 2010
SOURCE: INEC (2010)

by farmers or fishermen, emerging groups of women began to transform them into handicrafts across the various cantons in the province (Figure 11.4).

As can be seen in Figure 11.4, female artisans are present in all the cantons of the province. Among them are women utilizing shellfish waste, shells, and snails. There are also bakers, hairdressers, seamstresses and banana fiber workers. Most of these female artisans are located in Machala, followed by Santa Rosa, Huaquillas, and Pasaje.

As has been pointed out, with the advent of the financial crisis in 1999, unemployment, precarious work, and migration all increased, both in Ecuador overall and in the province of El Oro specifically. However, there was a potential inherited by the women of that province, a range of ancestral artisan knowledge and skills, including knowing how to treat banana stems, convert them to fiber, and weave this fiber to produce items such as hats and handbags. These are factors of identity of the province, which allow the emergence of this initiative based on the principles of solidarity and the motivation to generate income in a self-managed manner.

4   Establishment and Emergence of the AMA

During the first decade of the twenty-first century, new currents of thought, alternative economic models, and novel public policies started to be applied and the women's movement began to occupy an unusually strong position in

Latin America compared to previous times. Ecuador is no exception in this respect.

Within this framework, in 2008, a group of 32 women from the different cantons and parishes of the province of El Oro, who had a wealth of organizational experience at the provincial level and ancestral knowledge about the use of the banana stalk, decided to form the Association of Agro-artisanal Women (AMA), with its headquarters in the parish of El Retiro. They are women, linked above all to agricultural activity, but also to the services, and time, they provide and dedicate to this activity. These women are located mainly in the parish of El Retiro de Machala and in the cantons of Santa Rosa and Pasaje, as can be seen in the map illustrated in Figure 11.5.

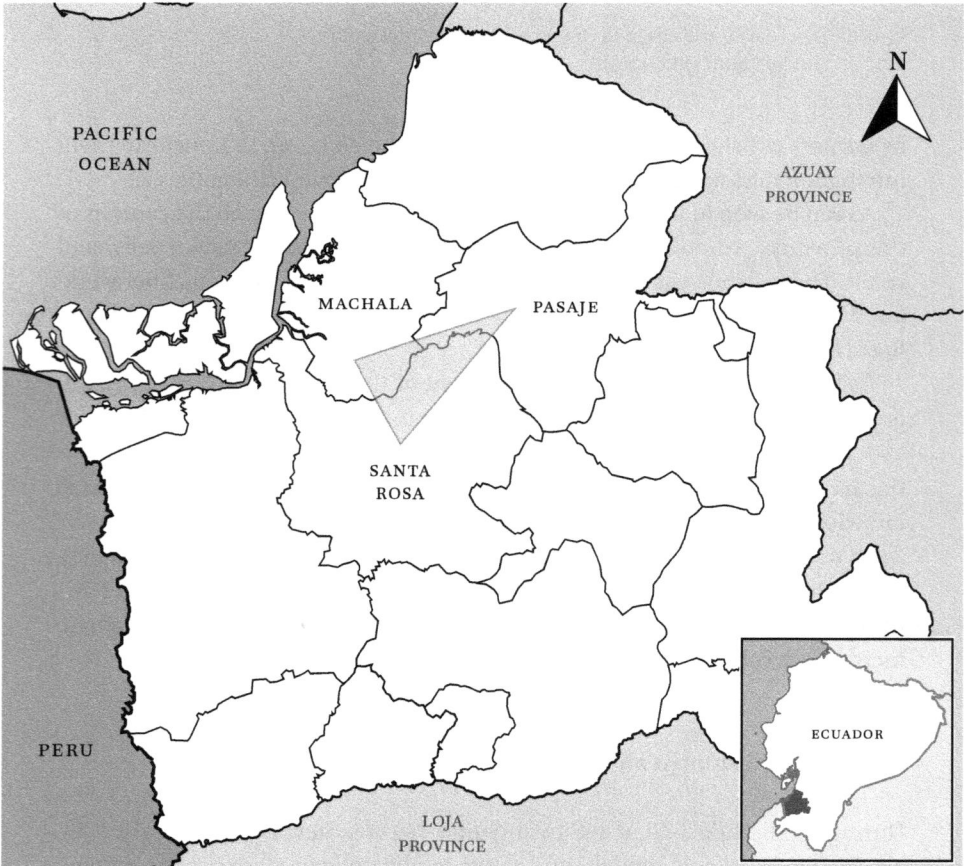

FIGURE 11.5 Ubication of the women of AMA within El Oro province, Ecuador

The women of these cantons are constituted as a de facto solidarity organization, defining their objectives as processing, marketing products with banana fiber, training in handicraft techniques, disseminating women's rights, achieving their empowerment, and thus improving their and other women's living and working conditions (F. Mendía, personal communication, October 10, 2018).

Some of the female artisans who established the AMA in 2008 had participated in mobilizations since 1990 in defense of their rights to a life without violence, for equal access to productive resources, as well as for municipal and provincial public policies to strengthen productive activity and economic autonomy.

5   The Road Travelled

The AMA has designed various strategies and initiatives since its establishment to broaden its field of action, which not only contemplate the installation of artisan workshops but also the diffusion of women's rights, their empowerment, and making them visible as economic actors who contribute to homes and local development.

In this way, the Association strengthened alliances with other women's organizations in the south to develop joint agendas as well as with non-governmental organizations, such as the Yerbabuena Foundation, the Technical University of Machala, and the ESPOL Polytechnic University, for training in the improvement of production methods, marketing, and women's rights. With these inputs, they have strengthened their management capacities and have influenced governmental authorities at different levels from the local through to the national (Fundación Yerbabuena 2009).

Developments have allowed them to have legal recognition and support, including with respect to acquiring sewing machines and furnaces, allowing them to increase production as demand increased. At the same time, they also now have access to participation in national and international fairs.

Moreover, by virtue of their experiences accrued over time, the artisans have become trainers and they give workshops in Ecuador. They were also invited to the EARTH University in San José, Costa Rica. This has allowed them to position themselves in the foreign market. The main organizational milestones are summarized in Figure 11.6.

The AMA has endured and been consolidated by the conjunction of key factors, such as ancestral knowledge, solidarity in production and marketing, and democratic participation in decision-making, as elaborated on in what follows.

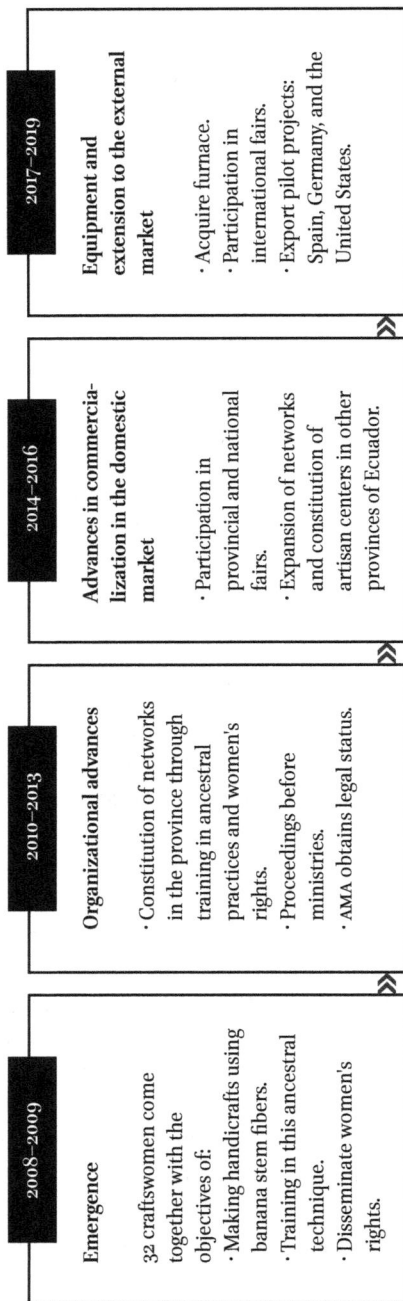

FIGURE 11.6 Chronology of the road traveled by AMA

SOURCE: F. MENDÍA (PERSONAL COMMUNICATION, OCTOBER 10, 2018)

6   Shared Ancestral Knowledge

In the case of banana artisans, ancestral knowledge is key. Although not part of Western knowledge, it is equally valid (Foucalt 2002) and reflects the inheritance from grandfathers and grandmothers who were designing techniques to transform the stem of this tree, called *chanta*, into handicrafts. This has been the fundamental pillar to take the initiative in developing this activity. Felicia Mendía, President of the AMA points out:

> Our grandparents used the chanta (banana stalk) to make baskets, fans, to tie loads in the mules and other things. We continued with these practices, we trained to improve this technique and also offer other products such as hats and handbags.
>
> F. MENDÍA, personal communication, October 10, 2018

It is this knowledge that has been transferred from generation to generation. Rural women in the province are central to this transference and workshops provide a forum for disseminating knowledge to other women, who are later incorporated as part of the Association.

7   Solidarity in the Production and Marketing of Handicrafts

To study the dynamics of craftsmanship, it is necessary to approach the cultural and economic dimensions in a complementary way. Similarly, it is important that production and commercialization processes are analyzed from their interrelations.

The beginnings of the craft production processes are decided jointly, based on customer orders, which are the result of efforts made also by those responsible for marketing in the AMA.

The raw material used to process the fiber is the stem of the banana. This can be regular banana, *orito* or *silk*. What can be obtained from a stem depends on its thickness and height. If it is a thick stem, 15 channels (layers) wide and 2 meters high, up to 4 hats or 4 wallets can be made.

The artisanal work begins with the acquisition of the stem, supplied by a farmer after the banana harvest has concluded. The farmer delivers it free of charge to the artisan, who carries out her work in the way summarized in Figure 11.7.

The handicrafts obtained from the production process are hats in natural or dyed fibers for men and women, bags and wallets for women, various types of

| Trained craftswoman obtains the banana stalk and takes it to her house for processing. | The stem is then cut into sheets and classified to decide what will be used to make which products. | The sheets are left to dry, then cleaned and cut into fibers that serve as fabric. | The fabric is then worked on the basis of a design. | Other natural fibers are chosen and incorporated. | The craftsmanship is packed. |

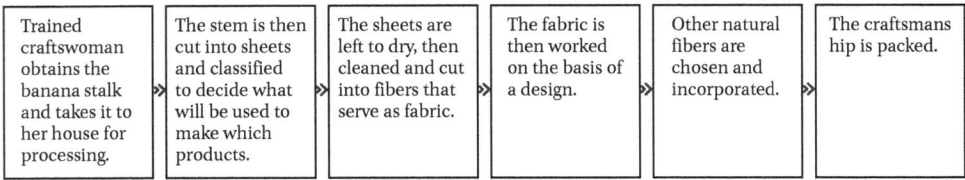

FIGURE 11.7 Production process using natural banana fiber
SOURCE: AMA'S CRAFTSWOMEN (PERSONAL COMMUNICATION, OCTOBER 2018)

baskets and necklaces made of natural fiber combined with another natural resource such as *tagua*, as well as pencil holders, picture frames, purses, key rings, and dolls.

It is important to emphasize that after a period of training, empowerment on the part of the artisans, as well as by virtue of the results of the sale of handicrafts, this work has begun to be valued and the participation of the artisans' companions and daughters has ensued. Family members who initially said that the activity of the artisans was to collect garbage, have changed their opinion; now this activity is appreciated and, in many cases, family members participate in the collection of the banana stem. Also, as noted above, the banana producers give away stems free of charge after the harvest, which has allowed an integration of both the community and the family.

Through marketing and management initiatives, support has been obtained from provincial and cantonal authorities, as well as from some non-governmental organizations, for promotion and transportation to national fairs. This has opened-up the wider domestic market to the artisans. Recently, this has also involved participation in the 'Exporta Fácil' program with pilot exports to other countries, places where they have had access to quotas of up to 50 handicrafts. The artisan market spaces of the AMA are as shown in Figure 11.8.

The price of a hat traded in the external market is twenty-five dollars and the costs are broken down in Table 11.1.

Responsibilities for commercialization are delineated in the directives of the Association and campaigns pursuant of the diffusion of their products are made through fairs and catalogs. After orders arrive from clients, the production task is assigned to a group of craftswomen who already have the fibers and a delivery term is established.

However, according to interviewees, an issue arises in terms of access to credit, since in spite of fulfilling quality requirements for exportation, barriers remain because of cumbersome procedures. At the same time, it is necessary for places to be assigned for the exhibition and sale of crafts in airports, other transport hubs, and tourist sites, to extend the market.

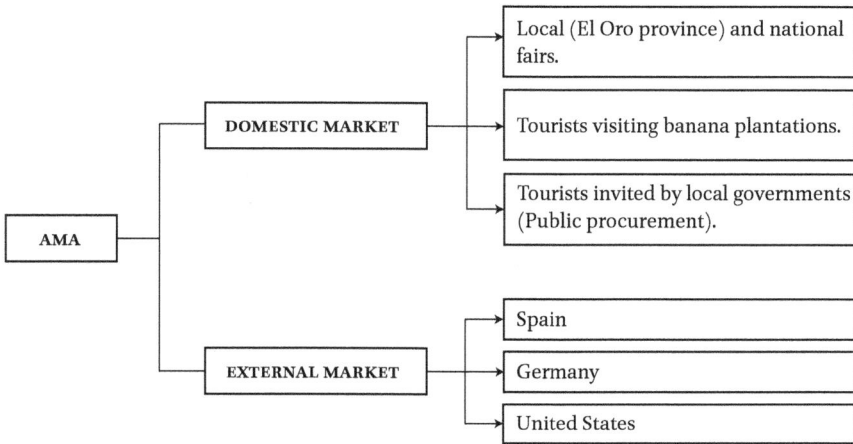

FIGURE 11.8 Market spaces of the AMA
SOURCE: AMA'S CRAFTSWOMEN (PERSONAL COMMUNICATION, OCTOBER 2018)

TABLE 11.1   Costs and prices of an artisanal hat

Item	Value
Payment to the craftswoman	$17.00
Payment for the finish	3.50
Payment for the *tafilete*	1.00
Cost of packaging	1.00
Membership fee	2.50
Selling price	$25.00

SOURCE: AMA'S CRAFTSWOMEN (PERSONAL COMMUNICATION, OCTOBER 2018)

8   Paid and Unpaid Work: Craftsmanship and Care

Feminist economics as a critical theory that questions the exclusion of care work and community work from the scope of the economy, leads us to address the visibility of the multiple jobs that artisans take on every day to show that the contributions of women are not only in terms of goods captured by the market, but also in terms of the provision of non-market services that generate welfare and contribute to sustaining life.

The 32 producers of the AMA are diverse in terms of age, ranging between 25 and 77 years. Alongside their artisanal activities—which may not

TABLE 11.2   Daily work of the AMA craftswomen

Work	Number of craftswomen	%
Crafts and care	10	31
Crafts, food sales, and care	4	13
Crafts, trade, and care	4	13
Crafts, studies, and care	3	10
Crafts, packing, and care	2	6
Crafts, teaching, and care	2	6
Crafts, local leadership, and care	2	6
Crafts, office work, and care	1	3
Crafts, cleaning. and care	1	3
Crafts, pharmacy, and cares	1	3
Crafts, dressmaker, and care	1	3
Crafts, jam sales, and care	1	3
TOTAL	32	100

SOURCE: AMA'S CRAFTSWOMEN (PERSONAL COMMUNICATION, OCTOBER 2018)

be consistent, depending on the orders—other activities are also pursued (Table 11.2).

Table 11.2 shows that members do not exclusively develop crafts but combine such work with other paid and unpaid jobs. All women combine craftwork with care with around two-thirds of the women additionally taking on paid work or studies.

These data show the existence of an overload of work, which is corroborated by testimonies from the interviewees. That is, women devote more hours to care work, in relation to male family members. Accordingly, the need for state investment in care centers has been raised so as to allow women to free up time for both training and artisan tasks, which would enhance their skills.

9   Democratic Decision-Making

From a participative perspective—which is one of the principles of the solidarity economy and was promoted from the establishment of the organization—decisions concerning production, commercialization, and organization are taken on the basis of elections. F. Mendía (personal communication, October 10, 2018) states:

> Democracy in our organization is expressed because we ask the opinion of all the members for the decisions of production and allocation of orders. We reach agreements and compromises and what they point out is respected. When something is difficult, we put it to the vote and that is how decisions are taken.

Being registered with the Superintendence of Popular and Solidarity Economy (SEPS) and following the legally established regulations, the Board of Directors is formally elected every two years, based on a secret ballot. In these elections, the President, Secretary, Members, and Supervisory Board are also appointed.

Rotation in management is a challenge for the Association and actions have been defined to implement training programs for new leaders. Lorgia Cuenca, one of the members, points out that when organizing promotional events or participation in fairs, it is necessary to cover tasks such as collecting requests, dealing with a dissemination agenda with the media. and preparing promotional materials. It is also necessary that there are trained partners to assume these responsibilities (L. Cuenca, personal communication, October 10, 2018).

10   Weaving Networks of Artisan and Feminist Knowledge

AMA's artisans are not concentrated exclusively in the province, but have established networks and artisanal banana fiber centers elsewhere in Ecuador, especially in areas where bananas are produced and where this resource can be harnessed by women (Figure 11.9). Here, together with training in the production and marketing of handicrafts, they disseminate women's rights, demand their fulfilment, and set joint agendas at the national level.

Alongside these efforts, the AMA has decided to integrate other craftswomen from those cantons where they are working in cognate areas of production.

The constant work, the training to provide a seedbed for new AMA centers, and the incorporation of new designs have allowed the organization to meet international quality standards. Likewise, the fact that members have access to fair payment for their work and make decisions collectively has strengthened and positioned them at the family, community, and provincial levels. In recent years they have been called to participate in debates at the parish and cantonal levels, as well as in elections at the parish level which has resulted in them gaining elected representatives.

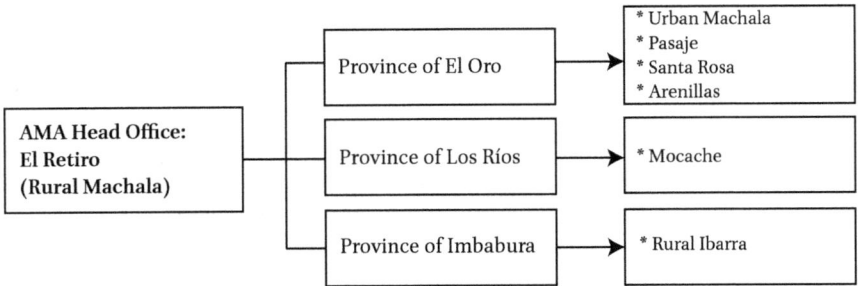

FIGURE 11.9 The AMA's network
        SOURCE: AMA'S CRAFTSWOMEN (PERSONAL COMMUNICATION, OCTOBER
        2018) NOTE: * AMA ARTISAN CENTERS.

The work of a decade has left its fruits. The outputs produced have a viable brand because they are authentic and because they have met all the quality requirements demanded to access markets. Indeed, this has allowed pilot exports to other countries with the support of Pro Ecuador (an initiative of the Vice-Ministry of Export and Investment Promotion of Ecuador).

Key facts showing the recognition of the organization and its products at provincial and regional levels can be delineated as follows (AMA 2017):

- Awarded with the Medal of Merit 'Matilde Hidalgo de Procel,' Manta, March 2010.
- Awarded best women's organization in productive entrepreneurship (Ecuador's zone 7) by the Institute of Popular and Solidarity Economy, Loja, 2013.
- Recognition by the Ministry of Justice for the organization's role the fight against violence against women, 2017.

In spite of these achievements which testify to the motivation and work of the members of the Association, there is still plenty of room for creating a more favorable policy environment. Among these are policy initiatives aimed at helping handicrafts become part of the identity of the province. In the province of El Oro there is currently no widespread artisan identity and it is proposed to create this identity through emphasizing the role of artisans in conserving heritage. The banana fiber hat should become the symbol of the heritage of the province of El Oro, say members of AMA.

Another concrete demand is for policies at the local government level to grant strategic premises for the sale of craft items in busy places such as airports and other transport hubs, as well as in Machala, the capital of the province.

In addition, it is necessary to democratize the system for credit provision operationalized by the public bank *BanEcuador*, promoting equitable policies vis-à-vis access to finance, with preferential interest rates for artisans who produce goods using ancestral knowledge. Further, there is ample scope for soliciting support from the Ministry of Foreign Affairs, to help promote authentic crafts made by securing exhibition spaces in Ecuadorian embassies in different countries around the world.

To this must be added the need for local governments to implement policies and funding mechanisms to finance infrastructure for care, namely nurseries and senior centers, in places where artisans are active and organized. Mechanisms for access to social security, where artisans do not have access to alternative means, are also necessary.

Finally, there is a need to strengthen the work of banana fiber artisans, which would have the effect of increasing employment amongst women, advancing their empowerment, and strengthening solidarity economy initiatives in the province of El Oro and throughout Ecuador.

11   Conclusions

The emergence of the Association of Agro-Artisanal Women (AMA) in 2008 was a response to factors specific to the economic and political situation in the province, the region, and Ecuador more generally. Among these are the abundance of natural resources used in the production of handicrafts (banana stalk), the cultural heritage that is the ancestral knowledge to transform the stalk into fiber and then into fabric, the organizational advancements observed with respect to women of the southern border coming together, and the legal framework provided by the Constitution that was approved in the same year as the emergence of the Association and that for the first time recognizes the activities of the solidarity economy.

The strategies developed by the members of the AMA since 2008 have allowed them to remain a significant force for change, empowerment, and sustainability through dissemination of ancestral knowledge and women's rights, joint action plans with other banana artisans in the province and Ecuador more widely, democratic decision-making for production processes, marketing and fair payment for work based on the principles of solidarity, and the ability to negotiate with local and national governments.

The results of these practices developed by the members of the Association have contributed to the strengthening of this new form of economics, the solidarity economy, which in turn contributes to local development, as well as to individual empowerment, given the spaces of debate that have been created among the members, the knowledge of their rights and the contribution to the family economy, which allows recognition of their work and progress in autonomy. However, due to the sexual division of labor, this handcraft work is combined with other remunerated and non-remunerated activities and especially with care activities. This results in women being overloaded with work as evidenced by the time use data for the province. Therefore, the craftswomen are faced with a situation in which inequality still persists particularly in relation to care work, and this problem is compounded by weak or non-existent infrastructure in some of the cantons to free up time and enhance the work of the craftswomen.

The leadership forged by the organization, based on democracy, collective work and solidarity, has helped generate a power base at the local level. Important and interesting in this respect is the fact that some of the AMA's members have been elected through popular vote to serve on Parish Boards. This then provides a framework for going beyond the local level, and even advancing to the national level, for the purposes of making the agenda and requirements of artisanal craftswomen visible to a broad away of decision makers. This experience of bringing to life the notion of a solidarity economy shows us that, with an organization strengthened on the basis of solidarity practices, with ancestral knowledge in artisan production, and with management skills, it is possible to build another way of doing business: an economy with justice and equity at its foundations. These advances, however, require comprehensive public policy support that incorporates the proposals of the AMA and cognate organizations, in terms of their demands for access to productive resources such as credit, and product exhibition centers, as well as budgets to establish infrastructure for child care centers and senior centers. The justification for the implementation of these policies is broad, because they are rights established in the Constitution and because the artisans of the south not only produce goods with an economic value but also a cultural value by virtue of the fact that these women are carriers and disseminators of ancestral knowledge which is part of the heritage of Ecuador.

References

Asociación de Mujeres Agroartesanales. (2017). *Perfil de la Asociación de Mujeres agroartesanales.* AMA.

Banco Central del Ecuador. (2002). *Setenta y cinco años de información estadística. 1927–2002.* BCE.

Carrasco, C. (2003). "La sostenibilidad de la vida humana: ¿un asunto de mujeres?" In M. León (Ed.), *Mujeres y Trabajo.* ALAI, CLACSO, REMTE.

Comité de Desarrollo de Mujeres de Frontera. (2001). *Líneas estratégicas de acción.* CEDIME & Konrad Adenauer.

Foucalt, M. (2002). *La arqueología del saber.* Siglo XXI Editores.

Fundación Yerbabuena. (2009). *Informe de proyectos con organizaciones de mujeres.*

Gaiger, L. (2007). "La economía solidaria y el capitalismo en la perspectiva de las transiciones históricas." In J.L. Coraggio (Ed.), *La economía social desde la periferia. Contribuciones latinoamericanas.* Editorial Altamira.

Instituto Nacional de Estadística y Censos. (2010). *Censo Nacional de Población y Vivienda.* INEC.

Instituto de Patrimonio Natural y Cultural & Ministerio de Industrias y Productividad. (2010). *Estudio propuesta para el posicionamiento de la artesanía patrimonial del Ecuador: Informe final.* Ediciones La Tierra.

Jain, D. (2013). "Incorporación de la perspectiva de género en el progreso económico." In C. Calderón-Magaña (Ed.), *Redistribuir el cuidado: el desafío de las políticas.* ECLAC, United Nations.

Kay, C. (2009). "Estudios rurales en América Latina en el período de globalización neoliberal: ¿una nueva realidad?" *Revista Mexicana de Sociología* 71(4): 607–645.

Larrea, C. (1987). "Auge y crisis de la producción bananera (1948–1976)." In C. Larrea (Ed.), *El Banano en el Ecuador. Transnacionales, modernización y subdesarrollo.* Corporación Editora Nacional.

Nobre, M. (2015). "Economía solidaria y economía feminista. Elementos para una agenda." In M. Nobre, N. Faria, and R. Moreno (Eds.), *Las mujeres en la construcción de la economía solidaria y la agroecología. Textos para la acción feminista.* Sempreviva Organização Feminista.

Pérez, A., Vásconez, A., and Gallardo, C. (2008). *El tiempo de ellos y de ellas. Indicadores de la Encuesta Nacional del uso del tiempo 2007.* INEC & CONAMU.

Singer, P. (2000). *A economía solidaria no Brasil: a autogestão como resposta ao desemprego.* Editora Contexto.

Index

www.ingramcontent.com/pod-product-compliance
Lightning Source LLC
Chambersburg PA
CBHW070912030426
42336CB00014BA/2387